BRIDGING TROUBLED WATERS

BRIDGING TROUBLED WATERS

China, Japan, and Maritime Order in the East China Sea

JAMES MANICOM

GEORGETOWN UNIVERSITY PRESS
Washington, DC

Library of Congress Cataloging-in-Publication Data

Manicom, James.
Bridging troubled waters : China, Japan, and maritime order in the East China Sea / James Manicom.
pages cm
Includes bibliographical references and index.
ISBN 978-1-62616-035-4 (paperback : alkaline paper)
1. China—Foreign relations—Japan. 2. Japan—Foreign relations—China. 3. China—Military relations—Japan. 4. Japan—Military relations—China. 5. International cooperation. 6. Sea-power—China. 7. Sea-power—Japan. 8. Sea-power—East China Sea. 9. East China Sea—Strategic aspects. I. Title.
DS740.5.J3M357 2014
341.4′50916457—dc23

∞ This book is printed on acid-free paper meeting the requirements of the American National Standard for Permanence in Paper for Printed Library Materials.

15 14 9 8 7 6 5 4 3 2 First printing

Printed in the United States of America

Contents

Illustrations

Maps

Figures

Tables

Acknowledgments

THIS WORK BEGAN as a PhD dissertation in international relations at Flinders University in Adelaide. Therefore, thanks are due first and foremost to my supervisor, Andrew O'Neil, who has supported my work since 2004 and continues to provide mentorship and friendship. The School of Political and International Studies at Flinders University provided an exciting and diverse intellectual environment for postgraduate study. Thanks are due to faculty members who provided feedback on my work, including Richard DeAngelis, John Fitzpatrick, Maryanne Kelton, Haydon Manning, and Michael Sullivan. Richard Leaver functioned as a second supervisor and used his expertise to sharpen the discussion of many of the issues. Stephen Fildes of the Spatial Information Systems Laboratory at Flinders University drew the excellent maps. Greg Austin, Jean-Marc Blanchard, Steve Chan, Chris Chung, Harvey Starr, Robert Sutter, and Mark Valencia all provided valuable guidance on key arguments in this stage of the project.

My first field trip to China and Japan would have been a complete failure if not for John Bradford, the International Office at Flinders University, the late Francis Reagan, Xi Yanbin of the International Affairs Office of the Chinese Academy of Social Sciences, and of course, the interviewees who agreed to discuss a controversial and topical national security issue. My field trip to Japan in 2011 would not have been possible without the support of the Japan Foundation and the helpful staff in its Toronto office. The field trip would have been a failure if not for the assistance of Robert Dujarric, Ohnishi Fujio, Akimoto Kazumine, Akiyama Masahiro, Andrew Oros, Alessio Patalano, and the Ocean Policy Research Foundation. The trip would not have been possible without the kind understanding of David and Kathy Thorne.

I am grateful for the financial support provided by the Endeavour International Postgraduate Research Scholarship of Flinders University, the Social Sciences and Humanities Research Council of Canada, and the

Japan Foundation. I am particularly grateful to Bernie Frolic, Joe Wong, and the Asian Institute in the Munk School of Global Affairs at the University of Toronto for helping to smooth the transition from Australia to Canada.

Various iterations of this project were presented at the 2006 Oceanic Conference on International Studies, the 2006 and 2007 meetings of the Australasian Political Studies Association, the 2010 National Bureau of Asian Research Policy Assembly, the 2011 meeting of the Canadian Political Science Association, and the 2013 meeting of the International Studies Association. Ideas were also presented at the University of Adelaide, Macquarie University, the Chinese University of Hong Kong, the University of Toronto, Temple University Japan, and the University of Leeds. I am indebted to the participants at these conferences for their helpful comments.

This manuscript was written during my two-year postdoctoral fellowship at the Balsillie School of International Affairs in Waterloo. Thanks are due in particular for the friendship, support, and intellectual guidance of Whitney Lackenbauer, Mark Raymond, and David Welch. A special thank you is due to the staff of the Centre for International Governance Innovation, particularly David Dewitt and Fen Hampson, who allowed me the time to put the finishing touches on the manuscript during my time there.

Several colleagues suffered through reading part or all of the manuscript, including Ben Habib, Andrew O'Neil, Alex Stephens, Vlado Vivoda, and David Welch. I am indebted to Todd Hall for the title. Don Jacobs is a very patient editor at Georgetown University Press and is supported by an excellent editorial staff. Don also managed to find two excellent reviewers who offered detailed, constructive, and thought-provoking comments on the manuscript. I also benefited from the insights of June Teufel Dreyer, Taylor Fravel, and Kazuhiko Togo.

Parts of chapter 2 appeared in "The Interaction of Material and Ideational Factors in the East China Sea Dispute: Impact on Future Dispute Management," *Global Change, Peace and Security* 20, no. 3 (October 2008): 375–97. Parts of chapter 5 appeared in "Sino-Japanese Cooperation in the East China Sea: Limitations and Prospects," *Contemporary Southeast Asia* 30, no. 3 (December 2008): 455–78. Parts of chapters 4 and 6 appeared in "Japan's Ocean Policy: Still the Reactive State?" *Pacific Affairs* 83, no. 2 (Summer 2010): 307–26. I am grateful to these publishers for permission to use this material here.

Finally, a special debt is owed to my friends and family, particularly Caroline, my lovely and patient wife.

Acronyms

ANRE	Agency for Natural Resources and Energy, Japan
ASDF	Air Self-Defense Force, Japan
ASEAN	Association of Southeast Asian Nations
CMS	China Maritime Surveillance
CNOOC	China National Offshore Oil Company
CCP	Chinese Communist Party
DPJ	Democratic Party of Japan
DWF	distant water fishery
EEZ	exclusive economic zone
EFZ	exclusive fisheries zone
FLEC	Fisheries Law Enforcement Command, China
JCG	Japan Coast Guard
JDA	Japanese Defense Agency
JDZ	joint development zone
LDP	Liberal Democratic Party, Japan
LTC	Law on the Territorial Sea and the Contiguous Zone
MAFF	Ministry of Agriculture, Forestry, and Fisheries, Japan
METI	Ministry of Economy, Trade, and Industry, Japan
MFA	Ministry of Foreign Affairs, China
MOFA	Ministry of Foreign Affairs, Japan
MSA	Maritime Safety Agency, Japan
MSDF	Maritime Self-Defense Force, Japan
MSR	marine scientific research
MVM	maritime value matrix
NFFC	National Federation of Fisheries Cooperatives, Japan
ODA	official development assistance
PLAN	People's Liberation Army Navy, China
PRC	People's Republic of China

PMZ	Provisional Measures Zone
SLOC	sea line of communication
UNCLOS	United Nations Convention on the Law of the Sea

Introduction

Disorder at Sea?

ON SEPTEMBER 7, 2010, a Chinese fishing boat collided with a Japanese Coast Guard (JCG) vessel in the East China Sea. The collision took place near a group of islands called Senkaku in Japan and Diaoyu in China. Totaling an area of 7 square kilometers, the five islets and nearby rock formations are 120 nautical miles northeast of Taiwan and approximately 120 nautical miles southwest of Okinawa. As all three of these governments claim sovereignty, all argue their fishermen are entitled to fish near the islands. The ensuing diplomatic crisis paralyzed the China–Japan relationship as Beijing decried the recklessness of the Japanese vessel and the detention of the Chinese crew by the JCG. Tokyo argued that the JCG was enforcing Japan's maritime rights against a reckless captain who was fishing illegally. Japanese authorities subsequently released the captain without filing criminal charges, but not before China appeared to curtail the export of rare earth elements—a vital input in Japanese manufactured electronics—and anti-Japanese demonstrations raged across several Chinese cities. The administration of Kan Naoto was accused of backing down in the face of naked Chinese aggression. Nevertheless, the incident caused Washington to restate its view that though it did not take a position on the sovereignty of the disputed islands, they did come under the purview of the United States–Japan alliance.

Two years later, tensions again surfaced when the governor of Tokyo, the outspoken conservative politician Ishihara Shintaro, attempted to purchase the Senkaku/Diaoyu Islands from their private owner. To prevent the islands from falling into the hands of a man bent on ruining the Sino-Japanese relationship, the central government of Japan bought the islands for itself. Despite these seemingly benign intentions, Chinese society was incensed. Chinese consumers boycotted Japanese goods, the Chinese government dispatched armed ships to the islands, and Chinese nationals turned on their own for using Japanese products.[1]

These incidents mark the low point of the China–Japan maritime relationship. Both claim sovereignty over the Senkaku/Diaoyu Islands, assert their entitlement to exercise maritime jurisdiction in the surrounding sea area—including the exploitation of marine resources, such as fish and hydrocarbons—and are influenced by domestic political considerations when dealing with crises. In this context it is striking that China and Japan have managed to avoid a military conflict over the islands. This makes the relationship between China and Japan one of the most intriguing in contemporary world politics. The two countries are culturally similar in many ways, yet they are incapable of moving on from historical tragedies; they are economically integrated, yet they seem to be on the brink of a strategic rivalry.[2] In light of the correlation between territorial disputes, rivalry, and war, the management of territorial tensions between China and Japan has considerable importance for the wider bilateral relationship.[3] Indeed, it is now widely anticipated that the tensions surrounding the Senkaku/Diaoyu Islands will trigger a conflict between China and Japan in the East China Sea.[4] This book challenges this conventional wisdom: It explores the origins, depth, and durability of Sino-Japanese maritime cooperation; explains why it has varied across issues and over time; and proposes ways to get the cooperative aspects of the maritime relationship back on track. There is, in fact, more cooperation in the bilateral maritime relationship than is commonly appreciated.

The range of challenges that confront China–Japan relations vary widely.[5] At the political level, disputes over history textbooks, Japanese politicians' visits to the Yasukuni Shrine, Beijing's manipulation of popular anti-Japanese sentiment, and the ongoing process of competitive regionalism are evidence of a politically "cold" relationship.[6] Strategic mistrust plagues the relationship. Beijing is acutely aware of the role that Japan and its US ally would play in a potential Taiwan Strait conflict, and China's military modernization worries Japanese policymakers.[7] Of course, there are grounds for optimism in the economic relationship. China's economic links with Japan predate its opening to the global economy, and many Chinese look to Japan as a model of export-led economic growth. Japan, meanwhile, has cultivated economic relations with China as a means to assure the emergence of a responsible power with a stake in the international order. As a result, integrated production networks, robust direct investment, and bilateral trade underwrite stability in the bilateral relationship.[8]

Nevertheless, the sovereignty dispute over the Senkaku/Diaoyu Islands has plagued the relationship since 1970. Both states made claims to the islands following a report issued by the United Nations–funded Economic Commission for Asia and the Far East, which found that the seabed of the East China Sea "may be one of the most prolific oil reserves in the world."[9] Claims to the islands plagued the negotiations ahead of the normalization of bilateral relations in 1978, and during the 1990s Japanese nationalist groups triggered diplomatic spats by traveling to the islands.[10] In 1996, both parties ratified the UN Convention on the Law of the Sea (UNCLOS), which raised the profile of the seas surrounding the Senkaku/Diaoyu Islands for both states, not least because it created overlapping claims to maritime zones.

The entitlement to rents from the sea created by UNCLOS has made the ocean more useful to coastal states, whereas advances in undersea mining techniques have made once inaccessible resources commercially viable. China's and Japan's economic expansion has simultaneously increased local and global demand for the living and nonliving resources of the sea. Likewise, this economic growth has led to associated rises in military spending, which, due to reliance on the global maritime supply chain, is disproportionately spent on naval assets.[11] This growing maritime awareness is occurring in a complex international political environment. UNCLOS has led to contested jurisdictional entitlements that coexist with overlapping claims to maritime space and competing claims to island territories. Although international law makes it incumbent upon states to settle their disputes peacefully, more often than not states prefer to delay formal negotiations and take steps to strengthen their claims by behaving as though their claims are "correct."

Consequently, military encounters between Chinese and Japanese aircraft and naval and coast guard vessels have been occurring with increased regularity as both states exercise jurisdiction over their claimed maritime space. Chinese marine research and coast guard vessels routinely enter Japanese-claimed waters with growing frequency. As a product of tension over Chinese natural gas installations near the Japanese-claimed area, Chinese enforcement ships have confronted Japanese resource survey ships. Likewise, Japan has tried to keep Chinese protesters and fishermen away from the Senkaku/Diaoyu Islands, with moderate success. Invariably, however, the application of Japanese law against Chinese nationals near the islands brings accusations of illegitimacy from Beijing on the grounds that Chinese citizens are entitled to land on Chinese territory. This pattern has fostered distrust that extends to interactions in uncontested waters as well. On more than one occasion, a Chinese helicopter has flown perilously close to a Japanese destroyer monitoring Chinese naval activity on the high seas. The Sino-Japanese maritime relationship seems to confirm much of the pessimism expressed by some scholars that disputes over resource-rich maritime space are inherently prone to conflict.[12]

However, increased recognition of the material value of the East Asian seas has not translated into explicit conflict between China and Japan. Rather, the two have a track record of cooperation on tense maritime issues in the areas of fisheries exploitation and conservation and hydrocarbon resource exploitation, and one of limited cooperation regarding marine surveys.[13] There is even evidence that they are capable of managing crisis-like tensions in disputed waters. For instance, in 2001, the JCG sank a suspected North Korean spy ship as it fled Japanese waters into the East China Sea. Chinese condemnation was swift and strident.[14] Yet despite elevated tensions over the political symbolism of Japan's first use of force since World War II, China and Japan avoided escalation, and they even managed to agree on the raising of the vessel by the Japanese.[15] Furthermore, the sovereignty dispute over the Senkaku/Diaoyu Islands was generally well managed for much of the past forty years.

Although there is no doubting the importance of the maritime realm for bilateral relations, its impact on future stability is uncertain. On one hand, the East China Sea is likely to be the medium through which a Sino-Japanese military rivalry will be played out. Both countries have become more active naval powers. Although much has been written about China's "Mahanian" turn in naval strategy, it may be Japan that has most altered its strategic posture due to the dispute. Following the detection of the Han submarine in territorial waters in November 2004 and the tension over the Chunxiao gas field in 2007, Japanese ocean specialists, combined with the media, embarked on a lobbying campaign designed to reform Japan's legal institutions with reference to its ocean domain.[16] This marked a clear assertive turn in Japanese maritime policy.

On the other hand, the dispute has not visibly disrupted the trade relationship, one of the most profitable and dynamic in the world; hence, leaders have little incentive to pursue cooperation according to this logic. Scholarly interpretations of China's behavior toward its territorial disputes suggest that Chinese leaders are more likely to compromise on a territorial dispute if they believe it will result in greater internal political stability.[17] This makes the East China Sea dispute an intriguing case, as vocal minorities in China have called for a more assertive stance toward Japan with regard to the Senkaku/Diaoyu Islands, often criticizing Beijing's posture.[18] Although this appears to provide the basis for a more assertive stance, Beijing has also exercised restraint. As a consequence of these seemingly conflicting dynamics, the East China Sea dispute should be considered a least-likely case study in cooperation that may shed light on similar disputes.[19]

This book explores the Sino-Japanese maritime relationship and makes the case that cooperation will endure. This may sound unsurprising in the context of the deep economic interdependence between the two and the deterrent effect of the United States–Japan alliance, but neither of these conditions has prevented maritime tensions.[20] Indeed, these factors explain the absence of conflict over maritime space, but they do not explain why China and Japan have at times incurred costs to cooperate, rather than delay, management of their maritime disputes. Indeed, the cooperative track record between China and Japan in the maritime realm is often overshadowed by the cyclical tensions between the two. Why have China and Japan come so close to war in their disputed waters, yet persistently backed down? How have policymakers successfully negotiated three agreements on issues arising from their overlapping maritime claims? Why have these agreements failed to prevent further tensions? There is no doubt that the importance of maritime areas to Chinese and Japanese leaders is growing. The ocean is seen to provide resources for national development, a medium over which to project power and a domestic legitimizing issue wherein gains are made at the expense of the "other."[21] Despite these conditions, this book maps out how cooperation in the Sino-Japanese maritime relationship has been achieved in the past and how it can be achieved in the future.

How Important Is the Sea?

Disputed territory, as distinct from disputed seas, is clearly a politically salient issue to policymakers and citizens. According to Paul Huth, if leaders expect significant political support for pressing a territorial claim, they are more likely to do so, even if the territory under dispute is strategically irrelevant. Similarly, if they believe that failing to support a long-standing claim could incur domestic political costs, they are reluctant to seek a settlement and may even escalate the dispute if their domestic standing is weak.[22] Democratic states are not necessarily more cooperative; they are less likely to make territorial compromises when the issues at stake are politically salient or when to do so would be domestically unpopular.[23] Thus, the decisions surrounding disputed territories rely not simply on the economic value of a given territory to a state but also on ruling elites' perceptions of their domestic political fate.

This is somewhat unsurprising. Publics feel a strong attachment to national territory because it provides the container within which the "nation" resides.[24] On issues of territorial integrity, therefore, the impact of national identity on foreign policy is similar to that of public opinion on foreign policy.[25] National identity informs a society's perception of its environment and, by extension, the parameters of its domestic and international interests.[26] Polities are more likely to mobilize when confronted with a slight to their territorial identity, and this can limit leaders' willingness to cooperate.[27] Although the material value of disputed territory is certainly one reason for this, the intangible value of territory and the role it plays in a nation's sense of self is another. Existing debates over the importance of disputed space distinguish between easily divisible plots of land, land containing separatist groups, strategically important land, and "sacred spaces."[28] However, these distinctions do not translate well into the analysis on disputed maritime space because a given contested space can simultaneously possess none, some, or all of these characteristics. Assessing the importance of maritime space to policymakers thus presents a daunting analytical challenge.

Furthermore, though the relationship between national identity and territory is fairly straightforward, it is considerably less obvious in the maritime domain. For instance, international lawyers consider territory and maritime space to be distinct concepts; states have sovereignty over land and limited jurisdiction over the sea. An island is clearly part of one's country, but the waters around it are not typically assigned much importance; scholars typically assume that maritime space is not inherently useful to states or at a minimum is less important than disputed land.[29] In this view "territorial issues are generally salient for both tangible and intangible reasons, whereas maritime and river issues generally lack the intangible dimension and are less salient overall."[30] Maritime space, therefore, does not engender the ideational and political salience required to become indivisible.[31] As UNCLOS was being drafted, many analysts were sanguine about the prospects of the settlement of possible overlapping boundaries.[32]

On the contrary, however, in reality maritime disputes are far from peripheral. Despite their lack of intrinsic value, disputes over "useless islands" have been a recurring source of tension worldwide.[33] Maritime space has long been a source of discord among nation-states, particularly over rights to fisheries. These disputes remain the most frequent source of military conflict between democratic states.[34] Some scholars expected the institutionalization of the ocean regime under UNCLOS to reduce the likelihood of conflict over maritime boundary issues. However, recent research suggests that "UNCLOS members challenging the maritime status quo are more likely to employ militarized force to pursue their issue-related goals."[35] The value of maritime space is thus a function of humanity's "social construction" of the world's oceans.[36]

Maritime Space in the China–Japan Relationship

As a matter of international law, China and Japan disagree on the fundamental legal principle upon which to base maritime delimitation claims. China claims a continental shelf for the whole of its natural prolongation as far as the Okinawa Trough and has submitted evidence to this effect to the United Nations.[37] UNCLOS also allows exclusive economic zone (EEZ) claims of 200 nautical miles—which are favored by geographically disadvantaged states with little or no continental shelf, like Japan. In the event of an overlap with a neighboring state, Japan claims an EEZ as far as a median line bisecting the claims. China does not recognize Japan's median line in the East China Sea, because it was declared "unilaterally."

This disagreement over delimitation lies at the core of Sino-Japanese maritime tensions, but it stems from the sovereignty dispute over the Senkaku/Diaoyu Islands. Both China and Japan claim the islands on irredentist grounds.[38] China claims that the islands were named and used by China during the Ming Dynasty, whereas Japan argues that the islands were *terra nullius* when it occupied them in 1895. Sovereignty over the disputed Senkaku/Diaoyu Islands could push any final delimitation line in a favorable direction for the owner—westward for Japan and eastward for China.[39] Maritime tensions did not visibly disrupt the relationship until the publication of the aforementioned UN report in 1969, after which the issue became politically salient under very particular circumstances.

Indeed, the relationship between the importance of maritime space and the China–Japan bilateral relationship has been quite varied. For instance, despite its heavy reliance on imported oil, Japan has not embarked on large-scale offshore development in the East China Sea, even when oil prices were relatively high. China, an emerging fisheries power, agreed to share jurisdiction over fisheries in the East China Sea with Japan in 1997, despite the fact that this led to a reduction in catch levels and a dramatic increase in the unemployment rate among Chinese fishermen. Simultaneously, China has resisted sharing jurisdiction over the exploitation of the resource in the seabed in the same area. Japan has tacitly accepted the presence of Chinese marine survey, intelligence gathering, and military vessels in its waters, in stark contrast to its violent response to North Korean vessels that have been spotted without permission. Likewise, Japan has tacitly accepted, and in some cases funded, Chinese development of the East China Sea's resources, yet reacted sharply to one such effort in May 2004.

Despite these paradoxes, most explanations of these issues fall back on the direct link between the salience of a particular dimension of disputed maritime space—be it resources, nationalism, or strategic value—and link that importance to confrontational behavior.[40] By contrast, this book advances a more nuanced explanation of the pattern of Sino-Japanese interaction at sea that begins with the assumption that policymakers seek to achieve objectives in their contested maritime space, and that these functions are informed by an assessment of how policymakers perceive the salience of their maritime environment. Viewed this way, the Sino-Japanese maritime relationship is certainly characterized by brinkmanship, but not without a considerable degree of cooperation.

Cooperation and the Salience of Maritime Space to China and Japan

This book is concerned with the origins, nature, and durability of cooperation between China and Japan on issues where there is some degree of conflicting interest between them. China and Japan have arrived at agreements to manage tensions in four areas of their disputed maritime space—over the Senkaku/Diaoyu Islands in 1978 and 1996, over fisheries in 1997, over marine research in 2001, and over gas and oil exploration in 2008. It could be argued that these do not amount to cooperation, but instead are merely temporary peaks in an ongoing strategy of provocation and delay as the two jostle for the upper hand in their maritime boundary dispute.[41] However, this perspective overlooks the fact that on each occasion Beijing and Tokyo have articulated some kind of consensus on a point of difference and, however briefly, have adjusted their behavior in accord with the actual or anticipated preferences of the other party.[42] The cases of cooperation explored in the pages that follow cover the spectrum between explicit, formal, treaty-based cooperation to informal *notes verbale*, to tacit points of consensus. The comparison of cooperative dynamics across these cases within a common issue area, such as disputed maritime space, should shed light on the dynamics of cooperation under these scope conditions. Most important, in light of the deterioration of the bilateral maritime relationship since 2010, this book can shed light on pathways to renew the cooperative nature of Sino-Japanese maritime relations.

The subsequent failure or lapse of a cooperative agreement is an analytically separate, but related, question. Each agreement merely addressed the symptoms, not the causes, of the underlying problem created by the delimitation dispute in the East China Sea. As a result, the latter two agreements, over survey activity and resource development, have failed to build a sustained adjustment to behavior. This inconsistent pattern of behavior is one appealing factor about exploring cooperation between China and Japan; there is variation along the dependent variable. A second appealing factor is that the challenges created by disputed maritime boundaries, such as the contested jurisdiction in the East China Sea, are not limited to the security realm or the economic realm.[43] Traditionally, the academic literature on cooperation has classified issues subject to cooperation under different issue "structures." Security issues, for instance, are characterized by concerns over relative gains, which militate against cooperation.[44] Economic and trade issues, by contrast, are more germane to absolute gains, which facilitate cooperative outcomes.[45] The challenge of analyzing maritime space is that the challenges that arise from contested claims to maritime jurisdiction contain a host of issues that do not fit within this dichotomy. Some policy challenges, such as the sustainable exploitation of living and nonliving resources, are reminiscent of collective action problems among states with a shared interest in sustainable efforts. Yet, under certain conditions, these issues have gained a zero-sum character. By contrast, the strategic interaction between the two powers at sea is developing a more aggressive tone; yet both have backed down when confronted. This has not precluded reaching cooperative agreements, but it appears to have limited their implementation. There is thus a rich variety of cooperative behavior for analysis.

Structure of the Book

Chapter 1 outlines the analytical framework that underwrites the analysis in the subsequent case study chapters. There is little consensus in the literature about what drives state policy toward disputed maritime boundaries, given that these present a variety of challenges to policymakers that are of greater and lesser degrees of salience. Chapter 1 outlines the maritime value matrix, a 2X2 matrix that categorizes how leaders perceive the importance of maritime space to their national objectives.[46] The matrix makes two sets of distinctions. First, it distinguishes between the material and symbolic aspects of disputed maritime space. Second, it distinguishes between those aspects of disputed maritime space that are understood by both parties and those that are unique to one claimant. This allows the matrix to derive expectations of issues that are more or less germane to cooperation. By illustrating the function of disputed space for leaders, the analysis identifies factors or constituencies that affect leaders' perceptions of the costs of cooperation over continued inaction. Policymakers weigh these costs against their reference point, or their interpretation of the "normal" state of affairs in the maritime relationship. By deconstructing the salience of maritime space for policymakers, the book offers insights into how mixed-stake territorial problems can be managed.

The case studies were selected because they are the only incidents when Beijing and Tokyo tacitly or explicitly altered their preferences in accord with those of the other party. One possible case that was considered and discarded was the North Korea spy ship incident of December 2001. China allowed Japan to raise the sunken ship from its waters, which could be interpreted as an alignment of preferences. However, this case was discarded because it appears to be a case of crisis bargaining, rather than an issue of maritime jurisdiction. Each case follows a change in the Sino-Japanese maritime relationship, which resulted from China's emergence as a maritime power. This shift necessitated changes in how China and Japan interacted over their maritime realm.

The first case study explains how China and Japan managed tensions over the Senkaku/Diaoyu Islands and finds evidence of tacit cooperation. The second case study explores the management of fisheries issues following the ratification of UNCLOS by China and Japan in 1996 and argues that successful cooperative outcomes stem in large part from long-standing interaction between policymakers. Chapter 4 explores the circumstances that led to an agreement governing research activities at sea in 2001 and explains why, in light of subsequent Chinese violations, the agreement failed to solve the problem. Chapter 5 explores the confrontational dynamics over the disputed Chunxiao gas field located in the middle of the East China Sea. The analysis of the circumstances surrounding the 2008 agreement indicate once again the importance of interaction between policymakers and highlight the importance of decoupling material issues from symbolic ones.

The findings suggest that, contrary to pessimistic assessments, the two countries have been able to cooperate on contested jurisdiction when material issues have been separated from the more symbolic aspects of their relationship. Nevertheless, the legacy of ideational connections to maritime space led to coercive rather than reciprocal approaches to cooperation. In all cases cooperation occurred following domestic pressure in Japan for a more assertive posture, which in the case of marine research and hydrocarbon resource development underwrote coercive strategies such as the application of sanctions, threats to proceed unilaterally, and military posturing. Cooperation follows crisis—typically, after Japan awakes to changes in its maritime environment brought about by China's rise. Greater frequency of interactions between Chinese and Japanese negotiators is consistent with more successful, and more binding, cooperative outcomes. China and Japan are able to manage escalatory pressures through recognized and established practices aimed at managing tensions through a cooperative process that seeks to remove or sidestep issue areas that are the source of tension. The fisheries agreement was the most successful, and it followed more than fifty years of interaction between Chinese and Japanese authorities. By contrast, the marine survey agreement, which has been the least successful, was the product of three meetings between officials. Strategic concerns, which are characterized by both material and symbolic importance, confront the highest barriers to cooperation.

Chapter 6 identifies the prospects for future cooperation vis-à-vis the residual issues of interaction at sea and resource development. It proposes a trade-off that allows each party to meet its objectives for disputed space, without sacrificing its claims to maritime jurisdiction. The book concludes with two main findings, one theoretical, one empirical. As to the former, the separation of symbolic from material territorial functions is analytically useful (if artificial) inasmuch as it allows the analyst to observe the primary drivers and limits of cooperation. Symbolic functions of disputed space often limit cooperation over purely material objectives, but they are insufficient to provide a rationale for the escalation of a dispute. Simultaneously, policymakers can be capable of cooperation over the material aspects of disputed space if they can separate these from symbolic concerns. There is thus cause for optimism in the management of sensitive issues in the Sino-Japanese relationship, provided the leaders of each state can exercise the necessary leadership to manage their respective nationalist pressures. The central empirical finding is also counterintuitive. China, more often than Japan, has incurred costs to its claim to pursue cooperation. China's willingness to compromise was a function of its perceptions of Japanese willingness to escalate the issue. China thus cooperates to protect the gains it had made: to defend a perceived threat to the status quo. This, in turn, provides a rationale for a more proactive Japanese posture toward its maritime realm, which it has been pursuing since 2005. Ultimately, the book proposes a way to avoid major conflict between Asia's two dominant indigenous maritime powers. This is critical because "how Japan and China handle their maritime disputes, and their maritime strategic posture, should be a guide to the disposition of the two governments toward each other in military strategic affairs."[47]

Notes

1. Qin and Wong, "Smashed Skull Serves as Grim Symbol of Seething Patriotism."

2. This description stems from He, "Ripe for Cooperation or Rivalry?" 162–97.

3. Colaresi, Rasler, and Thompson, *Strategic Rivalries in World Politics*; Vasquez, "Distinguishing Rivals," 531–58; Rasler and Thompson, "Explaining Rivalry Escalation to War," 503–30.

4. Rudd, "East Asia . . . A Maritime Balkans"; Pomfret, "Risk of War in the Far East"; Zhou, "Sino-Japan Ties Not Easy to Improve"; Rachman, "Shadow of 1914 Falls over the Pacific."

5. Wan, *Sino-Japanese Relations.*

6. Taniguchi, "Cold Peace," 445–57; Feng, "Factors Shaping Sino-Japanese Relations"; Kojima, "Japan's China Policy," 33–47.

7. Wu, "End of the Silver Lining," 119–30; Mochizuki, "Japan's Shifting Strategy toward the Rise of China," 739–76; Roy, "Stirring Samurai, Disapproving Dragon," 86–101.

8. Fan, "Searching for Common Interests between China and Japan," 375–82; Xia, "Prospects of China–Japan Relations," 204–21.

9. Emery et al., "Geological Structure," 40–41.

10. Tretiak, "Sino-Japanese Treaty of 1978," 1235–49; Cheng, "Normalization of Sino-Japanese Relations," 245–72.

11. Ball, "Arms and Affluence," 78–112; Bitzinger, "New Arms Race?" 32–37.

12. Salameh, "China, Oil and the Risk of Regional Conflict," 133–46; Valencia, "Energy and Insecurity in Asia," 85–106; Calder, *Asia's Deadly Triangle.*

13. Valencia and Amae, "Regime Building in the East China Sea," 189–208; Gao and Wu, "Key Issues in the East China Sea," 34–38.

14. Xin, "'Justifiable Defense' Irregular."

15. For the Chinese and Japanese version of events, respectively, see Shih, "Casting Doubts on Japan's Sinking of Suspicious Ship"; and JDA, *Defense of Japan 2002,* 125–26. For the details, see Tkacik, "How the PLA Sees North Korea," 163–64.

16. Akiyama, "Use of Seas and Management of Ocean Space," 1–28; Manicom, "Japan's Ocean Policy," 307–26.

17. Fravel, "Regime Insecurity and International Cooperation," 46–83.

18. Chung, *Domestic Politics,* chap. 3.

19. On the least likely cases, see George and Bennett, *Case Studies and Theory Development,* 120–22; and Eckstein, "Case Study and Theory in Political Science," 118–19.

20. Manicom and O'Neil, "Sino-Japanese Strategic Relations," 213–32.

21. He, "History, Chinese Nationalism and the Emerging Sino-Japanese Conflict," 1–24; ICG, "Northeast Asia's Undercurrents of Conflict."

22. Huth, *Standing Your Ground,* 182; Walter, "Explaining the Intractability of Territorial Conflict," 137–53; Chiozza and Choi, "Guess Who Did What," 251–78.

23. Huth and Allee, "Domestic Political Accountability," 775–80; Hensel, "Contentious Issues and World Politics," 106.

24. Anderson, *Imagined Communities*; Hobsbawn, *Nations and Nationalism,* 177. On debates surrounding the formation of national identity, see Haas, "Nationalism," 505–45; and Brown, *Contemporary Nationalism.* On the explicit relationship between identity, territory, and war, see Midlarsky, "Identity and International Conflict," 25–58.

25. Risse-Kappen, "Public Opinion, Domestic Structure and Foreign Policy," 479–512. This is not to suggest that the two are identical.

26. Prizel, *National Identity and Foreign Policy,* 14.

27. Allee and Huth, "When Are Governments Able to Reach Negotiated Settlement Agreements?" 13–32.

28. For these distinctions, see Hassner, *War on Sacred Grounds,* 43.

29. Huth, *Standing Your Ground,* 26.

30. Hensel et al., "Bones of Contention," 138–39.

31. Goddard, "Uncommon Ground," 35–68; Newman, "Real Spaces, Symbolic Spaces," 3–34.

32. Buzan, "Sea of Troubles?"

33. This term comes from Kimura and Welch, "Specifying 'Interests,'" 233.

34. Mitchell and Prins, "Beyond Territorial Contiguity," 169–83; Hellman and Herborth, "Fishing in the Mild West," 481–506.

35. Nemeth et al., "Ruling the Sea," 3.

36. Steinberg, *Social Construction of the Ocean.*

37. Greenfield, *China's Practice in the Law of the Sea,* 119. See Division for Ocean Affairs and the Law of the Sea, "Submission by the PRC Concerning the Outer Limits of the Continental Shelf," December 14, 2012.

38. Suganuma, *Sovereign Rights.*

39. Valencia, "East China Sea Dispute," 127–67. This is contingent on what effect each party determines the islands to have on delimitation.

40. See, e.g., Hsiung, "Sea Power, Law of the Sea," 133–53; Cole, "China and Japan Turn the Screw," 2–5; and Maritime Forces Pacific, Royal Canadian Navy, "Strategic Isles of the East China Sea."

41. Fravel, "Explaining Stability," 144–64.

42. This definition of cooperation is based on Axelrod and Keohane, "Achieving Cooperation under Anarchy," 226.

43. One effort has catalogued fifty-one factors that complicate solutions to a disputed ocean boundary. See Johnston and Valencia, *Pacific Ocean Boundary Problems.*

44. Grieco, *Cooperation among Nations.*

45. Grieco, "Anarchy and the Limits of Cooperation," 151–71.

46. Finnemore, *National Interests in International Society.*

47. Austin and Harris, *Japan and Greater China,* 99.

CHAPTER ONE

Cooperation and the Value of Maritime Space

THIS IS A BOOK about the ebb and flow of cooperation between two rivals over disputed maritime space. The analysis compares five attempts at cooperation in the East China Sea in the areas of disputed sovereignty, fisheries management, marine surveys, and hydrocarbon resource development, and it draws lessons for remaining challenges in the Sino-Japanese maritime relationship. The theoretical concern relates to the impact of the value of disputed space on cooperative efforts between rival states. The findings may shed light on some of the most pressing issues in East Asian international relations. Why are disputes over tiny rocks seen to be intractable? Why does cooperation over fisheries endure and cooperation over resource exploitation stagnate? The answers to these questions can inform expectations and policies about ongoing dispute management processes and cooperation over emerging issues in the Sino-Japanese maritime relationship.

This focus on cooperation represents a new approach to the study of China–Japan maritime relations. Recurrent political tensions and several close calls between Chinese and Japanese ships are oft-cited evidence that China and Japan cannot cooperate over disputed maritime space.[1] Although Chinese and Japanese leaders face powerful economic disincentives for conflict, this does explain why the two have actively sought to cooperate over different aspects of disputed maritime space. Maritime tensions between the two are related to the growing importance of the ocean to both states' development goals.[2] In addition to the material value of the sea brought by living and nonliving resource exploitation, the Senkaku/Diaoyu Islands have taken on a domestic political relevance that is built on nationalist discourses between the two states, which extends to constituencies within government. Moreover, in recent years, the East China Sea has become a strategically vital area for policymakers in Beijing and Tokyo. China's strategy for the "near seas" is inextricably linked with Beijing's posture toward Taiwan and the question of national reunification.[3] Japan by contrast does not trust that its economic fortunes, which rely on open seas, could be assured if China were the dominant regional navy. In light of this Sino-Japanese rivalry, the fact that the two have managed to avoid overt conflict over their maritime boundary dispute is noteworthy.[4] As is illustrated below, many analysts interpret this importance as creating incentives for conflict between the two.

In light of these apparent incentives for confrontation, an explanation of Sino-Japanese maritime behavior must be rooted in the salience of disputed space to policymakers. The theoretical framework outlined in this chapter links the importance of disputed space with policymakers' objectives for that space. Questions of territoriality are of utmost importance to states in an anarchic international system. Contested boundaries also raise issues that do not threaten the integrity of the state, but that may threaten the interests of constituencies within the state, as well as the domestic political prerogatives of leaders themselves. As a result, there is a great degree of variance in the salience of disputed maritime space to policymakers. Furthermore, this salience may not be identical between two states. States may both have an interest in a material aspect of a disputed space, but for reasons of onshore resource wealth, or trade relationships with other states, may have a less acute need. This would surely affect the salience of this material issue to policymakers. Likewise, policymakers who have invested a great deal of their domestic credibility in the resolution of a symbolic political issue are more likely to take risks to ensure that comes to pass than policymakers who have not. Any assessment of the salience of disputed space to state leaders needs to be able to account for these differences. The importance of space, filtered through the domestic and international framing exercises conducted by both parties, informs policymakers' interpretation of the territorial status quo and in turn affects their reaction to perceived challenges to it.

Debates over the Salience of Maritime Space

According to Jean-Marc Blanchard, states derive both material and ideational functions from disputed territories, which are derived from how they perceive its value. These functions, in turn, inform state objectives toward a given territory.[5] These need to be identified in order to understand a cooperative interaction in which two states agree to compromise on some aspect of disputed space that affects state goals.[6] However, the importance of maritime space has not been well integrated into explanations of the Sino-Japanese maritime relationship. Some argue that the East China Sea dispute is driven by material factors, such as resource demand or geopolitical calculations, while others stress ideational factors, such as national identity and domestic political legitimacy. These works have typically not taken the long view and instead have reflected the state of the dispute at the time of writing. Throughout the 1990s, before the discovery of commercially viable hydrocarbons but at the height of nationalist activity, the ideational school was dominant. Subsequently, as China began to exploit resources in the East China Sea, the material dimension became more accepted as a motive. Consequently, little research has been done on the interaction between these two motives because they have not occupied the same temporal space.[7]

According to the ideational perspective, compromise cannot be pursued for fear of alienating nationalist constituencies in their respective societies.[8] Political elites in Japan and Taiwan have exploited the dispute for domestic political gain during the electoral cycle.[9] Cooperation is further complicated by deteriorating mutual perceptions of the other. Japanese people have become increasingly wary of their authoritarian neighbor, and Chinese popular perception of Japan has deteriorated as a consequence of a legitimizing exercise by the Chinese Communist Party (CCP).[10] Likewise, Japanese politicians earn political currency by visiting national symbols such as the Yasukuni Shrine to demonstrate their support for an assertive, independent Japan. This in turn feeds the Chinese perception that Japan is unrepentant for its past invasions of China.[11]

Viewed through Robert Putnam's two-level games thesis, Chien-peng Chung argues that compromises on China's territorial disputes have occurred when there has been little opposition from domestic constituencies.[12] Consequently, formal negotiations on the Senkaku/Diaoyu dispute have not occurred because of the high degree of nationalist attachment, and conflict has been avoided because the islands are not believed to be valuable in a material sense.[13] Cooperation is thus only expected on material aspects of disputed space, like fisheries.[14] Therefore, "the prominence of political morality in Sino-Japanese relations comes at the cost of a pragmatic attitude toward issues of contention."[15] This sentiment is politically significant on two levels. First, it could be indicative of genuine popular opposition to the interests of the rival state, which in turn could constrain policymakers' attempts to control the escalation of political tension or pursue settlement options. Second, these nationalist sentiments are not limited to the general public but are also scattered throughout the policy apparatus in both countries. This creates sections of government that may have suspicious or hostile views of the other state, which in turn affects these bureaucratic arms' preferred policy outcomes. According to Michael Yahuda, these mutually reinforcing negative images have created a lack of empathy for the other, which in turn has hindered the creation of institutions or constituencies that publicly favor improved relations, as predicted by the liberal internationalist notion of interdependence.[16] Consequently, due to their long-standing inimical historical relationship, Chinese and Japanese leaders appear to confront numerous political barriers to territorial settlement.[17]

Likewise, those that emphasize the material salience view it as an incentive for conflict. Policymakers in both countries believe that the ability to use their ocean domain to their advantage is integral to the future prosperity of their state. Japan is one of the world's largest consumers of fish products, and formerly was the world's greatest fishing nation. That distinction has recently passed to China, which has emerged as a global fishing power to meet domestic demand that has risen with standards of living. Although bilateral fisheries management between the two has a long pedigree, overfishing and transboundary fish stocks have created a disincentive for management of fishing in disputed waters. In semi-enclosed seas such as the East and South China seas, as well as the Sea of Japan, this created a raft of overlapping areas of coastal state authority. According to this view, overlapping maritime claims created by UNCLOS are highly volatile due to the growing energy needs of Asian states and a concomitant growth in defense spending.[18] China and Japan are both sufficiently desperate for energy that either party would consider the use of military force to secure access to East China Sea resources.[19] According to Selig Harrison, China's growing energy needs will force it to drill in the East China Sea, regardless of whether or not Japan agrees to jointly develop the resources buried there.[20] Analysts argue that the resource value of the East China Sea as a whole indicates that it could provide for the long-term energy security of either party.[21] Even those who view energy security as an area of nascent cooperation between the two are pessimistic about the likelihood of cooperation over resource development in the East China Sea.[22] This perspective is strengthened by a growing "energy nationalism" across Asia and by the fact that neither Japan nor China displayed an interest in the sovereignty of the Senkaku/Diaoyu Islands until a bullish energy assessment was released in 1969.[23]

A third conception of value is focused on the strategic importance of maritime space. Rising military spending is evidence of state resolve to use military force to secure access to resources.[24] China's impressive economic growth is predicated on secure sea lanes and access to affordable seaborne resource imports, which has seen a departure from China's historically continentalist orientation.[25] Chinese strategists now talk in Mahanian terms about the importance of coastal defenses, sea lines of communication (SLOCs), and blue water naval aspirations.[26] Japan, for its part, has always been concerned about the security of its sea lanes, and the protection of these served as the pretext for expanding the operational scope of Maritime Self-Defense Force (MSDF) missions in the 1980s. Japan has historically been willing to free-ride on the global SLOC security provided by the US Navy, but the emergence of China as a naval power presents a challenge to Japanese interests that are geographically well within the operational radius of the MSDF. This has led to a proliferation of maritime activity in the confined and contested space of the East China Sea. Because navies from both states are increasing their operational parameters and capabilities, the possibility of an incident near the disputed gas fields is elevated.[27] Some scholars view the dispute as a rationale for the acquisition of more advanced military hardware, while others argue that these resource considerations are subservient to a broader strategic rationale for a more robust maritime presence in the region by both parties.[28] In either case, it is clear that Chinese and Japanese military and civilian agencies are becoming more active on East Asian waters, which militates against cooperation.

The latest phase of East China Sea tensions suggests that this development bodes poorly for stability. In 2010, Chinese vessels chased Japanese survey ships from contested waters and the Chinese navy held a series of naval training exercises in waters south of Okinawa. Japan did not contest the legalities of the exercises, but it protested the close proximity with which a Chinese helicopter passed its destroyer.[29] Likewise, a Japanese survey vessel was pursued and harassed by a Chinese vessel while conducting a resource survey in a contested area of the East China Sea.[30] The fact that Chinese vessels conduct similar activities in waters near Japan that it does not claim is a source of irritation for Japanese officials. One could argue that a new phase is emerging in the dispute in which the defining characteristic of the dispute will be tensions over the interaction between government vessels of all stripes in contested waters. As with other aspects of disputed space, however, there are important cooperative processes here that are often overlooked, which are outlined in chapter 6.

Therefore, according to the current literature, the importance of disputed space yields one policy outcome: confrontation. This approach naturally has a number of shortcomings. First, the ideational argument assumes that the disputed islands are worthless in a material sense to Chinese and Japanese leaders.[31] The reduction in the territorial imperative for Asian states is thus related to a reduction in the material value of land in developing Asian economies.[32] However, the disputed Senkaku/Diaoyu Islands are linked by UNCLOS to the wider resource wealth of the East China Sea, as well as to questions about the conduct of vessels at sea. The former concern is illustrated by the discovery of commercial resources in the East China Sea in 2003, which triggered a new phase of the dispute in which policymakers in Beijing and Tokyo, rather than nationalist groups or hard-line politicians, raised tensions over the area. The latter concern is illustrated by disputes over jurisdictional authority regarding marine research activities and naval activity in contested waters, which has a direct bearing on the national security of both states. This is important because the benign predictions of the ideational school assume that elites are disinterested in the material value of the East China Sea. Rather, by 2005, both elites and the populace at large perceived the salience of the East China Sea through a conflated material and ideational lens.[33] Furthermore, leaders may choose to incur costs to their own domestic standing in order to pursue cooperation. For example, when nationalist fervor over the islands reached a fever pitch in 1996, elites in China weathered nationalist criticism to prevent deterioration of relations with Japan.[34] There may be limits to the influence of "othering" on cooperation.

Second, the material perspective views China as the more insecure state with regard to energy security, and thus the more aggressive, despite the fact that it is less reliant on oil and gas imports than Japan.[35] The fact that Japan has pursued an equally state-centric approach to energy security and has greater import reliance than China is overlooked. Few scholars expect Japan to pursue an assertive posture toward offshore resource development. However, this is precisely what Japan did upon discovering a Chinese drilling installation in the East China Sea in 2004.

Existing approaches do a poor job of conceptualizing the impact of issue salience of disputed space on decision making. The importance of disputed space to state leaders is dynamic, not static. Different aspects of a disputed space may have more or less value to state leaders at a particular time and under particular conditions. For example, China and Japan did not dispute the material dimension of the East China Sea during the early to mid-1990s, possibly because the hydrocarbon potential was not proven, global prices were low, and neither party's foreign policy agenda was characterized by acute energy insecurity. However, under different conditions, between 2004 and 2008, this aspect of the dispute became quite active. The ideational perspective, that the dispute was driven by nationalism, held for much of the 1990s and early 2000s. However, as the nationalist sentiment provoked by popular anti-Japanese feelings became a liability for the CCP following anti-Japanese protests in April 2005, Beijing was careful to rein in this sentiment following the agreement on joint development in June 2008.[36] This book unites two models of territorial value to conceptualize how state leaders value maritime space at a given time and, by extension, identify their objectives for disputed space.

Choosing to Cooperate

Policymakers face three choices when confronted with challenges to their territorial sovereignty—or maritime jurisdiction: They can cooperate, escalate the dispute, or do nothing.[37] Of course, all three options may not be available at a given time. It is conceivable that any one of these choices could be impossible in a practical sense. There may be a number of structural and proximate reasons why one or another may not be an option at a given time, and this is true in the case of China and Japan. Escalation and cooperation require diplomatic and military capabilities that a state may or may not have at its disposal. Doing nothing may incur accusations of apathy from domestic audiences. Therefore, the importance of maritime space is linked to policymakers' perception of the opportunities and constraints presented by the maritime milieu.

This book is concerned with how policymakers choose cooperation when challenged by a perceived shift in the status quo, how their rival chooses to reciprocate, and how the two align their preferences, however briefly. This is achieved by comparing the dynamics of cooperation across four issue areas in an effort to understand why leaders incur material and ideational costs to pursue cooperation over their disputed maritime space. The explanation of cooperation between adversaries contained in this book is structured along three variables that order the empirical content of the book. The first variable considers the decision to cooperate and is a function of policymakers' assessments of the territorial status quo and its relationship to their objectives for the disputed space. The second considers the depth of the resulting agreement—the process by which leaders align their preferences. The third considers the agreement's durability.

Although the literature on cooperation is extensive and covers a wide range of behaviors, a common definition endures. Cooperation occurs when states explicitly or tacitly "adjust their behavior to the actual or anticipated preferences of others through a process of policy coordination."[38] This book assumes that states initiate this decision process in response to a perceived territorial challenge that affects how policymakers perceive their maritime environment. States' behavior is informed by how policymakers perceive the salience of the dimension of maritime space that has been challenged—fisheries, resources, islands, navigation—by the rival claimant relative to the costs of inaction.

The book is not concerned with the dynamics of either escalation or delay. Recent work suggests that cooperation, particularly the kind of dispute management efforts pursued by China and Japan, can be better conceptualized as delay rather than meaningful cooperation.[39] Delay is to do nothing beyond reiterating claims through public declarations, offering neither concession nor using force.[40] States can delay by participating in negotiations, while refusing to compromise. However, this description places a very high empirical bar for knowing whether cooperation is meaningful or simply a delaying tactic. Short of accessing the internal discussions of Chinese leaders, there is no way to know how genuine their efforts at cooperation are. Interviews with Japanese officials suggest a mixed picture of their perspective on Chinese intentions. Japanese hawks doubt the substance of Chinese overtures, but officials involved in the execution of these agreements interpret their intentions as genuine, even if they have become more skeptical as the agreements have stagnated.[41] As for Japan, delay seems like a strategy that is beyond the capacity of Japanese leaders, who have often been accused of being reactive rather than proactive in their ocean policy.[42] Defining delay in this way also obscures some of the more interesting questions about cooperation. All cases of cooperation discussed herein reflect an effort to adjust behavior to the preferences of the other; what differs is their origin, depth, and durability, the study of which may reveal important clues for future cooperative efforts. In the case of China, there is simply no way of knowing if cooperation is in fact delay, and delay seems to be a strategy that is beyond the capacity of Japanese leaders. Cooperation must be taken at face value.

The dynamics of escalation are not considered for three reasons. First, a number of compelling structural conditions militate against the escalation of Sino-Japanese maritime disputes.[43] These include the deep economic interdependence between the two,[44] the deterrent effect of the United States–Japan alliance, constitutional restrictions on the use of force in Japan,[45] the stated Chinese foreign policy priority of maintaining a peaceful external environment, and the norm against war for the purposes of territorial aggrandizement.[46] None of these conditions has prevented maritime tensions from recurring, nor have they amounted to sufficient incentive to embark on lasting cooperation.[47] Although these factors may explain the absence of conflict over maritime space, they do not explain why China and Japan have at times incurred costs to cooperate, rather than delay resolution of their maritime disputes. Furthermore, the case studies that follow indicate that in addition to these structural limits on escalation, there are a number of proximate barriers to escalation in each case.

Second, in light of these structural barriers to escalation, there are few empirical data upon which to draw to argue that conflict escalation is a realistic choice entertained by policymakers in Beijing or Tokyo. Nevertheless, China and Japan have engaged in dangerous signaling via their military forces and have at times made abstract threats. This book thus views threats and demonstrations of force as types of coercive cooperation, which are used to signal red lines in an ongoing process of territorial bargaining over disputed space.

Third, "escalation" over maritime space is more difficult to conceptualize than that over disputed territory. The ocean cannot easily be conquered and occupied by a state through force, a typical indicator of escalation. User states, including nonparties to the dispute, retain access rights to maritime space, such as navigational freedom and the ability to lay submarine cables. Deviation from this norm would bring with it widespread international condemnation and risk intervention by the United States—witnessed, for example, in the Gulf of Sidra in 1986. The fact that maritime space cannot be "captured" in the conventional sense further reinforces the characterization of state behavior as degrees of cooperation, rather than a simple cooperation/conflict dichotomy.

Therefore, rather than seeing maritime space as something that states seek to control exclusively, and in the interest of taking cooperation at face value, it is more useful to think of boundary and jurisdictional issues in terms of a status quo defined by articulated geographic claims and established norms of behavior, which can be challenged by states that try to push boundaries or exercise jurisdiction in new ways to expand their influence over the area, or prevent their adversaries from achieving new influence over the area. States may be as motivated to prevent a further deterioration of the status quo as they are to try to roll it back.

Cooperation and Challenges to the Status Quo

Viewed as competing perceptions of a status quo, the politics of disputed maritime space become larger than simply questions of domestic and foreign policy. Rather, they relate to a state's perception of its security environment writ large. According to the literature on psychological explanations of state behavior, a state's perception of the status quo is defined by its reference point.[48] In a territorial context the status quo is relatively easy to define because territory can be divided by claims to borders or boundaries. The exercise is more complicated in the maritime realm because international laws governing ocean space allow it to be shared by other states and because states often have different interpretations of their entitlements under the Law of the Sea.[49] A state's reference point can be identified by analyzing not only reactions to claims made vis-à-vis the boundary itself, but also policymakers' expectations of what functions the disputed space serves, such as fishing or holding a military exercise. Policymakers might interpret their reference point defined not only by the location of a boundary line but also in response to shifting norms of acceptable behavior at sea.

Policymakers' perception of a changing status quo is a function of the importance of the particular dimension of maritime space that has been challenged.[50] This interpretative process has a number of inputs. Central policymakers may not perceive a challenge to the status quo as such until they interact with domestic groups that are sensitive to the challenge in a given issue area. Domestic interests therefore help policymakers frame the stakes in a territorial contest. Like all policy decisions, state "interests" or "objectives" for disputed maritime space are informed by leaders' own prejudices and by organizational or bureaucratic inputs—which may or may not have their own agendas—as well as by calculations of how the issue can benefit both the state in question and the leadership in power.[51]

State objectives for disputed maritime space can be observed by the way actors convey the issues—in this case, maritime boundary issues—to other actors. The concept of "framing"—the messages delivered by political elites to their constituents that inform expectations—is a useful mechanism to observe this process empirically. Policymakers will attempt to frame certain issues for public or government consumption in an effort to manage expectations and better insulate themselves from domestic criticism in the event of a perceived policy failure. Alternatively, policymakers actively try to shape the expectations of the domestic climate in such a way that would increase their acceptance of a given outcome.[52] How issues are framed by policymakers can yield clues as to their preferences regarding a potential boundary negotiation.[53]

Beyond their government's version of the stakes, costs, and benefits of an international agreement, domestic constituencies are also affected by alternative "frames" such as perspectives and ideas from other actors such as the media, industry associations, lobby groups, nongovernmental organizations, and opposition political parties. These actors advance alternative versions of the reference point in a process called "counterframing."[54] Analysis of such processes allows a scholar to identify a state's reference point vis-à-vis a given function of disputed maritime space. The process by which leaders become aware of shifts in the reference point illustrates the salient stakes, or territorial value, to that claimant. As illustrated by the case studies, cooperation can be a risky and high-cost strategy for Chinese and Japanese leaders that could have implications for a state's jurisdictional claim and could bring domestic consequences.

Despite the relative opacity of elite decision-making processes in both China and Japan, inferences can be drawn from open sources. The way media and bureaucracies frame the salience of disputed space is integral to understanding how these messages are interpreted by leaders and the public. For this book, twenty-six interviews were conducted with Chinese and Japanese officials and scholars who were close to the issues studied herein. The political sensitivity of territorial issues severely limited the number of willing interview subjects.[55] Collectively, these sources inform inferences about value of disputed space to leaders.

Challenges to the maritime order between China and Japan were triggered by China's emergence as a maritime power, which challenged Japan's satisfaction with the maritime status quo between them. For instance, China's rise as a fisheries state challenged Japan's status as a fisheries power. Greater operational latitude and frequency by Chinese military and civilian vessels as well as China's offshore energy production activities challenged Japan's perception of what it could and could not achieve in its maritime environment. Viewing Japan's reaction as motivated by a challenge to its reference point explains the motivations for Japan to react—as opposed to doing nothing—but it does not explain the depth and durability of cooperation, which are analyzed as separate processes.

Studying Cooperation: Origins, Depth, and Durability

As noted above, the analysis is organized along three variables that affect two questions. First, why do two states decide to pursue cooperative means to achieve their interests versus accepting the costs of the noncooperative status quo? Second, what explains the depth and durability of this cooperation? The first key variable is whether or not an agreement was reached and, with it, the dynamics of the decision by the rival to reciprocate. States use a variety of approaches to elicit cooperative behavior from a rival. As noted by Lisa Martin, cooperation can be reciprocal or coerced.[56] In his seminal work *The Evolution of Cooperation*, Robert Axelrod argues that cooperation can be achieved through a strategy of reciprocity defined as "helping out a colleague and getting repaid in kind." According to this view states can achieve greater benefit from reciprocating cooperative overtures with further cooperative overtures.[57] Martin has labeled this behavior "co-adjustment," the condition under which states choose to cooperate when to do otherwise leads to a suboptimal outcome.[58] As long as states continue to reciprocate, cooperation endures. The frequency of interaction on a given issue can improve the odds of achieving a consensus.

Cooperation may also be pursued coercively when the states have asymmetric interests.[59] Coercive cooperation is the use of costs or side payments to gain the cooperation of an adversary. States use a variety of instruments of power to raise the costs of noncooperation to their adversary. This extends to diplomatic remonstrations, threats, sanctions, and even military statecraft short of the use of force. Although this behavior is typically classified as assertive or escalatory, it may in fact occur in support of a cooperative goal. China and Japan have used both reciprocal and coercive strategies to encourage cooperation when confronted with challenges to their perception of the status quo in the maritime space between them.

The second variable is the depth of the resulting agreement. Cooperation in international relations covers a wide range of phenomena—including formal, legally binding treaties; the exchange of *notes verbale*; and informal, tacit recognition of the other party's red lines. The depth of cooperation includes a bargaining dynamic in which both parties inject negotiations with their preferences for the status quo.[60] This includes the process by which the two sides discuss the implementation of the deal and draw up monitoring mechanisms and enforcement protocols once the terms of cooperation are struck.[61] During this stage policymakers create the institutions that strengthen the durability of cooperation, reduce the incentives to cheat, and prevent defection.[62] In a maritime context, implementing cooperation often refers to reaching a consensus on which components of a state's sovereignty or jurisdiction will be delegated to another actor, or which aspects will be jointly regulated, or what norms of behavior will govern a particular issue area.

Finally, the durability of cooperation speaks to the success of a given agreement. Does the agreement prevent future political tensions over an issue? Or does one party seek to defect or redefine the agreement in ways that render it moot by allowing tensions to resurface? Does the agreement prevent the fulfillment of objectives in other issue areas in the disputed maritime space? How is the agreement received by domestic actors? This variable also hinges on the postagreement political environment and the ways in which the new status quo is perceived by both parties. If, in the course of negotiations, new facts emerge that suggest that the two parties interpret the terms of the agreement differently one party may seek to defect early in order to avoid contributing to a less favorable status quo. Interactions in a given issue area can also affect durable cooperation. Positive interactions on a particular issue area can institutionalize expectations about behavior, and can mitigate the conditions of anarchy. Under these conditions defection is punished by a loss of prestige and belonging to the group dynamic.[63] By contrast, negative interactions can have the opposite effect by reinforcing assumptions about anarchy.[64] State leaders that have an insecure, "realist" worldview will behave as if this is the case, and in so doing they will invite this behavior from other states.[65] In any event, behavior in all three phases of cooperation is informed by policymakers' perception of the salience of the disputed space. Locating the salience of maritime space in a claimant's national agenda requires a method of assessing the impact of these different dimensions on a claimant state.

Conceptualizing the Salience of Disputed Space

The decision to cooperate over an aspect of disputed maritime space is a function of the perceived costs of cooperation measured against the perceived costs of inaction, informed by policymakers' interpretation of the salience of disputed space.[66] As noted above, the literature on the East China Sea dispute, and territorial disputes generally, views a linear relationship between the value of space and tension. However, the historical record of Sino-Japanese maritime relations does not reflect the singular militarized pursuit of the material value of disputed ocean areas. Moreover, this perspective oversimplifies the problems that arise from disputed maritime boundaries because it does not account for situations in which states pursue these interests cooperatively. Likewise, the argument that ideational pressures, such as nationalism, increase the disincentives for cooperation cannot explain instances of cooperation that are marked by the outpouring of nationalist sentiment. This section outlines the maritime value matrix (MVM) as a way to conceptualize the salience of disputed maritime space to leaders at a given time.

The MVM draws two distinctions related to the importance of space. First, maritime space is important for both tangible and intangible reasons, although as noted above explanations of state behavior have tended to emphasize the impact of one over the other. The second distinction considers which aspects of disputed space are salient to both parties, and which aspects are only salient to one party. The MVM locates the areas of common and disputed interest vis-à-vis a given disputed issue in the maritime relationship. This in turn informs the analysis of the sources of cooperation by identifying the incentives and disincentives for cooperation. This exercise orders subsequent discussions of the competing interpretations of the importance of disputed spaces between claimant states and their interpretation of the territorial status quo.

At its most basic level territory is important for both tangible reasons, such as providing foodstuffs and resources for exploitation, and intangible reasons, such as the formation of a group identity, as distinct from "others."[67] Tangible territorial aspects include security from external danger, the provision of basic needs for survival, the accumulation of wealth such as resources, and a space in which citizens exist and interact.[68] Territory also has a symbolic or intangible function for its inhabitants. It is a homeland; a source of historic, religious, or cultural security; and a source of independence and prestige that in turn creates a sense of exclusive attachment that excludes "others."

Most of these functions are clearly unique to land territory, but many of these types of value are evident in disputed maritime space as well. The East China Sea is home to potentially vast hydrocarbon resources that could improve energy security for both claimants. Both claimants rely on fish protein from the sea in their diets. Similarly, control of the East China Sea would confer a significant military advantage because it would enhance the ability to disrupt SLOCs and project power ashore. Also, the disputed Senkaku/Diaoyu Islands have become part of regime legitimization and nation-building strategies in Tokyo and Beijing, which in turn gives maritime issues a high degree of domestic political prominence.[69]

However, the distinction between tangible and intangible importance only tells half the story because it treats salience as constant across both claimant states. In the maritime realm significant technological, logistical, and geological barriers exist to the pursuit of state goals, which increase or reduce the importance of a given maritime issue to a given claimant. National defense, resource exploitation, and policing are all more difficult on sea than on land. These actions require capabilities that are not widespread throughout the international system, and the absence of any one of these capabilities on the part of a claimant may affect the value of the disputed territory to policymakers.[70] Not all aspects of disputed space are necessarily valued equally by both parties, and this is especially true in the case of disputed maritime space.

In an effort to conceptualize the political value of territory to each claimant, Goertz and Diehl have drawn a distinction between intrinsic and relational value.[71] Intrinsic value is the salience of territory that is of universal importance across all states; it can be equally comprehended by both actors. Intrinsic value may refer to the presence of exploitable resources, the value of the territory as a potential market for goods, and the advantages brought by control of the territory itself and its population, including new strategic opportunities related to ownership.[72] By definition, intrinsic value is appreciated by both claimant states. Intrinsic value is not expressed in material units, such as dollars or barrels per day; it is not a question of scale but of reciprocated acceptance. For instance, the fact that seafood demand is higher in China by virtue of its greater population does not in itself imply that China values fisheries more than Japan. Rather, both parties accept that the other has a legitimate interest in fishing the waters of the East China Sea.

Relational value refers to importance that is subject to the orientation of a particular claimant that makes the territory more valuable to one party than the other. Close geographic proximity to a national homeland area would raise a territory's value to one claimant.[73] Of particular importance, relational value does not only apply to immaterial or symbolic characteristics. There may also be a unique material aspect that benefits one state over another.[74] For instance, advances in resource extraction techniques may make previously inaccessible oil resources exploitable, or may lead to the discovery of new frontier resources such as methane hydrates. Thus, previously worthless maritime space can become more important. However, a rival claimant may lack these technological capabilities, which would reduce its ability to extract these resources. This could affect the importance it attaches to the area and, by extension, state policy. Faced with geological barriers, or in the absence of required technologies, a state may adopt cooperative policies to access disputed resources that it otherwise could not. The perception of the legitimacy of a rival claim is an important indicator of relational value. For instance, while a rival claimant may also claim the territory on similar grounds, because irredentist claims contain an inherent legitimacy deficit, they are classified as relational. If these claims are perceived to be legitimate by the other party, they would adopt an intrinsic quality as both parties appreciate their symbolic importance to the other. These two approaches to territorial value are illustrated by the MVM in figure 1.1. The MVM yields a logic about the practicability of cooperation over aspects of disputed maritime space that can be ordered along a spectrum (figure 1.2), which in turn generates hypotheses on the origin, depth, and durability of cooperation over disputed maritime space.

FIGURE 1.1
The Maritime Value Matrix

	Intrinsic	*Relational*
Tangible	**Intrinsic-tangible:** Material value perceived as legitimate by both parties.	**Relational-tangible:** Material value perceived as legitimate by one party.
Intangible	**Intrinsic-intangible:** Symbolic value perceived as legitimate by both parties.	**Relational-intangible:** Symbolic value perceived as legitimate by one party.

FIGURE 1.2
The Spectrum of Cooperation

Explicit cooperation	→		*Tacit cooperation*
intrinsic-tangible	intrinsic-intangible	relational-intangible	relational-tangible

According to this logic, issues in the upper-left-hand corner of figure 1.1 (intrinsic-tangible) are those about which there is a shared interest over something that is divisible. Resource wealth, for instance, can be divided between claimants through joint development agreements, production-sharing agreements, or purchase swaps.[75] By this logic, cooperation over these "intrinsic-tangible" issues should be straightforward because tangible issues are material and their intrinsic nature means that they are relatively easily divided. All else being equal, the political salience of this issue should be relatively marginal, given that it relates to mundane economic concerns and not to matters of national security or national identity. The resulting hypothesis is as follows:

> H1: Cooperation over intrinsic-tangible (economic) issues will be pursued reciprocally, and will result in a formal and enforceable agreement that will yield lasting cooperation.

By contrast, issues located in the lower-right-hand corner of figure 1.1 (relational-intangible) are more challenging. Neither state recognizes the legitimacy of the other's claim to the issue; moreover, intangible issues are not easily divisible. These issues are indivisible either because policymakers perceive them to be so a priori, or because policymakers adopt this position in the course of bargaining over disputed space.[76] Issues contained within this subset include the very notion of sovereignty and jurisdiction and the ideational basis upon which a state forms its national identity. These are issues complicated by an "in" group–versus–"out" group dynamic between the two state identities.[77] As a function of these sensitivities, attempts at coercive cooperation are futile; cooperative efforts are thus necessarily reciprocal. However, cooperation could undermine some vital aspect of the state's ideational fabric and impose serious costs on state leaders if cooperation is framed in sovereignty terms.[78] Policymakers thus have little incentive to publicize agreements with the rival claimant if they wish to cooperate at all. Similarly, as a function of this domestic salience and the informality of the issue at hand, these cooperative agreements can be subject to the whims of insecure leaders. Accordingly:

> H2: Cooperation over relational-intangible (contested-symbolic) issues will be pursued reciprocally, result in informal cooperation with little enforcement, and be tenuous at best.

Issues in the upper-right-hand corner of figure 1.1 (relational-tangible) are tangible, and thus divisible, but claims are not recognized as legitimate by the rival state. Their divisibility is thus complicated by the fact that neither party recognizes the entitlement of the other to the issue at hand. As illustrated above, issues contained within this subset include the perceived strategic value of disputed space and thus relate to national security concerns—a first-order priority for states in the international system. The logic of the MVM expects that cooperation over this issue area will be coercive, with the party that is reacting to the new status quo attempting to compel its rival to the bargaining table. Agreements are likely to be informal as the more dominant party likely perceives the emerging strategic environment to be to its advantage. Finally, these agreements are not likely to be lasting as long as the supplicant is perceived by the challenger to be weaker. Cooperation over these "relational-tangible" issues is likely to be colored by concerns over relative gains and is thus more complicated than the former two issue subsets:

> H3: Cooperation over relational-tangible (strategic) issues will be pursued coercively, result in informal agreements, and be short-lived.

Finally, cooperation over issues contained within the lower-left hand corner of figure 1.1 (intrinsic-intangible) is facilitated by a shared recognition of legitimacy or entitlement (intrinsic), yet is complicated by the fact that intangible issues are not readily divisible. These issues are not complicated by in group–out group dynamics, but by the mechanics of sharing the issue. These issues lie near the cooperative end of the "cooperative spectrum" illustrated in figure 1.2, but they are not considered in this study because there is no evidence of their existence in the Sino-Japanese maritime relationship. The exercise of jurisdiction in disputed space, properly formulated, can be a positive-sum game if the parties agree on the nature of what is being shared. For instance, Peru and Ecuador established "peace parks" as part of a border agreement, which were under Ecuadorian control but Peruvian sovereignty.[79] Further, recent research on reconciliation reveals that states are capable of moving beyond historical narratives to foster a shared historical narrative.[80] Whether such dynamics will eventuate with reference to the maritime disputes between China and Japan is a matter for the conclusion of this book.

Of course, these issue areas do not exist in a vacuum but often occupy the same space and time. Interaction effects between these can pollute or facilitate the cooperative process by adding costs via perceived issue linkage or by creating the opportunity for trade-offs in other issue areas. Figure 1.3 places the issues at stake in the East China Sea dispute in the context of the MVM.

This operationalization of different aspects of disputed space represents ideal types; as the overall salience of the East China Sea has increased, it has become more difficult to define some issues, such as exercising maritime jurisdiction, as being purely tangible or intangible. As noted above, disputed maritime boundaries raise a variety of issues around which states form goals based on the function performed by maritime space. Some aspects of maritime boundary issues, such as the importance of the boundary claim itself or the rules and norms governing the activities of ships at

FIGURE 1.3
Aggregate Value of the East China Sea

Intrinsic-tangible: Economic	**Relational-tangible: Strategic**
• Resource value of Xihu Trough • Fisheries resources • Employment in the fisheries industry • Marine survey data	• Command of the East China Sea (China) • Navy operational experience (China) • China's Maritime Expansion (Japan) • Exercising maritime jurisdiction
Intrinsic-intangible: Shared-symbolic • Void	**Relational-intangible: Contested-symbolic** • Disputed Senkaku/Diaoyu Islands • Sharing maritime jurisdiction post 2005

sea, can easily be construed as vital to the national security of a claimant state. Simultaneously, other aspects, such as fisheries regulation or hydrocarbon resource exploitation, remain important but do not have a direct bearing on state security. Both parties can appreciate the desire to exploit hydrocarbon resources; it thus has an intrinsic and a tangible dimension. However, under certain conditions this concern can be framed as a strategic concern by interested constituencies, in which case it would adopt a relational quality, while remaining a tangible issue. Furthermore, some aspects of these issues might be more or less salient to leaders in different claimant states, and this in turn affects the degree to which there is a commonality of interest between parties and by extension the prospects for cooperation between claimant states. The MVM therefore presents a useful analytical tool to identify the source of cooperative behavior.

This book considers each case of cooperation by assessing the importance of disputed space to China and Japan through the lens of the MVM. Chapter 2 explores Chinese and Japanese efforts to manage their dispute over the Senkaku/Diaoyu Islands, an issue characterized by the contested-symbolic attachments to national sovereignty. Chapter 3 explains cooperation over fisheries, an economic issue, and finds a highly successful cooperative agreement underwritten by an alignment of interest, a long track record of interaction, and a high degree of institutional activity on the issue. Chapter 4 explores a case of cooperative failure over marine survey activity, an activity with mixed salience to China. Despite a sharp difference in preferences, China and Japan were able to reach an agreement on marine scientific research in February 2001, partly because of coercive efforts by Japan. However, this agreement remained weak; and because no enforcement mechanism was in place, the agreement subsequently lapsed. The final case of cooperation, over hydrocarbon resource development, is a hybrid case. Japan's efforts to coerce China into an agreement yielded a dramatic concession by Beijing when it agreed to consider a joint development zone in the East China Sea that included the Japanese claimed median line. Nevertheless, the agreement remains unfulfilled.

Alternative Explanations of Cooperation

The pattern of Sino-Japanese interaction at sea presents challenges for international relations theory. The two countries have avoided conflict over their disputed maritime boundary and the associated challenges that arise, yet they have resisted a settlement of the underlying issues; they have cooperated, yet they have engaged in military posturing and saber rattling at sea. Mainstream theories of international relations provide some insight, yet they do not offer a complete explanation. Japan and China have taken embryonic steps toward the building of a maritime regime over fisheries issues and marine research, as well as military confidence building.[81] However, these efforts have been only moderately successful, and in one case they failed completely. Recurring games have yielded a lasting solution in only one case: the issue of fisheries. The reasons for this defection may lie in the weakness of the agreements reached or in the way in which Beijing and Tokyo have calculated their interests in light of changing circumstances. Put another way, China and Japan have been more effective at solving the "collective action problem" than the "enforcement problem."[82] This pattern defies explanation by existing theories of international relations.

The constructivist preoccupation with the ideational construction of interests does not explain the apparent instrumental nature of policymakers' mobilization of historical grievances. Popular nationalism in both states appears to have created a situation in which, under certain circumstances, Chinese and Japanese leaders are constrained from pursuing lasting cooperation by audience costs.[83] Nevertheless, they have been able to overcome these pressures at times and reach points of consensus in two cases overcoming outpourings of nationalist sentiment.[84] Likewise, constructivist insights can account for Chinese intransigence on territorial questions, which are consistent with China's "images" of its geographic makeup, but not Chinese compromise on these issues.[85]

Rationalist explanations expect limited cooperation between adversaries in areas of peripheral importance, but the maritime space between China and Japan is vital to both parties.[86] Similarly, assumptions such as strategic restraint under conditions of deterrence may explain delay, but they do not explain cooperation over maritime boundary issues between rivals. Some scholars have argued that China and Japan have actively encouraged the deepening of economic links in order to mitigate the tensions that arise from the dispute over the Senkaku/Diaoyu Islands.[87] Further, according to Beth Simmons, states settle territorial disputes when there are significant opportunity costs to be borne by their continuation, such as lost trade volume.[88] Although these dynamics may be at play in the Russo-Japanese dispute over the Northern Territories, they are certainly not a factor in the East China Sea dispute.[89] The trade relationship has not prevented the recurrence of cyclical tensions and has even been damaged by these tensions.

Indeed, pessimism regarding cooperation in the East China Sea dispute appears to be well founded because it displays none of the conditions for peaceful territorial settlement identified by Arie Kacowicz. The power distribution between the two parties is not asymmetric; the trend is toward parity. The two parties have opposite styles of government—one-party authoritarian rule versus a liberal democracy. Only Kacowicz's final condition, "a convergence of norms and rules of international law and morality sustained by the parties in relation to a disputed territory," may apply with regard to the impact of UNCLOS on the fisheries dispute.[90]

Conclusion

This book makes three contributions to the fields of international relations and East Asian politics. First, by exploring Sino-Japanese security cooperation in the maritime realm, the book contributes to the literature on security cooperation between adversaries. Chinese and Japanese interaction over their contested maritime space is an ideal case study because there is variation along the dependent variable: the depth and durability of each instance of cooperation.

Second, the book advances the study of territorial disputes by unpacking the notion of "value" and assessing the impact of different territorial functions on state behavior. The incomplete nature of cooperation in the maritime realm could be explained by the ideational and political limits placed on cooperation between China and Japan. Nevertheless, they have been able to overcome these pressures at times and reach points of consensus. The MVM transcends the level-of-analysis problem by offering a holistic analysis of the salience of maritime space, whether as a function of domestic political utility or of international strategic importance. The theory thus avoids the determinism of the analyses noted above; there is nothing preordained about the behavioral outcomes of two states embroiled in a maritime territorial dispute, even two with a bilateral relationship as tumultuous as that of China and Japan.

The book's third contribution is empirical. It builds on recent scholarship regarding China's posture toward its territorial disputes and develops an understanding of its attitude toward maritime space.[91] The inquiry also offers an opportunity to assess the impact of ocean politics in Japan that goes beyond the traditional fixation on sea lanes.[92] Japanese leaders have become far more aware of the importance of the maritime domain, and this has significant implications for the maritime order in East Asia.[93] From a regional perspective, the book builds on recent work on the geopolitical underpinnings of disputed maritime boundaries in East Asia in an effort to assess the direction of Chinese and Japanese maritime policy and the prospects for the establishment of a stable maritime order in East Asia.[94] Finally, the research findings will inform American policymakers interested in China's maritime posture, particularly in light of recent events on East Asian seas.

Notes

1. See, e.g., White, "Caught in a Bind"; Suzuki, "Japan and China's Masochists"; and Calder, "China and Japan's Simmering Rivalry," 129–39.
2. Wirth, "Ocean Governance, Maritime Security," 223–45.
3. Manicom, "China's Strategy in the East China Sea."
4. A rivalry is defined as "as a relationship between adversaries who identify each other as threatening competitors and enemies. Once these perceptions emerge, subsequent interactions will be characterized by suspicion and hostility which can lead to misperception, expectations of bad faith behavior and exaggerations of hostility." Rasler and Thompson, "Contested Territory," 149.
5. Blanchard, "Linking Border Disputes and War," 692.
6. Welch, *Painful Choices,* 26–27.
7. One exception is Emmers, *Geopolitics and Maritime Territorial Disputes.*
8. Mack, *Island Disputes in Northeast Asia*; Valencia, "Domestic Politics."
9. See Chung, "The Diaoyu/Tiaoyutai/Senkaku Islands Dispute," 135–64; and Deans, "Contending Nationalisms," 119–31.
10. See, e.g., "Commentary Accuses Japan of Historical 'Cover-Ups,'" Xinhua News, July 24, 1996; Gries, *China's New Nationalism*; Zhao, *Nation-State by Construction*; and Wang, "National Humiliation," 783–806.
11. Suganuma, *Sovereign Rights.*
12. Chung, *Domestic Politics,* 8–9.
13. Chung, "Resolving China's Island Disputes," 53.
14. Bong, "Flashpoints at Sea?" chap. 2.
15. Odgaard, "Perception, Pragmatism and Political Will," 136.
16. Yahuda, "Limits of Economic Interdependence," 162–85.
17. Berger, "Set for Stability?" 405–28; Buszynski, *Asia Pacific Security.*
18. The classic works of this nature are Klare, *Resource Wars,* 109–37; Calder, *Asia's Deadly Triangle*; and Valencia, "Energy and Insecurity in Asia," 85–106.
19. Hsiung, "Sea Power, Law of the Sea," 133–53.
20. Harrison, "Quiet Struggle in the East China Sea," 271–77.

21. Jiang, "East Asia's Troubled Waters, Part I"; Ding, "China's Energy Security Demands," 36.

22. Lai, "China's Oil Diplomacy," 535.

23. Emery et al., "Geological Structure," 3–41. The energy nationalism literature includes, among others, Herberg, "Asia's Energy Insecurity," 339–77. For early recognition of the energy issue in the Senkaku/Diaoyu Islands dispute, see Li, "China and Offshore Oil," 143–62; and Harrison, *China, Oil and Asia.*

24. Bussert, "Oil May Be Focal Point of Sino-Japanese Dispute," 33–36; Cole, *Great Wall at Sea,* chap. 3.

25. Ross, "Geography of the Peace," 81–118.

26. Holmes and Yoshihara, *Chinese Naval Strategy in the 21st Century.*

27. Cole, "Chinese Naval Modernization and Energy Security," 11.

28. On the first point, see Hughes, "Japanese Military Modernization," 109; and Dreyer, "China's Military Strategy regarding Japan," 25. For the latter view, see Yoshihara and Holmes, "Japanese Maritime Thought," 23–51; and Woolley, *Japan's Navy.*

29. "Chinese Navy Helicopter Circles MSDF Ship Again," *Mainichi Shimbun,* April 22, 2010.

30. For background, see Manicom, "Beyond Boundary Disputes," 46–53.

31. For an exception, see Blanchard, "China's Peaceful Rise," 230–35.

32. Wang, "Territorial Disputes and Asian Security," 381.

33. Manicom, "Interaction of Material and Ideational Factors in the East China Sea Dispute," 375–91.

34. Downs and Saunders, "Legitimacy and the Limits of Nationalism," 114–46.

35. E.g., in 2008, the year the two states created a joint development zone in the East China Sea, only 9.87 percent of China's total energy consumption came from imported oil. Japan, meanwhile, relied on imported oil for 48.5 percent of its total energy consumption. In 2012, these ratios only converged slightly, with Chinese reliance at 10.2 percent and Japanese at 42 percent. Author's calculations based on BP, *BP Statistical Review of World Energy 2008*; and BP, *BP Statistical Review of World Energy 2012.* However, China's relationship with the United States, which polices the global SLOC chain, contributes to its sense of energy insecurity. On these concerns, see Lanteigne, "China's Maritime Security," 147–49. Furthermore, China became a net importer of natural gas in 2007.

36. Chen, "Anti-Japanese Protesters Assail Beijing's Gas Pact."

37. This assumption has most recently been employed by Fravel, *Strong Borders, Secure Nation,* 12–13. This assumption is common in the literature on territorial disputes and dates to Huth, *Standing Your Ground,* 30.

38. Keohane, *After Hegemony,* 51–52. Milner notes this definition is a point of consensus in the literature. Milner, "International Theories of Cooperation," 468.

39. Fravel, "Explaining Stability in the Senkaku (Diaoyu) Islands Dispute," 144–64.

40. Fravel, *Strong Borders, Secure Nation,* 12.

41. Author interview "R," June 29, 2011, Tokyo; author interview "S," June 30, 2011, Tokyo.

42. Manicom, "Japan's Ocean Policy," 307–26. See also Potter and Sueo, "Japanese Foreign Policy," 317–32.

43. Wan, *Sino-Japanese Relations*, chap. 13.

44. Koo, "Senkaku/Diaoyu Dispute and Sino-Japanese Political-Economic Relations," 205–32.

45. See Midford, *Rethinking Japanese Public Opinion and Security*; Katzenstein and Okawara, "Japan and Asia-Pacific Security," 97–130; and Soeya, "Japan: Normative Constraints Versus Structural Imperatives," 198–233.

46. See Zacher, "Territorial Integrity Norm," 215–50.

47. Manicom and O'Neil, "Sino–Japanese Strategic Relations," 213–32.

48. Levy, "Prospect Theory and International Relations," 283–310; Welch, *Painful Choices*, 42.

49. Bateman, "UNCLOS and Its Limitations," 27–56.

50. Berejekian, "Gains Debate," 789–805. Some of this language may seem familiar to students of prospect theory, and the model borrows the notion of a reference point and issue framing from this literature. However, the model does not try to associate the psychological "frame" of policymakers (as gain vs. loss) with a willingness to incur risks, nor does it try to draw causal links between psychological frames, risk acceptance, or aversion and state behavior.

51. Huth and Allee, *Democratic Peace and Territorial Conflict*; Gourevitch, "Squaring the Circle," 349–73.

52. Mintz and DeRouen, *Understanding Foreign Policy Decision Making*, 149; Hudson, *Foreign Policy Analysis*, 91.

53. Levy, "Prospect Theory and the Cognitive-Rational Debate," 36. On domestic ratification of international agreement, see Putnam, "Diplomacy and Domestic Politics," 427–60.

54. Mintz and DeRouen, *Understanding Foreign Policy Decision Making*, 154.

55. For this reason, the interview subjects are identified only by a letter, city, and date of interview.

56. This section assumes the existence of a difference of interest. As Keohane notes in cases where interests are aligned, or in harmony, there is no cooperation to be had. This typology seems to include the "coincidence" outlined by Martin, *Coercive Cooperation*, 27.

57. Axelrod, *Evolution of Cooperation*, 5.

58. Martin, *Coercive Cooperation*, 30.

59. Ibid., 27.

60. This is a formulation of the classic bargaining problem articulated by Nash and Schelling. See Nash, "Bargaining Problem," 155–62; and Schelling, *Strategy of Conflict*.

61. Fearon, "Bargaining, Enforcement and International Cooperation," 274.

62. O'Neal and Russet, "Classical Liberals Were Right," 267–94.

63. Acharya, *Constructing a Security Community in Southeast Asia*. See also Adler and Barnett, *Security Communities*; and, most recently, Kupchan, *How Enemies Become Friends*.

64. Grieco, "Realist Theory and the Problem of International Cooperation," 600–24.

65. Wendt, "Anarchy Is What States Make of It," 410.

66. This book uses salience, value, and importance interchangeably when discussing the weight policymakers assign to an aspect of maritime space in general terms, unless otherwise specified, i.e., "economic value."

67. Starr, "Territory, Proximity, and Spatiality," 392. This is similar to the "concrete and symbolic" distinction employed by the "issue-based" approach to the analysis of war, articulated by Diehl, "What Are They Fighting For?" 333–44.

68. Newman, "Real Spaces, Symbolic Spaces," 5–12.

69. Blanchard, "China's Peaceful Rise," 230.

70. Starr and Most, "Substance and Study of Borders," 581–620.

71. Goertz and Diehl, *Territorial Changes and International Conflict,* 12.

72. Ibid., 14–17.

73. Ibid., 17–20.

74. Some conflate relational with intangible value. See Koo, "Scramble for the Rocks," 30; and Starr, "International Borders," 8. However, the authors clearly state that "intrinsic importance relates to the value that territory has for all parties to a territorial dispute . . . relational importance refers to the different significance attached to the territory by the parties in the territorial exchange." Goertz and Diehl, *Territorial Changes and International Conflict,* 66–67.

75. Ong and Hamzah, "Disputed Maritime Boundaries," 41.

76. On the first point, see Hassner, *War on Sacred Grounds,* chap. 3. On the second point, see Toft, *Geography of Ethnic Violence*; Hassner, "The Path to Intractability," 107–38; and Goddard, "Uncommon Ground," 35–38.

77. Mitzen, "Ontological Security in World Politics," 341–70.

78. Some have called these "justice stakes." See Welch, *Justice and the Genesis of War*; and Albin, *Justice and Fairness in International Negotiation.*

79. See Jervis, "Realism, Neoliberalism, and Cooperation," 303.

80. See He, *Search for Reconciliation*; Lind, *Sorry States*; and Suh, "War-Like History or Diplomatic History?" 386.

81. Valencia, "Maritime Confidence and Security Building," 27–45; Drifte, "From 'Sea of Confrontation' to 'Sea of Peace, Cooperation and Friendship'?" 27–51.

82. Fearon, "Bargaining, Enforcement and International Cooperation," 269–305.

83. Fearon, "Domestic Political Audiences and the Escalation of International Disputes," 577–92; Weeks, "Autocratic Audience Costs," 35–64.

84. Downs and Saunders, "Legitimacy and the Limits of Nationalism," 114–46; Manicom, "Sino-Japanese Cooperation in the East China Sea," 455–78.

85. Carlson, *Unifying China, Integrating with the World,* chap. 3; Fravel, "Regime Insecurity and International Cooperation," 46–83.

86. Glaser, "Realists as Optimists," 129.

87. Koo, "Senkaku/Diaoyu Dispute." 205–32.

88. Simmons, "Capacity, Commitment, and Compliance," 832–33; Simmons, "Rules over Real Estate," 823–48.

89. Linge, "Kuriles," 116–32.

90. Kacowicz, "Problem of Peaceful Territorial Change," 219.

91. Wiegand, "China's Strategy in the Diaoyu Islands Dispute," 170–93; Fravel, *Strong Borders, Secure Nation*; Chung, *Domestic Politics*; Austin, *China's Ocean Frontier*; Lo, *China's Policy towards Territorial Disputes.*

92. Graham, *Japan's Sea Lane Security.*

93. Manicom, "Japan's Ocean Policy," 307–26.

94. Emmers, *Geopolitics and Maritime Territorial Disputes.*

CHAPTER TWO

The Collapse of Cooperation over the Senkaku/Diaoyu Islands

THE SENKAKU/DIAOYU ISLANDS lie at the center of Sino-Japanese maritime relations. Claims to the islands emerged following the publication of a bullish report on the hydrocarbon wealth of the East Asian seabed in 1969. This chapter examines the origins of the dispute and traces the evolution of the perceived value of the islands to Chinese and Japanese policymakers. The islands were initially useful as the basis for a claim to maritime space, but over time they became an important nationalist symbol in the bilateral relationship. Nevertheless, the two sides managed tensions via two points of consensus: Deng Xiaoping's modus vivendi in 1978 to shelve the sovereignty issue; and a tacit understanding reached after 1996 not to allow nationalist groups to affect bilateral relations.

The islands have been at the center of a number of small-scale political crises since both parties made competing claims to the islands in the early 1970s. Crises over the islands typically emerged from secondary political actors that attempted to link the issue to their broader nationalist agenda, including assertive foreign policy preferences. Following each crisis Beijing and Tokyo were able to limit the political fallout, and by 1996 Chinese and Japanese leaders reached an informal understanding that provocations from nationalist actors could be ignored. This was supported by a mutual recognition of Deng Xiaoping's maxim that the sovereignty question should be shelved and the emphasis placed on joint resource development. These informal understandings began to collapse in 2002 as growing interest in the economic value of the islands as the basis for claims to maritime space coincided with a preoccupation with the contested-symbolic value. Dramatic confrontations over the islands between 2010 and 2013 mark the end of tacit cooperation over the sovereignty question. Nevertheless, a close examination indicates that, as always, quiet dispute management efforts endure, although leaders confront stronger disincentives for cooperation than at any point in the history of the dispute.

The East China Sea dispute can be divided into three phases.[1] The "dispute onset phase," between 1969 and 1978, established a territorial status quo: Japanese occupation and administration of the Senkaku/Diaoyu Islands, which was challenged by China. The second period, the "crisis management phase," was characterized by three high-profile diplomatic incidents in the 1990s, during which China and Japan struggled to balance their bilateral relations against domestic nationalist pressure.[2] The dispute entered a new phase starting in the late 1990s, when the Chinese and Japanese governments became more attuned to the immediate implications of the territorial dispute vis-à-vis their ability to use the ocean areas that surrounded the islands. This phase is characterized by a new territorial status quo, under which China exercises a greater degree of indirect control over the disputed maritime area, through resource production facilities and an expanded naval presence, yet in practice accepts Japanese occupation of the islands. It is as yet premature to determine whether Chinese efforts to remake the status quo around the islands themselves after September 2012 amount to a new phase of the dispute. China's efforts to exercise its claimed jurisdiction around the islands reflect similar efforts in other parts of the East China Sea that date to the late 1990s.

The Dispute's Onset

The Senkaku/Diaoyu Islands dispute erupted between Taiwan and Japan in the wake of the publication of the Emery Report in May 1969. Named for its lead investigator and issued by the United Nations–funded Economic Commission for Asia and the Far East, the report found that the seabed of the East China Sea "may be one of the most prolific oil reserves in the world."[3] The report triggered a scramble to lock up resources amid a flurry of sovereignty claims. Nevertheless, policymakers were able to establish a territorial status quo that downplayed the significance of the islands relative to more pressing imperatives in the bilateral relationship.

Setting the Territorial Status Quo

As a function of the Emery Report, interest in the resource wealth of the area was such that claims over maritime jurisdiction actually preceded sovereignty claims to the islands. In July 1970, Taiwan claimed jurisdiction over the continental shelf area based on the principle of the natural prolongation of its territory, and it then entered into an oil concession arrangement with Gulf Oil.[4] It claimed sovereignty over the Senkaku/Diaoyu Islands in September 1970. Japan protested Taiwan's concessions on the grounds that they overlapped with existing Japanese interests.[5] Japan issued its own declaration of sovereignty, on September 12, 1970, which claimed the islands as part of the Ryukyu Islands chain. The Senkaku/Diaoyu Islands, which were then under the administration of the United States, would be returned to Japan with the reversion of Okinawa in 1972. Tokyo immediately began to assert its authority over the islands; it argued that Taiwan's oil concessions were illegal and did not prejudice Japan's rights to the continental shelf. Tokyo was supported in this effort by the Okinawan government.[6] In September 1970, the Okinawan authorities removed a Taiwanese flag that had been placed on Uotsuri/Diaoyu Island, the largest of the islands, and the Japanese Maritime Safety Agency (MSA) increased its efforts to turn away Taiwanese fishermen from the area.[7] On March 8, 1972, the Japanese Ministry of Foreign Affairs (MOFA) outlined its legal claim to the islands. It claimed that the islands were *terra nullius* in 1895 when they were incorporated into Japan, and that Japan has demonstrated effective occupation of them since.[8] Under pressure from its oil companies, Tokyo pressed Taiwan and South Korea—which claims the northern tip of the East China Sea—to enter into joint development negotiations predicated on shelving the sovereignty issue.

Trilateral meetings toward this goal came to an abrupt end when Beijing expressed its objections via the *People's Daily* in December 1970. China claimed sovereignty over the islands and condemned the Japanese and Taiwanese efforts to jointly develop their resources as an attempt to steal Chinese resources.[9] In 1971, Beijing claimed the islands based on historical usage dating back to the Ming Dynasty, when they were used as navigation points by sea voyagers from Taiwan. Beijing's statements were particularly strident. Actions and sentiments attributed to the "Chinese people" were mentioned five times, and the basis of the Japanese claim was characterized as "gangster logic."[10] Further bellicose rhetoric came at a UN ocean conference in March 1972, when the Chinese representative called the Japanese occupation of the islands "a glaring act of aggression."[11] As Ma Ying-jeao points out, the establishment of oil concessions was integral to this early phase. However, Japan did not pursue the resource wealth in the seabed at that time due to the Chinese threat, which delayed the implementation of the joint development agreement with South Korea until 1978. The territorial status quo, of Japan administering the islands while ignoring Chinese claims to sovereignty, was set.

Deng's Modus Vivendi: Reinforcing the Status Quo

On April 12, 1978, between 80 and 100 fishing vessels appeared near the Senkaku/Diaoyu Islands; some occupants were lightly armed, and the vessels were draped in white banners declaring Chinese sovereignty over the Senkaku/Diaoyu Islands. The incident is the first example of secondary political actors in China and Japan influencing territorial politics between the two and concluded with the consensus to shelve the sovereignty issue.

Negotiations toward diplomatic normalization between China and Japan had stalled due to differences over the tone and severity of the antihegemony (i.e., anti-Soviet) clause. The Chinese sought a strong declaration because the Soviet Union represented their most immediate strategic threat; but the conservative, pro-Taiwan faction of Japan's Liberal Democratic Party remained hesitant. A strong declaration could exacerbate relations with a superpower with which Japan had several conflicting foreign policy concerns, including the close proximity of the Soviet military, the Northern Territories territorial dispute, and the opportunities for energy imports from the Russian Far East. In an effort to scuttle the Treaty of Peace and Friendship, these conservatives publicly pressed the government to include the Senkaku/Diaoyu Islands in the agenda of the normalization talks on April 7, 1978.[12] In response Deng dispatched the flotilla of fishing vessels to the islands in an effort to demonstrate China's claims. The reply from nationalist segments of Japanese politics was animated. In Tokyo, conservative Diet members tabled a resolution condemning the Chinese move in the strongest terms, while locally the Okinawa Prefectural Assembly called for the Japanese government to defend Japan's national sovereignty.

China's move reflects similar factional politics. The incident was an effort by Deng Xiaoping to shore up his nationalist credentials against conservatives who opposed his wider reform program, while not endangering the treaty negotiations by sending regular military forces to the islands.[13] If Deng had confronted the Japanese over the islands, the treaty would have been scuttled, but to have accepted the rhetoric emanating from Tokyo and Okinawa would have appeared soft. The result was a show of force disguised as a fisheries protest. To manage tensions, Deng subsequently characterized the incident as an "accident" to visiting pro-China members of the Japanese government, and ensured that Chinese representatives in

Japan reiterated both their interest in Japanese trade and their support of the Japanese position on the Northern Territories question.[14] In October 1978, Deng traveled to Tokyo to sign the Treaty of Peace and Friendship and issued his modus vivendi that the sovereignty dispute should be shelved for future, wiser generations to solve and that the two sides should focus on the joint development of resources.[15]

When Deng Xiaoping uttered his famous phrase, he was in fact repeating existing Chinese policy. The Chinese had first indicated that the dispute could be shelved in 1972, and in January 1975, they promised not to raise the issue during the treaty negotiations.[16] The fact that an understanding had been reached three years before the 1978 incident raises the question of whether the Chinese perceived the actions by conservatives in 1978 as a change in Japanese policy. Tretiak notes that Prime Minister Fukuda Takeo did not inflame domestic nationalist passions as he could have, which had the added bonus of dispelling Chinese concerns that he did not want the treaty to proceed.[17] This is evidence that policymakers on both sides sought to keep the issue in check, which in turn strengthens the interpretation that the Chinese "fisheries protest" was aimed at constituencies in China. By accepting Deng's overtures, Fukuda permitted both sides to save face.[18]

Deng's statement represents an innovative effort at dispute management. By pledging to shelve the issue Deng implicitly removed any justification for a challenge to Japanese control by the Chinese government. Both parties perceived that they had agreed on a status quo that served both states' interests. This statement was interpreted in Japan as a pledge that further incidents involving Chinese vessels near the islands would not occur and that China had in effect recognized Japanese sovereignty over the islands.[19] The two sides engaged in a number of attempts to pursue cooperative resource development in the sea area between them, but they were repeatedly stymied by the sovereignty question.[20] As a consequence, leaders in both capitals came to expect that neither party would attempt to alter this set of circumstances. Secondary political actors have had other ambitions, however. In August 1978, a Japanese nationalist group erected a primitive lighthouse on Uotsuri Island.[21] That MOFA revoked the Ministry of Transport–approved license for the construction of a lighthouse indicates Tokyo's interest in downplaying the issue at such a sensitive time—the Treaty of Peace and Friendship had been concluded but not signed.

Crisis Management

The construction of the lighthouse in 1978 was a harbinger of things to come. However, as nationalist actors continued to be a nuisance, Beijing and Tokyo were able to fall back on Deng's modus vivendi as a point of consensus to reassure each other that policymakers did not seek to alter the territorial status quo. Although it was possible to keep tensions over the disputed islands from completely disrupting the bilateral relationship, a period of tension was often a prerequisite. This was in no small part due to the fact that, following UNCLOS's entry into force in 1994, policymakers in Beijing and Tokyo were not disinterested in the islands themselves. A critical aspect of any territorial dispute is the dogmatic reassertion of one's claim when challenged, which was dutifully carried out by leaders in Beijing and Tokyo during each crisis.

The 1990 Incident

The upsurge of nationalist activities in 1990 was sparked by an application from Nihon Seinensha (Japanese Youth Federation) to have the lighthouse built in 1978 recognized by the MSA as an official navigational marker.[22] Sanctioning such an installation could be perceived in China as an attempt by Japan to consolidate its occupation of the islands. Nationalists from Taiwan, including athletes bearing a mock Olympic torch, attempted to land on the islands in protest but were repelled by the MSA. The incident was captured on Taiwanese television and sparked anti-Japanese demonstrations across Taiwan and calls to ban Japanese products. On October 18, Beijing condemned the lighthouse and demanded that Tokyo control its nationalist groups.[23] Tensions eased when Japanese prime minister Kaifu Toshiki declared that Tokyo would not recognize the lighthouse. Taipei attempted to dissuade further visits by stating that it would not protect Taiwanese citizens going to the island.[24] Beijing reiterated its claim to sovereignty in person through Vice Foreign Minister Qi Huaiyaun on October 27 in Tokyo.

Nationalists continued to influence the dispute after tensions subsided. Beijing was criticized by overseas Chinese nationalists for not being more forceful in its objections. Rather than taking the initiative, the Chinese Ministry of Foreign Affairs' (MFA's) assertions of sovereignty had been in reply to questions from a Taiwanese reporter. Throughout the crisis Beijing attempted to restrict nationalist expression through media blackouts and restricted demonstrations on the Mainland.[25] However, demonstrations occurred outside the Japanese Embassy in Hong Kong. Domestic Chinese activists were troubled by these restrictions because they had been expected to be given permission to demonstrate against Japan. This in turn increased criticism of the CCP for its approach to the dispute.[26]

It is unclear whether the MSA's initial decision to recognize the lighthouse in response to Nihon Seinensha's application was the product of deliberate endorsement of the nationalist agenda or merely the product of bureaucratic inertia.[27] It may be that not all sectors of the Japanese government were equally aware of the sensitivity of the islands. For example, the Ministry of Transport acquiesced to the 1978 lighthouse construction, over MOFA's objections, and had twice refused to recognize it as a navigational aid because it was not up to standard. It would be difficult to argue that the MSA would not be sensitive to the implications of recognizing the lighthouse in 1990. Indeed, one interviewee suggested that the Ministry of Transport's decision to recognize the lighthouse in 1990 was driven by its interest in reinforcing Japan's effective occupation of the islands, whereas MOFA was motivated by the "China School" in the Asian Affairs Bureau, which had historically favored a soft line for Japan's China policy.[28] In any case, the incident illustrates that elites in both states worked to limit destabilizing provocations from nationalists both inside and outside government. Japanese authorities intervened when it appeared that the incident would cause friction with Taiwan. Whatever the reason for the MSA's decision, Tokyo calculated that recognition of the lighthouse was not worth the negative political fallout with Taiwan. For its part, Beijing incurred criticism from overseas nationalists for its unwillingness to escalate the issue with Japan.

The 1992 Incident

Tensions resurfaced in February 1992 after China passed its Law on the Territorial Sea and Contiguous Zone (LTC), which outlined its rights and responsibilities pertaining to the newly created maritime zones under UNCLOS, which China had signed in December 1982. The LTC reiterated China's claims to its claimed territories in the South China Sea and the Senkaku/Diaoyu Islands. Japan's primary concern was that the LTC breached the agreement to shelve the dispute. Japan's prime minister, Miyazawa Kiichi, immediately opposed the claim and described the dispute as a "closed case" that should be left to future generations, as had been suggested by Deng in 1978.[29] CCP general secretary Jiang Zemin defended the move at a meeting with Miyazawa in early April, where he said that the law did not contravene the shelving arrangement but expressed hope that relations would be not damaged.[30]

Problematically, the LTC was passed at a particularly sensitive time in the Sino-Japanese relationship.[31] Chinese policymakers were seeking to end their international isolation after the Tiananmen Square incident. To this end, they were in the process of organizing reciprocal visits between Jiang Zemin and the Japanese emperor.[32] However, Japan's conservatives, who also opposed the emperor visiting China, seized on the LTC as an effort by China to seize the islands. Conservative opposition was so strident that the government issued special protection to those officials working on the issue for fear that they would be targets of violence.[33] These political machinations in Japan were mirrored by bureaucratic politics in China. It is widely suspected that the islands were included in the LTC against the wishes of the MFA and as a result of intense lobbying by the military, particularly the navy.[34] This debate appears to have concerned how best to press China's sovereignty claims. The MFA maintained that including reference would upset the political relationship with Japan, but military delegates of the National People's Congress argued that it was required to maintain China's claim.[35] Certainly, for China to have claimed the islands in the South China Sea and not those in the East China Sea would have been interpreted by Japan as a renunciation of China's claim.

Neither government had an incentive to see the LTC issue escalate. The People's Republic of China (PRC) had an interest in positive relations with Japan, particularly in light of the international condemnation that followed the Tiananmen Square incident, and wanted to ensure the success of the Emperor's visit. Miyazawa wanted improved relations with China and had invested a great deal of personal political capital to ensure the Emperor's visit occurred. He thus downplayed the significance of the LTC in the face of conservative outrage. MOFA spokesperson Hashimoto Hiroshi explained the LTC as an effort by China to clean up its domestic legislation and stated that both sides understood the sovereignty dispute was shelved.[36] Beijing made public assurances that the LTC did not represent a change in policy and that China still wanted positive relations with Japan. Nevertheless, the tensions over the LTC are indicative of the dynamics during this phase of the dispute. Both governments were willing to manage nationalist pressures for the sake of bilateral relations, but secondary political groups on both sides advocated more hard-line policies; the military on the Chinese side and the political right in Japan.

The 1996 Incident

The nationalist outbursts and subsequent diplomatic confrontation over the Senkaku/Diaoyu Islands in 1996 marked a new low in the East China Sea dispute. Like its predecessors, the 1996 incident was sparked by nationalist reaction to a central government policy decision; in this case Chinese and Japanese ratification of UNCLOS. There are signs the internal political climate in China and Japan was conducive to manipulation by secondary political groups. Some analysts have observed that, similar to the 1990 dispute, China was in the midst of a nationalist propaganda campaign, this time due to the missile exercises over Taiwan in March.[37] Throughout 1996, Beijing encouraged the celebration of China's achievements since its economic opening in 1978. As Avery Goldstein remarked in retrospect, "Beijing did not have to massage public opinion much at all to evoke the desired response in support of government policy."[38] In Japan, newly elected Liberal Democratic Party (LDP) leader Hashimoto Ryutaro was seeking to strengthen his party's fortunes after three years in a coalition. Given the party's conservative base and the likelihood of a lower house election at some point that year, some demonstration of Hashimoto's nationalist credentials was to be expected.

In China the National People's Congress ratified UNCLOS on May 15, 1996, and reaffirmed its sovereignty over the islands claimed in the 1992 LTC.[39] As China did not explicitly claim the Senkaku/Diaoyu Islands, Japan did not protest China's declaration, whereas the Philippines and Vietnam—claimants to islands in the South China Sea—did.[40] Japan ratified UNCLOS and announced the delimitation of its EEZ and continental shelf on June 7, 1996, although it did not draw baselines around the islands or claim an EEZ from them.[41]

As Japan's EEZ bill was being considered in the Diet, Nihon Seinensha constructed a lighthouse on Kita Kojima/Bei Xiaodao, a small island in the Senkaku/Diaoyu Islands, sparking an expression of "grave concern" by MFA spokesperson Cui Tiankai.[42] Nevertheless, he reiterated China's pledge to seek a solution through "friendly consultation" and expressed hope that both sides would exercise restraint.[43] This occurred the same day that Hashimoto expressed his support for China's bid for membership in

Island and constructed a Shinto shrine. The act was denounced by Chinese nationalists and caused both states to reassert their claim, somewhat routinely.[54] The first successful landing by Mainland Chinese protesters occurred on March 24, 2004, when seven activists from the Federation for Defending the Diaoyu Islands were arrested by the JCG for landing on Uotsuri/Diaoyu Island, where they attempted to plant a Chinese flag. The protesters were detained in Okinawa briefly and deported, but not before the situation deteriorated. Rhetoric from both capitals was strong but measured. Prime Minister Koizumi Junichiro stressed calm and said that the protesters would be dealt with under Japanese law. Beijing meanwhile reiterated its claim to the islands and labeled the detention of the activists illegal. These measured replies were soon drowned out by demonstrations of nationalism in Chinese streets and internet chat rooms and in Japanese newspapers.[55] Nihon Seinensha promised to conduct its own landing on the islands in response.[56] Conservative Japanese politicians, such as Ministry of Economy, Trade, and Industry (METI) minister Ishihara Nobuteru, called for Japan to strengthen its presence on the islands to reinforce its territorial claim.[57] Despite these tensions, elites on both sides intervened to manage the dispute. According to Chung, Beijing prevented subsequent visits by the group in April and July 2004, while Tokyo sought to limit the political fallout by banning Nihon Seinensha from visiting the islands.[58] The clearest evidence of elite intervention to manage tensions is that the Cabinet Office prevented the detained Chinese protesters from being prosecuted under Japanese law in Okinawa, which could have further escalated the situation.[59]

The 2004 landing marked the last time the two were able to manage tensions over the islands under the consensus reached after the 1996 crisis. Both Deng's modus vivendi and the agreement to manage nationalist tensions began to unravel as policymakers in both countries became more attuned to the importance of the islands and the surrounding maritime space. As a consequence of the jurisdictional entitlements of UNCLOS, Chinese and Japanese leaders became increasingly aware of the need to exploit their newfound maritime space. This development shifted elite, bureaucratic, and popular concern away from the sovereignty dispute over the islands and toward jurisdiction over maritime zones granted by their ownership. Problematically, nationalists extended their ideational attachment to the disputed maritime space as well as the islands themselves.[60] In this climate, leaders in both countries have less incentive to manage tensions over the islands.

From Disputed Islands to Contested Maritime Space

The latest phase of the China–Japan maritime relationship has been characterized by challenges over maritime jurisdictional issues brought about by UNCLOS and accentuated by China's rise as a maritime power. Subsequent chapters detail the ebb and flow of cooperative interaction over these issues. Two features of the last phase of tensions stand out. First, nationalist constituencies have begun to view the East China Sea itself with the same symbolic attachment as they do the disputed Senkaku/Diaoyu Islands. The 1996 lighthouse incident marked the first time that a popular nationalist group had undertaken an action in light of jurisdictional concerns, rather than as an expression of sovereignty over the islands. China did not make fresh claims to the islands in its EEZ declaration; it merely reiterated claims made under the LTC. Nevertheless, Nihon Seinensha's decision to build the lighthouse appears to have been based on a perceived need to demonstrate Japanese opposition to China's EEZ claim, given that Tokyo did not protest China's declaration.

Nationalist actors reinforced the salience of jurisdictional issues by challenging the political center to assert itself. In 1999, the Lower House Committee on Security, led by Nishimura, planned a visit to the islands to "demonstrate Tokyo's sovereignty" in light of a growing number of intrusions by Chinese vessels into Japanese waters.[61] This illustrates that nationalists viewed maritime jurisdictional issues to be as potent an anti-Chinese symbol as the disputed Senkaku/Diaoyu Islands themselves. Although Nishimura was a polarizing figure in Japanese politics, the planned aerial survey had broad support across the bipartisan committee. The self-defense forces' director-general, Hosei Norota, pledged to help the committee members make the trip on an MSDF aircraft. By contrast, in 1997, calls to have the MSDF mobilized to prevent incursions into Japan's territorial waters and landings on the islands were rejected by the head of the self-defense forces because defense against illegal entry was not within the MSDF's operational mandate.[62] The selective approach toward the use of military over coast guard assets in response to Chinese intrusions into Japanese waters is telling.

Second, the ratification of UNCLOS by Japan and China in 1996 increased the salience of maritime jurisdictional entitlements such as fisheries, marine research, and offshore gas and oil exploration for central policymakers in Tokyo and Beijing. Reports of Chinese vessels entering Japanese waters surfaced in the early 1990s but ceased after complaints from Tokyo.[63] However, the issue resurfaced in the latter half of the 1990s, and by 2000, it was no longer restricted to survey vessels because People's Liberation Army Navy (PLAN) vessels were also detected operating in Japan's claimed waters. By the late 1990s, Chinese thinking focused less on the disputed islands and became more concerned with "differences between China and Japan over maritime rights and interests and sovereignty in the East China Sea."[64]

The controversy surrounding China's exploration efforts in the Xihu Trough is one such difference over jurisdictional entitlements in the East China Sea. Chinese exploration vessels have been sighted in the vicinity of the Senkaku/Diaoyu Islands since the early 1990s.[65] Political tensions first surfaced in 2001, when Chinese survey vessels began crossing the median line more frequently to conduct resource surveys.[66] However, Chinese production efforts have not occurred near the Senkaku/Diaoyu Islands; rather, they are within its EEZ, just east of the Japanese-drawn median line. However, the proximity of China's Chunxiao gas field to Japan's claimed EEZ has raised concerns in Tokyo that China may be tapping resources on the Japanese side of the line.

The growing importance of both the tangible and intangible salience of the islands means that policymakers have fewer incentives to replicate the crisis management efforts of the 1990s. That the sightings of Chinese drill ships near the islands in the early 1990s did not trigger greater alarm can be attributed to an increase in the perceived economic and political importance of maritime space since 1996. These reduced incentives for cooperation have emerged against the backdrop of a rising number of confrontations between Chinese and Japanese vessels of all stripes both in the vicinity of the Senkaku/Diaoyu Islands and in the wider East China Sea. Both states' growing maritime awareness has created a pretext for a more active maritime enforcement capability. Furthermore, as a function of the growing tangible importance of disputed maritime areas, this capability is arguably a necessary dimension of state policy, but one that runs the risk of triggering a crisis in contested waters. This trend was most recently illustrated by China's reaction to the detention of a Chinese fishing boat captain following a collision with a JCG vessel in the territorial sea of the Senkaku/Diaoyu Islands in September 2010.

On September 7, 2010, a Chinese fishing boat collided with a pair of JCG vessels near the islands. The Chinese captain, Zhan Qixiong, was detained, arrested, held for seventeen days, and subsequently released by the Japanese authorities. In addition to numerous diplomatic protests, China dispatched its own fisheries patrol vessels to the area, suspended elite- and provincial-level contacts with Japan, canceled an MSDF port call to Qingdao, suspended a visit to the Shanghai expo by Japanese students, suspended talks on joint resource development in the East China Sea, arrested four Japanese citizens for espionage, and appeared to cut off rare earth elements exports to Japan. The Chinese media set about lionizing the captain by carrying reports about the trials and tribulations confronted by Zhan's family and attributing the death of his grandmother to his arrest.[67] His release was widely celebrated in state media.

Beijing's initial reaction to the collision was focused primarily on doing what was necessary to assert its claim to the disputed islands: It rejected the legitimacy of Japan's actions by demanding the release of the captain, ship, and crew. Nationalist demonstrations, which were expected, were relatively subdued. A limited demonstration occurred outside the Japanese Embassy in Beijing, and a larger demonstration occurred on September 18, to mark the anniversary of the Mukden Incident. Large-scale demonstrations occurred in Chengdu, Xian, Zhengzhou, and Mianyang on October 16–17, apparently in response to reports of nationalist demonstrations in Tokyo. Unlike previous anti-Japanese protests, such as those that occurred in response to Japan's UN Security Council bid in April 2005, these demonstrations were reportedly more violent as protesters scuffled with police in Wuhan and Chengdu.[68] Japanese policymakers interpreted the fact that the protests were confined to cities that did not have a Japanese consulate or other diplomatic presence as an effort by Beijing to control nationalist sentiment.[69] The heavy police presence surrounding the Japanese Embassy in Beijing suggests that the central authorities were prepared for protests in large cities like Beijing, Shanghai, and Chongqing, but that the scale of the protests in secondary cities caught them off guard.[70] The strident Chinese reaction is widely viewed as an attempt to avoid domestic criticism of the Chinese leadership.

Likewise, the collision was a watershed moment for the Japanese populace in terms of its negative perceptions of China.[71] The Kan Naoto administration was widely criticized for releasing the fishing boat captain instead of pursuing legal proceedings against him.[72] Japanese right-wing groups staged two large-scale protests in Tokyo on October 2 and 16. Both protests witnessed calls for a more assertive Japanese policy toward China and were heavily critical of the government. The release of a JCG video of the incident, which seemed to confirm the guilt of the Chinese captain, ensured that the Kan administration was heavily criticized when it released the captain in what was widely perceived as a political intervention in an ongoing legal matter. Nevertheless, some applauded the effort to reduce tensions.[73] Unlike previous crises, which were sparked by secondary actors, the 2010 dispute was caused by application of state authority in a disputed area and escalated by the ensuing outpouring of nationalist sentiment, which Beijing in particular was at pains to restrain. Japan exercised its sovereign prerogative to detain a vessel that in its view was fishing illegally and sailing recklessly in Japanese waters. By virtue of its claims to sovereignty over the islands, China does not recognize Japan's right to do so.

Since 2010, secondary actors have again sought to exploit the dispute for their own agenda. For example, the fisheries communities on Japan's southern islands have become outspoken advocates of Japanese claims. Yonaguni Island is composed of three small fishing villages and is the closest inhabited settlement to the Senkaku/Diaoyu Islands. Reports suggest growing concern on the part of its residents due to Chinese fishermen who frequent the waters near the islands.[74] On December 10, 2010, a city councilman from Ishigaki, Hitoshi Nakama, visited Minami Kojima/Nan Xiaodao—one the smaller Senkaku Islands—in an effort to assert his city's view that the islands should be visited by Japanese citizens.[75] One interview subject outlined a conservative turn in the politics of communities such as Ishigaki and Miyako, in which local politicians would accept a greater JCG presence designed to police illegal fishing by Chinese fishermen.[76] The disputed islands lie 100 miles away. In a move that echoes the moves by Shimane Prefecture to assert claims over Takeshima (disputed with South Korea), the Ishigaki Municipal Assembly unanimously voted to designate January 14 "Senkaku Day." This is the date when Japan claimed the islands in 1895. Local officials have also facilitated tours of the islands, despite the JCG's ban on vessels approaching the islands.[77]

The negative influence of secondary political actors is well demonstrated by the attempt by Tokyo governor Ishihara Shintaro to buy three of the Senkaku Islands from their Japanese owner in the summer of 2012. Although widely viewed as an unnecessary and escalatory gesture, the move was also popular.[78] After he issued his call in April 2012, donations poured in, totaling 1.3 billion yen by July.[79] This forced the Noda Yoshihiko administration to consider buying the islands for the state, if only to keep them out of Ishihara's hands. Chinese president Hu Jintao issued a personal warning to Noda not to proceed with the purchase at the Asia Pacific Economic Cooperation summit in Vladivostok in September 2012.[80] Nevertheless, the purchase proceeded as planned the next day.

Despite its benign intentions, the nationalization of the islands in 2012 was consistent with the strengthening of formal Japanese control over the islands, a process which may have hastened the erosion of both points of consensus. In 2002, Tokyo leased the islands from their private owner, which, according to one scholar, marks the first time a government initiated an action explicitly over the islands.[81] The move was denounced by China and Taiwan as an effort to strengthen Japan's hold over the territory.[82] Following its decision to ban Nihon Seinensha from landing on the islands in 2004, Tokyo subsequently passed a law banning anyone, of any nationality, from landing on the islands.[83] On February 9, 2005, Japan took formal possession of the islands, which in turn triggered small demonstrations in Beijing and, according to the Chinese state media, rekindled "the flames of war."[84] Two subsequent landing attempts by Chinese nationalists in 2006 and 2007 were turned away on the grounds that no one was permitted to land on the islands, but both interventions by the JCG were condemned by China.[85] In the latter case the group was barred from departing Hong Kong by local authorities, but was allowed to depart from Xiamen. Against this backdrop, it comes as no surprise that Beijing was either unwilling or unable to understand the nuance of Noda's decision to nationalize the Senkaku/Diaoyu islands, likely because of the state of the contested-symbolic value of the islands. From China's perspective, the move was the latest in a series of moves that formalized Japan's hold over the islands.

China's reaction to the nationalization suggests that it is either unwilling or unable to control its nationalist actors. According to the Japanese media, Chinese MFA officials met with Hong Kong–based activists after the 2007 attempted landing and requested that they cease their activities.[86] Nevertheless, as Tokyo deliberated whether to purchase the islands in the summer of 2012, this same group set out to land on the islands on the symbolic date of August 15. Although they were met by a considerable JCG force, several landed on the islands, and fourteen were arrested and promptly deported, just as they had been in 2004.[87]

Under these circumstances, it seems clear that the tacit cooperation over the islands has ended. The 2010 crisis witnessed the explicit rejection of both points of consensus by Japanese officials. The Japanese media described the action of arresting the captain as a breach of the post-1996 consensus; clearly, they too expected Japanese leaders to deport the Chinese nationals who had been detained near the islands, as they had in 2004.[88] Following the Chinese attempt to land on the islands in August 2012, Japanese activists, including several lawmakers, were able to land on the islands shortly after the Chinese attempt, despite a heavy JCG presence nearby.[89] This likely reinforced the perception in Beijing that the consensus to manage nationalist actors was over.

More controversially, Seiji Maehara, then minister of transport, stated in the Diet that Japan had never agreed to Deng's modus vivendi, a move that caught several experts off guard.[90] Despite the denials of retired diplomats, this now appears to be the position of the Japanese government, as reflected by its public material on the Senkaku/Diaoyu issue.[91] Likewise, Beijing does not appear to feel itself bound by Deng's maxim to shelve the sovereignty question. China has publicly articulated an effort to change the status quo around the islands.[92] Chinese vessels increased their presence around the islands after the 2010 crisis, and in August 2011, a fisheries vessel entered the territorial sea for the first time, possibly as a signal to incoming Prime Minister Noda. Since the 2012 nationalization Chinese vessels have regularly entered the territorial sea of the islands as part of "routine" patrols. The state media are explicit that this is an attempt to end Japan's effective occupation of the islands, by shifting from shelving to "keeping the dispute alive" by frequently patrolling the area and publicizing the validity of China's claim to the islands internationally.[93]

However, despite the explicit rejection of Deng's modus vivendi, there is evidence of continued management efforts. Efforts by the Chinese media to lionize the captain of the fishing boat were curtailed by Chinese central authorities. For instance, a Guangzhou weekly magazine named the captain one of the one hundred most influential men in China, but follow-up articles were canceled and, according to Hong Kong media, the staff of these publications were disciplined.[94] Likewise, although Chinese MFA spokesperson Jiang Yu characterized the visit by the two Ishigaki councilmen as "gravely" infringing on "China's territorial sovereignty," there were no efforts by Beijing to escalate the issue.[95] Finally, at the height of tensions in 2012, director-general-level discussions occurred between the two countries' foreign ministries.[96] Subsequent chapters bear out the importance of these interactions for fostering cooperation between China and Japan.

Conclusion

Despite the recent deterioration of relations over the Senkaku/Diaoyu Islands, cooperation between China and Japan historically rested on two points of consensus. The first was Deng Xiaoping's modus vivendi to shelve the sovereignty of the islands and to focus on joint development. This was reciprocated by Japanese leaders and enshrined a status quo that was beneficial for both sides. Both parties interpreted this to imply Japanese administration and occupation of the islands. China would not attempt to alter this status quo by territorial conquest, and Japan would not further consolidate its hold. Prime Minister Miyazawa framed his response to China's LTC in the context of Deng's maxim, which indicates that Japanese leaders were aware of what was expected by Beijing, despite efforts to officially deny the existence of any such arrangement.[97]

The second instance of cooperation was an informal agreement not to be provoked by nationalist groups. This emerged in the wake of the 1996 crisis and seems to have eroded between 2004 and 2010. Beijing's strident reaction to the detention of a Chinese fishing boat captain in September 2010—an issue to which the analysis returns in chapter 6—suggests that Beijing is no longer willing or able to downplay or ignore nationalist sentiment. The erosion of this consensus may also be attributed to the fact that, as illustrated in subsequent chapters, the anti-Chinese sentiment exhibited by Japanese conservatives, particularly as it relates to the maritime realm, has become a widespread sentiment across the Japanese government and public. China's reaction to the nationalization in 2012 stands in stark contrast to its ability to ignore Japanese nationalist provocations between 1997 and 2004.

These two agreements were focused on managing the tensions that arose from the contested-symbolic salience of the disputed islands, and this may explain the tacit, informal nature of the two countries' cooperation. As indicated by the MVM in chapter 1, the pursuit of such cooperation would have been difficult for both parties. Attempts to formalize either agreement would have incurred domestic political costs. It is thus unsurprising that both points of consensus unraveled as bilateral relations deteriorated and as the tangible and intangible aspects of disputed space became increasingly conflated for both policymakers and their constituents. Given that the islands are tied to wider claims to the East China Sea, policymakers became increasingly attuned to the potential tangible benefits brought by the sea area surrounding the islands and the rising ideational costs to compromise.

As a function of the contested-symbolic salience of the disputed issue, cooperation was never formal or robust. Consequently, it is no surprise that Deng's modus vivendi collapsed. Chinese elites perceived Japan's efforts to consolidate its hold over the islands as a violation of the agreement. Furthermore, by this stage, the ideational environment was such that renewed cooperation on this basis was impossible. Far too many actors had a stake in the contested-symbolic salience of the islands. Nevertheless, subsequent case studies suggest that under certain circumstances, Japan and China can overcome contested-symbolic barriers to cooperation provided there is an economic incentive.

Notes

1. Comprehensive background is given by Blanchard, "Island of Friction in a Sea of Problems."
2. Downs and Saunders, "Legitimacy and the Limits of Nationalism," 114–46.
3. Emery et al., "Geological Structure," 40–41.
4. This background draws from Anonymous, "East China Sea," 823–65; and Austin *China's Ocean Frontier*, chap. 6.
5. For the details, see Ma, *Legal Problems of Seabed Boundary Delimitation*, 32–35, 63.
6. Cheng, "Sino-Japanese Dispute over the Tiao-Yu-Tai (Senkaku) Islands," 242.
7. Li, "China and Offshore Oil," 146; Ragland, "Harbinger: The Senkaku Islands," 664–91.
8. Matsui, "International Law of Territorial Acquisition," 3–31.
9. Ma, *Legal Problems of Seabed Boundary Delimitation*, 50–51.
10. Statement of the Ministry Foreign Affairs of the PRC, quoted by Chiu, "Analysis of the Sino-Japanese Dispute," 15–17.
11. Lee, *Japan Faces China*, 109.
12. Tretiak, "Sino-Japanese Treaty of 1978," 1241.
13. Chung, *Domestic Politics*, 40. One scholar speculates that the incident reflected differences in Beijing over Japan policy and reflected an attempt by segments of the Chinese policy apparatus to disrupt the treaty negotiations. See Mendl, *Japan's Asia Policy*, 82.
14. Shaw, *Diaoyutai/Senkaku Islands Dispute*, 16.
15. Lo, *China's Policy towards Territorial Disputes*, 171–72.
16. Glaubitz, "Anti-Hegemony Formulas in Chinese Foreign Policy," 207. This was mostly likely an early concession by the Chinese in light of their predominant territorial concern, the status of Taiwan. See Cheng, "Normalization of Sino-Japanese Relations," 258.
17. Tretiak, "Sino-Japanese Treaty of 1978," 1243.
18. Ibid., 1244.
19. Chung, *Domestic Politics*, 40.
20. For the details, see Manicom, "Strategic Policy, Economic Opportunities and Cooperation," 38–44.

21. One analyst has argued that *Nihon Seinensha* "drove" the 1978 dispute but does not describe how. See Deans, "Contending Nationalisms in the Diaoyutai/Senkaku Dispute," 125.

22. Cheung and Smith, "Rocks of Contention," 19.

23. Downs and Saunders, "Legitimacy and the Limits of Nationalism," 127–33.

24. Chung, *Domestic Politics*, 42–43; Shaw, *Diaoyutai/Senkaku Islands Dispute*, 17–18.

25. Following the chaos of the anti-Japanese protests in China in the mid-1980s, Chinese leaders were more careful to control anti-Japanese sentiment. See Shirk, *China: Fragile Superpower*, 160–64.

26. Downs and Saunders, "Legitimacy and the Limits of Nationalism," 131–32.

27. See Deans, "Diaoyutai/Senkaku Dispute."

28. Author interview "B," February 1, 2008, Tokyo.

29. Miyazawa Kiichi, quoted in "Miyazawa Opposes China's Territorial Claim," Jiji Press English News Service, February 27, 1992.

30. Mendl, *Japan's Asia Policy*, 82; Hagstrom, *Japan's China Policy*, 126.

31. "Japan Regrets Timing of Chinese Claim on Islands," Kyodo News, March 2, 1992.

32. Kim, "Japanese Policy towards China," 229.

33. Ibid., 234–35.

34. Roy, *China's Foreign Relations*, 75; Drifte, *Japan's Security Relations with China*, 50.

35. Austin, *China's Ocean Frontier*, 313.

36. Drifte, *Japan's Security Relations with China*, 50.

37. Downs and Saunders, "Legitimacy and the Limits of Nationalism," 133–39.

38. Goldstein, "China in 1996," 34–35.

39. "PRC Declaration on Sea Baselines for Paracel Islands," *People's Daily*, May 16, 1996. China claimed a continental shelf and EEZ up to 200 nautical miles from its baselines, which were enshrined into law two years later. "PRC UNCLOS Ratification Statement," www.un.org/Depts/los/convention_agreements/convention_declarations.htm.

40. "Status of the Convention and Its Implementing Agreements," www.un.org/Dept/los/LEGISLATIONANDTREATIES/asia/htm.

41. See Roach, "China's Straight Baseline Claim," 1. There is conjecture on this point. Mark Valencia maintains that Japan uses the islands as a baseline for an EEZ claim. See Valencia, "China's Push for Offshore Oil"; and Valencia, "East China Sea Dispute," 127–67. However, Japan did not draw baselines around the islands until March 2008. See Division for Ocean Affairs and the Law of the Sea, Law of the Sea Information Circular no. 28, annex II.

42. Cui Tiankai, quoted in "Spokesperson Warns Japan over Lighthouse on Disputed Islands," *People's Daily*, July 18, 1996.

43. Cui Tiankai, quoted in "Foreign Ministry Spokesperson Discusses Diaoyutai Issue," *People's Daily*, July 25, 1996.

44. Hashimoto's visit, the first by a sitting Japanese prime minister since 1985, was likely a domestic electoral prerogative. By visiting the shrine on his birthday, Hashimoto avoided pressure to visit the shrine on the August 15. However, the

timing in the context of the escalating crisis over the islands served to further sour relations. According to one scholar, the brief nature of Hashimoto's visit indicated his reluctance to exacerbate Sino-Japanese relations. See Daiki. "Yasukuni Shrine Dispute," 209.

45. Downs and Saunders, "Legitimacy and the Limits of Nationalism," 135.

46. Ibid., 134–35.

47. Gries, *China's New Nationalism,* 123. The original was aimed predominantly at the United States.

48. Chung, *Domestic Politics,* 49; Downs and Saunders, "Legitimacy and the Limits of Nationalism," 135–36.

49. Downs and Saunders, "Legitimacy and the Limits of Nationalism," 136.

50. Chung, *Domestic Politics,* 58. This agreement has been described in other sources as Japan agreeing not to arrest protesters if China assured Japan that it would keep Chinese protesters from sailing to the islands. See "Nihon Senkaku Mitsuhyaku atta" [Japan had a secret agreement over the Senkaku Islands], *Aera, Asahi Shimbun Weekly,* October 25, 2010.

51. The MSA counted three attempts in 1997 alone. See MSA, "Annual Report on Maritime Safety 1998," 16.

52. "Senkaku Visit Riles Japan, China," *Asahi Shimbun,* May 6, 1997. The pledge occurred during the political campaign for the October 20, 1996, lower house elections.

53. Xue, "Foreign Ministry News Briefing."

54. Su, "Territorial Dispute over the Tiaoyu/Senkaku Islands," 46–50.

55. Curtin, "New Sino-Japanese Strain over Disputed Islands."

56. Donaldson and Pratt, "International Boundary Developments," 418.

57. "Japan Should Build Lighthouse, Heliport in Senkakus—Minister," Kyodo News, April 3, 2004.

58. Chung, "Resolving China's Island Disputes," 62; "Japan Bans Political Group from Sailing for Disputed Islands," Kyodo News, March 27, 2004.

59. "Japan Deported Chinese Protesters under Political Pressure," Kyodo News, April 2, 2004.

60. Manicom, "Interaction of Material and Ideational Factors in the East China Sea Dispute," 375–91.

61. Iitake, "Lawmakers Set Sights on Visit to Senkaku Islands."

62. Austin and Harris, *Japan and Greater China,* 102.

63. Austin, *China's Ocean Frontier,* 88.

64. Wu, "China's Regional Security Interests and Corresponding Strategic Countermeasures."

65. See "Japan Asks China to Investigate East China Sea Incident," Kyodo News, December 16, 1991; "Spokesperson: Vessel Leaves Disputed Area Near Diaoyutai Islands," Agence France-Presse, February 15, 1996; "Drillship Enters Senkaku Area," *Petroleum Economist,* March 1, 1996.

66. Harrison, "Quiet Struggle in the East China Sea," 274.

67. "Torture, Anger Overshadow Family Reunion Festival for Relatives of Detained Chinese Fisherman," Xinhua News, September 22, 2010.

68. "China Allows Rowdy Anti-Japanese Protests," Associated Press, October 18, 2010.

69. Author interview "O," Tokyo, June 20, 2012.

70. Manicom, "Growing Nationalism and Maritime Jurisdiction in the East China Sea," 9–11.

71. One prominent think tank described 2010 as the year of the "China shock"; Jimbo, *Japan's Security Strategy toward China*. See also "China: Towards a Less Cooperative, More Assertive Posture," in *East Asian Strategic Review 2011*, 109.

72. For a critical analysis of the discourses surrounding the incident, see Hagstrom, "'Power Shift' in East Asia?" 267–97.

73. "Kan Administration Criticized over Spat with China," *Asahi Shimbun*, September 28, 2010.

74. Fackler, "Japan Isle in Sea of Contention Weights Fist versus Open Hand"; Chino, "Yonaguni Island in Crisis."

75. Tritten and Sumida, "Local Officials Stir Dispute over Senkaku Islands."

76. Author interview "P," June 20, 2011, Tokyo. Plans are outlined by Chino, "Yonaguni Island in Crisis."

77. See "Lawmakers View Disputed Senkaku Islands," Kyodo News, June 11, 2012.

78. Japan's ambassador to China, Niwa Uichiro, was deeply critical of Ishihara's efforts; "Ambassador to China Slams Ishihara's Senkakus Plan," *Japan Times*, June 8, 2012.

79. "Tokyo Will Fight for Senkakus," *Yomiuri Shimbun*, July 8, 2012.

80. Shi, "Hu Warns Japan."

81. Hagstrom, *Japan's China Policy*, 151.

82. Liu, "Japan's Sinister Designs in Illegally Leasing Diaoyu Dao."

83. Marquand, "Japan–China Tensions Rise over Tiny Islands."

84. Liu, "Masses in Four Mainland Cities Stage Protests Defending the Diaoyu Islands."

85. "Barring of Diaoyu Offenders 'Unreasonable,'" *China Daily*, October 18, 2006; "China Slams Blocking of Activists," *Japan Times*, October 31, 2007.

86. "Newly Assertive China Wanted the Senkaku Stunt to Succeed," *Asahi Shimbun*, August 16, 2012.

87. "Noda Team Moves Swiftly to Curtail Senkaku Controversy," *Asahi Shimbun*, August 17, 2012.

88. "Japanese Article Says Tokyo Broke 'Secret' Islets Pact with China," Agence France-Presse, October 18, 2010. For a discussion, see Tiberghien, "Diaoyu Crisis of 2010," 70–78.

89. AFP-Jiji, "Rightwingers Land on Senkakus, Hoist Flags."

90. "Diet to See Video of Senkaku Run-in," *Japan Times*, October 28, 2010. For reactions, see Wan, "Japan's Party Politics and China Policy."

91. For a dissenting Japanese view, see Kuriyama, "Both Sides Need to Make Efforts to Maintain Status Quo." See also Japan Ministry of Foreign Affairs (MOFA), "Q&A on the Senkaku Islands."

92. "Diaoyu Islands Enters a New Stage," *Global Times*, December 14, 2012.

93. Chen, "Judging the New Game of the Diaoyu Islands."

94. Przystup, "Troubled Waters II," 5.

95. "Foreign Ministry Spokesperson Jiang Yu's Remarks," Embassy of the People's Republic of China in the Republic of Ghana, http://gh.china-embassy.org/eng/fyrth/t777814.htm.

96. "Chinese Foreign Ministry Official Visits Japan to Negotiate Diaoyu Island Dispute," *Zhongguo Xinwen She*, October 11, 2012.

97. Nevertheless, there was an effort to ensure ambiguity. MOFA issued a correction to Miyazawa's April 1992 reference to the shelving arrangement with Deng, saying that there was no such arrangement and that Miyazawa's statement invited misunderstanding. Hagstrom, *Japan's China Policy*, 124–25.

CHAPTER THREE

Cooperation on Fisheries, 1997–2000

CHINA AND JAPAN reached a compromise on their maritime jurisdiction in the East China Sea in November 1997, when they signed the China–Japan Fisheries Agreement. The final agreement was not completed until February 2000, and it came into force in June 2000.[1] The agreement is an example of reciprocal cooperation over an area of mutual interest. The MVM expects a robust agreement with enforceable protocols for managing fish stocks in the East China Sea. The agreement was not without resistance, however. Japan's long-standing opposition to the EEZ regime needed to be overcome in order to renegotiate its regional fisheries arrangements. Japan declared a 200-nautical-mile exclusive fisheries zone (EFZ, the precursor to the EEZ) in 1977 to protect its domestic fisheries from the expansion of Soviet maritime jurisdiction. However, as a function of its global fisheries interests, Japan sought to prevent regionwide adoption by exempting Chinese and South Korean fishermen in a quid pro quo to maintain Japanese access to their coastal waters.[2] Under the 1975 China–Japan Fisheries Agreement, resource management fell under the responsibility of the flag state, and Japanese coastal waters were treated as high seas for the purposes of Chinese and Korean fisheries vessels, although at the time this amounted to very little actual fishing.[3] This situation changed with the growth of China's fisheries industry, which allowed Chinese vessels unregulated access to Japan's coastal waters, whereas Japanese fishermen were bound by quotas and conservation measures in Chinese coastal waters. This challenge to Japan's reference point as a fisheries power was exacerbated by the fact that China benefited from Japan's reluctance to declare an EEZ.

This chapter first explores the value of the fisheries in the East China Sea using the MVM. The economic value of the East China Sea's fishery resources was important for both sides. China's rise as a fisheries power, combined with Japan's jurisdictional shortcomings, resulted in a growing number of confrontations between fishermen as Chinese fishing in Japanese waters increased. Furthermore, repairing the fisheries regime in East Asia risked inflaming tensions over the Senkaku/Diaoyu Islands. The second section explores the sources of cooperation between China and Japan. Several factors militated against a Japanese decision to redress the imbalance with China; opposition to the EEZ regime was deeply entrenched in the Japanese government, particularly in MOFA. Pressure from the fisheries lobby caused Japan to reverse its long-standing opposition to ocean enclosure in order to protect its offshore fisheries. Beijing was receptive to Tokyo's overtures because it sought to gain recognition of its maritime claims. The third section explores the depth of cooperation. The central bargaining challenge was that the narrow space of the East China Sea complicated the adoption of the EEZ regime, the mechanism that allows coastal states to regulate their own fisheries. Following several rounds of talks, and bolstered by more than fifty years of interaction on fisheries, the two sides arrived at an agreement in November 1997. The final section explores the durability of the Provisional Measures Zone created by the fisheries agreement and identifies further issues that were left unresolved.

The Value of the Fisheries in the East China Sea

The MVM illustrates that cooperation on fisheries in the mid-1990s is not surprising because both parties rely on protein sources from the East China Sea. Traditional concerns about food security made Japan particularly nervous about rising Chinese catch levels. Nevertheless, barriers to cooperation remained, not least the status of the Senkaku/Diaoyu Islands in any agreement. Also, due to Japanese policymakers' resistance to the EEZ regime since the notion emerged in the 1970s, they remained reluctant to act until pressured by special interest groups.

The Economic Value of the East China Sea's Fisheries to China

Beijing values the East China Sea's fisheries for economic reasons; it values fish products as a source of meat protein, and employment as a driver of national development. These are material aspects of maritime space, and the fact that Japan shared the same concerns indicates that they are seen as legitimate by both parties. The fisheries industry was targeted for dramatic expansion in the late 1970s and 1980s, and demand for fish products is sustained by eastern China's increasingly affluent population.[4] The East China Sea is home to fourteen traditional Chinese fishing grounds, including the vital Zhoushan Fishing Ground. Throughout the 1980s and 1990s, East China Sea's fisheries accounted for half of China's total annual catch of 25.3 million tons. According to the Food and Agriculture Organization of the United Nations (FAO), the East China Sea remains China's most important fishing ground, accounting for 34 percent of its total marine catch, with Zhejiang Province (home of Zhoushan) representing 22 percent of marine capture fisheries catch in 2004.[5]

The expansion of the fisheries industry during the reform period increased the importance of the industry to coastal communities. The number of motorized fishery vessels increased from 14,000 in 1970 to 200,000 in 1988, before leveling off at 249,000 in 1999. Employment in the industry grew from 1.25 million people in the 1980s to more than 20 million by the early 1990s.[6] The importance of employment in the Zhoushan fisheries area to Zhejiang's economy is evidenced by the implementation of the necessary cutbacks under the 1997 fisheries agreement. Rather than cut back on excess capacity and risk rising unemployment, the provincial authorities decided to police inshore fishing while promoting the distant water fishing (DWF) industry and coastal fish breeding.[7]

Chinese fishing in Japanese waters was driven by a number of factors. The development of China's DWF industry notwithstanding, most Chinese fishing vessels at the time were equipped with engines below 20 horsepower and designed for coastal fishing.[8] However, due to overfishing by Japanese vessels and Chinese coastal fishermen for much of the 1960s and 1970s, the share of the East China Sea's coastal areas in China's total catch began declining in 1981, when it peaked at 53.8 percent.[9] This drove Chinese vessels into Japanese coastal waters as the industry expanded. Furthermore, the Chinese authorities have struggled to enforce conservation measures on their coastal fishermen, partly due to the realities of the fishery environment in East Asia. Because many stocks are migratory, there is little incentive to enforce conservation in one's own EEZ when other states will not exercise the same responsibility when the fish migrate to their EEZ.[10] China's reluctance to manage its coastal fisheries and cut back its excess capacity is indicative both of the demand for fish products in China and the importance of the fisheries industry to coastal Chinese states.

The Economic Value of the East China Sea's Fisheries to Japan

Similarly, Japan values the East China Sea's fisheries as a source of protein and employment. Japan was the world's leading fishing nation, and the

East China Sea's fisheries have historically composed a significant part of Japan's total catch, which grew more important as a product of the emergence of the EEZ regime in the 1970s.[11] The Yellow Sea and East China Sea combined are one of Japan's eight offshore fishing sectors.[12] The expansion of state jurisdiction seaward—the "ocean enclosure movement"—threatened to reduce Japanese access to fishing grounds around the world and thus increased the importance of its offshore fishing sectors. Following its peak in 1973, at 41 percent of Japan's total catch, Japan's DWF catch fell from 2.45 million tons in 1978 to 800,000 tons in 1990.[13] This development highlights the relative importance of its offshore and coastal fisheries for Japan's fishery production. According to one expert, "except for a brief period in the early 1970s, when the distant water fisheries were thriving, the offshore fisheries have always tended to be the most important fisheries in Japan."[14] The East China Sea continues to play an important role in Japan's fisheries industry. However, the conservation measures applied to Japanese coastal waters under the 1975 China–Japan Fisheries Agreement combined with decreased access to DWF areas abroad reduced total Japanese fishery production from 12.2 billion tons in 1985 to 11 billion tons in 1990. This dropped even further by 1995, to 7.5 billion tons, a 32 percent decline driven by a 37 percent decrease in offshore and coastal fisheries production between 1990 and 1995.[15]

Fish protein continues to be in demand in Japan, despite rising prices and shifts to Western-style diets. Japan consumed 10.8 million tons of seafood in 1998, but due to catch reductions only 60 percent of this was provided by Japanese vessels.[16] As imports rose, so did unemployment among Japanese fishermen, due to industry restructuring and reductions in wages. The total number of fisheries workers has declined by 30 percent since 1995.[17] In absolute terms, the total number of fisheries enterprises decreased from 190,271 in 1988 to 163,169 by 1995. This contraction was felt most acutely in the offshore industry, whose total vessels decreased from 8,536 in 1988 to 6,964 in 1995.[18]

The salience of the East China Sea's fisheries is illustrated by the MVM depicted in figure 3.1. Despite the shared interest in exploiting these fisheries and ensuring the conservation of these resources, the Japanese side in particular viewed these concerns in a zero-sum fashion, as the next section of this chapter explains. The timing of the negotiations, the period 1995–96, also coincided with rising tensions over the Senkaku/Diaoyu Islands, as outlined in chapter 2. The salience of fisheries to both sides was accentuated by the rise of the Chinese fishing industry, which exposed weaknesses in the existing fisheries order.

FIGURE 3.1
Maritime Value Matrix, 1996

Economic:	Strategic:
• Fisheries resources • Employment in the fisheries industry	• Null
Shared-symbolic:	**Contested-symbolic:**
• Null	• Maintain claim to Senkaku/Diaoyu Islands

China's Challenge to Japan's Reference Point

By the mid-1990s, the balance of power between Chinese and Japanese fisheries had shifted toward greater parity, which challenged Tokyo's interpretation of the regional fisheries order. Hitherto, Chinese fisheries had not had the requisite capabilities to fish Japanese coastal waters to any serious extent, which led to the depletion of Chinese coastal waters because these were fished by both Chinese and Japanese fishermen.[19] This situation changed during China's reform period with the widespread adoption of modern fishing practices and a concerted effort to build the industry, including incentives such as tax breaks, funding allocations, and scientific research.[20]

Consequently, Chinese fisheries production increased dramatically, from 8.8 million tons in 1985 to 14.7 million tons in 1990 and 32.7 million tons in 1995, including a 33 percent increase between 1980 and 1985. Following the launch of China's DWF industry, total fishery production increased by 40 percent between 1985 and 1990 and by 55 percent between 1990 and 1995.[21] Although China's DWF fleet remained relatively backward by global standards—for example, it could not fish year-round like its Japanese counterpart—Chinese fishermen were able to challenge Japanese boats regionally.[22] By 2002, China's DWF industry had a fleet of 1,700 vessels and an annual output of 830,000 tons.[23] More extensive Chinese fishing in Japanese waters undermined Japanese supremacy in Northeast Asian fisheries. The shift exacerbated the steady decline of the Japanese coastal fisheries industry because it allowed China to exploit the loophole in the 1975 China–Japan Fisheries Agreement.

This situation led to a rise in the number of fishing disputes. As one observer has noted, overt fishing disputes between China and Japan were largely unheard of before diplomatic normalization between the two countries in 1978, due to the concern in both capitals of the potential for escalation. Somewhat ironically, diplomatic normalization and the end of Cold War tensions in Northeast Asia led to more frequent fishing disputes between coastal states, as states tolerated an increasing amount of illegal fishing by their own fishermen.[24] Chinese fishing in Japanese waters also exacerbated depletion, and many high-value species approached extinction. For example, the catch size of yellow croaker and hairtail peaked in the 1960s and has since been replaced with smaller, lower-value species such as mackerel and filefish.[25]

Unregulated Chinese fishing altered Japanese perceptions of the Northeast Asian environment in three ways. First, because Chinese fishing in Japanese waters was not illegal under the 1975 agreement, Japanese authorities could not regulate Chinese vessels. This was resented by Japanese fishermen, who often took it upon themselves to prevent Chinese fishermen from fishing in their waters; and Chinese fishermen retaliated.[26] Second, because of the unregulated nature of Chinese fishing in Japanese coastal waters, Chinese fishermen were able to use methods banned for Japanese fishermen, such as drift netting, which further angered Japanese coastal fishermen given that they had only recently had these conservation measures forced on them under the 1975 fisheries agreement.[27] Third, both led to increased tensions between rival fishermen, which led to more confrontations between Chinese and Japanese fishermen in Japanese waters.[28] In Northeast Asia's tense security environment, the potential for accidents in these policing actions is high and could have grave consequences for regional stability.

By the mid-1990s, the situation in Japan's coastal waters was critical. Chinese fishermen were more active off the Japanese coast than were Japanese fishermen, with deleterious effects on Japanese coastal fishermen and fish stocks.[29] The Chinese catch was exploding; China's catch in 1999 was 40.8 million tons, nearly double its catch in 1994.[30] By contrast, Japanese imports of fish products from China had been steadily increasing since 1992, and were often composed of fish caught in Japanese coastal waters by Chinese fishermen.[31] Many Japanese people adopted a zero-sum view of the situation: Japanese catches in its neighbors' waters were on the wane, and its neighbors' catches in its waters were on the rise.[32] The problem was exacerbated in the Japanese mindset by a simultaneous decline in DWF opportunities in light of the global acceptance of the EEZ regime. The threat to its coastal and offshore fisheries industry created an incentive for Tokyo to better manage fishery relations with Beijing.

The declaration of an EEZ, which placed resource management under the jurisdiction of the coastal state, would permit Japan to close the loophole in the 1975 China–Japan fisheries agreement. This, in turn, could meet both parties' territorial objectives by creating a sustainable, rule-based fisheries order that could reduce the frequency of incidents between fishermen. However, Japanese leaders were so wedded to the resistance of the EEZ regime that they were slow to recognize this solution.

Deciding to Cooperate

Both parties recognized their interest in accessing disputed fisheries resources and recognized that these concerns could be ameliorated by renegotiating the 1975 fisheries agreement on the basis of the EEZ regime. Nevertheless, Japanese policymakers remained reluctant for two reasons: Japan's long-standing opposition to ocean enclosure, and the risk of exacerbating territorial disputes with China. However, the perceived inequities of the emerging status quo in Northeast Asian fisheries, particularly rising imports from China, created a groundswell of domestic political pressure for the renegotiation of the fisheries agreement with China. The powerful fisheries lobby pressured the ruling LDP to ratify UNCLOS and renegotiate the agreement.[33] This pressure overcame the reluctance of some segments of the Japanese policymaking apparatus to fully embrace the new EEZ regime, and MOFA's reluctance to declare maritime zones that would likely be disputed by Japan's neighbors.[34] This pressure was integral to shaping Tokyo's perceptions of the reference point as one that no longer favored Japanese interests. China's decision was less complicated. As the state benefiting from the emerging status quo, Beijing viewed the renegotiation of the fisheries agreement in the context of potential delimitation negotiations that would confirm Chinese jurisdiction over its claimed 3 million square kilometers of ocean space. According to Yann-huei Song, China was reluctant to declare an EEZ in the absence of momentum from regional states for delimitation negotiations.[35] Failing this, Beijing could be assured that a renegotiated fisheries regime would reduce confrontations between fishermen and protect fragile resources.

Japan's Reluctance to Act

Japan's decision to cooperate was driven by domestic calls for a specific policy choice. Although there was no pressure on Japan to adopt a more confrontational posture, it is unclear what a more confrontational posture would have looked like. Without jurisdiction over fisheries in its offshore areas, there was little Japan could do to enforce authority it did not have. As a result of this proximate barrier to confrontation, the functional choice in this case was between doing nothing and cooperating. The former became an increasingly unpalatable policy choice due to domestic pressure.

Japan's inaction was based on its long-standing opposition to ocean enclosure. As a geographically disadvantaged state, with no continental shelf, Japan could have embraced the expansion of ocean jurisdiction permitted by UNCLOS. However, as the leading high seas fishery nation in the world, Japan opposed any steps to subject ocean space to any kind of sovereign authority because it recognized that this could reduce its fish catch on the high seas. During the 1960s, DWF vessels accounted for 5 percent of Japan's fleet, yet accounted for one-third of the total catch.[36] It was not until Japan lost access to 50 percent of its traditional high-seas fisheries zones, following American and Soviet EFZ declarations in 1976 and 1977, respectively, that Japan declared an EFZ of its own to protect its coastal fisheries. By the 1980s, Japan was fighting a losing battle against the trend toward ocean enclosure.[37] As a greater number of states asserted their jurisdiction over coastal waters fished by Japanese vessels, Tokyo sought to negotiate with these states for continued access.[38] To accomplish this, it needed to recognize coastal state jurisdiction over formerly high seas; and as a result, it eroded the very norm it was trying to protect.[39] Nevertheless, resistance to the EEZ regime was strong and widespread throughout Japan.

First, resistance to the EEZ was prevalent among the Japanese people due to their traditional sensitivities about food security.[40] Defined as "the ability of countries to meet target consumption levels" of a given food source, the security of fisheries products was historically assured by Japanese dominance as a global fishing power: Japanese consumers expected fish products to be available and affordable.[41] The ocean enclosure movement threatened Japanese food security.[42] According to one estimate, if all UNCLOS jurisdictional claims were granted, 90 percent of the global fisheries catch could be under coastal state jurisdiction.[43] This would inevitably lead to a reduction in catch levels. This sense of insecurity was heightened by the rise in Chinese catch levels throughout the 1980s and early 1990s. By the time fishery negotiations with China began in 1996, Japan's self-sufficiency ratio in fish meat protein was 56 percent, down from a peak of 113 percent in 1964.[44]

Second, Japan's fisheries industry and the Fisheries Agency in the Ministry of Agriculture, Forestry, and Fisheries (MAFF) lobbied against ocean enclosure in the 1970s. When Tokyo finally adopted the EFZ in 1977, it was able to do so only because it had the broad support of the DWF fisheries lobby, the Fisheries Agency, and the general public.[45] Following the EFZ declaration in 1977, MAFF was reluctant to renegotiate the fisheries order with China so soon after the agreement had been reached in 1975. Previous negotiations had been long, arduous processes, and the related ambiguities had resulted in thousands of seizures of Japanese boats by the Taiwanese and Mainland authorities and dozens of casualties.[46] In addition, MAFF and the fisheries lobby feared a reciprocal declaration by the Chinese and South Korean governments, which could have imposed limits on Japanese access to their coastal waters.[47] Therefore, by the time UNCLOS's ratification arose after the treaty went into effect in 1994, there was a great deal of bureaucratic resistance to the EEZ regime and renegotiation of the 1975 fisheries agreement.

Third, MOFA, which had argued in favor of adopting an EEZ in the 1970s, was reluctant to ratify UNCLOS in 1996. Because MOFA does not report to any domestic constituency, it is unconcerned with protecting domestic groups' interests—unlike MAFF. Its concerns relate to Japan's foreign policy and how it is perceived abroad.[48] For example, in the mid-1970s, one of MOFA's concerns was reconciling UNCLOS's territorial sea requirements with Japan's three nonnuclear principles, which were challenged by American nuclear-powered vessels that regularly passed through Japan's straits.[49] However, as the EEZ regime gained global and regional acceptance, MOFA argued that Japan did not want to appear intransigent in the face of global normative and legal change.[50]

By the mid-1990s, however, MOFA reversed this position amid concerns about how to handle the Senkaku/Diaoyu Islands issue.[51] The geographic realities in East Asia make maritime boundary disputes inevitable due to UNCLOS entitlements.[52] Further, there was concern that the EEZ regime would result in the conflation of national sovereignty with national jurisdiction, resulting in an increasingly zero-sum approach to fisheries management.[53] These concerns needed to be weighed against the benefits of exercising coastal state jurisdiction over fisheries. By declaring an EEZ,

Japan could assert its jurisdiction over the exploitation of fisheries resources up to 200 nautical miles offshore. Although this would certainly overlap with China's claims, UNCLOS could nevertheless provide the basis for a renegotiated fisheries agreement. If Japan included the disputed islands as base points in its EEZ declaration, it could risk political strife with China, which had claimed the islands in its 1992 Law on the Territorial Sea and Contiguous Zone.[54] Simultaneously, there was concern that if Japan did not include the islands in its EEZ declaration, the Chinese could argue that Japan had forfeited its title, which forms part of its EEZ claim in the southern part of the East China Sea.[55]

Finally, Japanese coastal fishery unions now favored ratification of UNCLOS as a way to protect their industry.[56] The de facto acceptance of the EEZ regime globally, which reduced access for Japan's DWF industry, reduced the political salience of the DWF industry. The futility of resisting ocean enclosure shifted the focus of the fisheries lobby from foreign fishing to the protection of the Japanese home waters.[57] In the words of National Federation of Fisheries Cooperatives (NFFC) managing director Noboru Azami, "If left unchecked, resources will be depleted . . . and it will be impossible to sustain the fishing business."[58] Indeed, Japan's DWF conglomerates had already begun to adapt to the EEZ regime by rationalizing their fleets and diversifying away from the fishery industry.[59] In doing so, the industry was choosing between the lesser of two evils. The rise of the ocean enclosure movement had threatened the future of the fishing industry in Japan, but the inequities of the 1975 agreement with China threatened the collapse of Japan's remaining fishing areas and, by extension, the offshore and coastal fishing industries.

This political pressure was highly public. At the NFFC's national convention in 1995, the largest coastal fisheries group, which was two thousand members strong, voted in favor of adopting the EEZ regime. This timely support occurred as the Diet was considering UNCLOS's ratification.[60] Political pressure also occurred in the streets of Tokyo when the NFFC and the Japan Fisheries Agency organized a rally calling for the establishment of a 200-nautical-mile EEZ. The rally was attended by more than six thousand people, including government officials, and by one estimate was the largest demonstration in Tokyo in twenty years.[61] The lobby also welcomed ratifications by other East Asian states. NFFC director Akira Sugawara described the South Korean EEZ declaration as "natural" and argued that the opportunity had arisen to renegotiate Japan's fishery agreements.[62] Japanese policymakers were aware of the potential impact of the Senkaku/

Diaoyu Islands dispute on the fishery negotiations, but by 1996, these concerns were regarded as less pressing than the protection of the Japanese offshore fishing industry. Japan ratified UNCLOS on June 7, 1996, and article 3 of its EEZ law asserts its jurisdiction over "exploring and exploiting, conserving and managing the natural resources."[63]

Japanese policymakers' perceptions of their policy options were significantly affected by the changing perceptions of relevant domestic actors. Japan's self-perception as a dominant fishing power was threatened by the rise of China as a competing fishing nation. China's emergence presented an acute challenge to Japan because years of Japanese policy inertia toward ocean enclosure had prevented Japan from exercising jurisdiction over its coastal waters. Japanese leaders chose to cooperate, reversing an entrenched policy, once domestic pressure made delay no longer politically viable.

China Reciprocates

In contrast to the Japanese stance, Chinese support for ocean enclosure is long standing. As a developing state with immense claims under the new regime, China was an ardent supporter of ocean enclosure throughout the UNCLOS negotiations. Like many developing states, Beijing advocated the maximum state jurisdiction over the maximum possible area for coastal states at the UNCLOS negotiations in the 1970s. This "maximalist" attitude went beyond the size of maritime zones, and extended to the degree of state authority over a given maritime zone. For instance, although the1958 Territorial Sea Convention set out an area for the purpose of policing adjacent to the territorial sea, China favored "the establishment of extensive zones for other purposes such as security and the protection of coastal fishery resources and national economic interests."[64] Furthermore, China has traditionally exercised jurisdiction over a vast area of ocean space for the purposes of conservation in the Yellow Sea and the East China Sea, and it has likewise created military zones that forbade the entry of foreign vessels.[65]

China's decision to renegotiate the 1975 fisheries agreement was a direct result of its decision to ratify UNCLOS in 1996, which extended a claim to more than 3 million square kilometers of ocean under its jurisdiction.[66] As a reflection of this interest, Beijing insisted that negotiations encompass both the issues of delimitation and of fisheries management.[67] When it became clear that boundary delimitation would be too complex and would delay the conclusion of a fisheries agreement, China agreed to focus on the fishery agreement and return to delimitation in due course.[68] As a rising fisheries power, China stood to benefit from a renegotiated agreement that reflected its reference point. It could expect that any agreement would reduce the frequency of confrontations between its fishermen and Japanese fishing vessels, while negotiating more stringent conservation measures. There is no evidence of serious domestic opposition within China to the expansion of Chinese maritime jurisdiction.[69] Cooperation was pursued reciprocally; Beijing recognized that a renegotiated agreement was consistent with its interests, defined in economic terms.

The Depth of Cooperation

The negotiations occurred against the backdrop of serious bilateral tensions over maritime issues, particularly during the tense summer of 1996, which witnessed the death of the Chinese activist David Chan amid elevated tensions over the islands. The fact that China and Japan had a decades-old bilateral fisheries relationship provided a climate of underlying support for the talks. The basis for negotiations was the EEZ regime outlined by UNCLOS, which had come into effect in 1994. The most serious concern was the issue of the Senkaku/Diaoyu Islands. Despite the reciprocal choice to renegotiate the fisheries agreement, territorial imperatives marred the process.

The process of ratifying UNCLOS was not without political tension. China's National People's Congress ratified UNCLOS on May 15, 1996, at which time China outlined the straight baselines that form the basis for its maritime claims.[70] It claimed a 200-nautical-mile EEZ and a continental shelf as far as the natural prolongation of the shelf, which were enshrined into law two years later. China also reaffirmed its sovereignty over the islands claimed in the 1992 LTC and reaffirmed its position that the coastal state could reserve the right to place limits on the innocent passage of warships through its territorial sea.[71] The 1992 LTC contained a claim to the Paracel Islands and Spratly Island groups in the South China Sea as well as the Senkaku/Diaoyu Islands.[72]

Less than a month later, Japan ratified UNCLOS and claimed an EEZ and continental shelf from its straight baselines. Its declaration is generally consistent with UNCLOS, except on the matter of dispute resolution, in which it adopts a median-line principle in the event of overlapping zones if no other line has been agreed upon.[73] According to Zou Keyuan, this reflected traditional Japanese attitudes toward overlapping EEZ claims and was consistent with the boundary drawn under Japan's 1977 Law on the 200-mile Fishery Zone.[74] Chinese leaders do not recognize the Japanese median line because it was drawn "unilaterally," without consultation with China.[75]

Neither side could compromise on the sovereignty on the islands, for two reasons. First, the islands were linked to each country's maritime claim in the East China Sea. Second, as illustrated above, to do so would have incurred tremendous domestic political costs due to the salience of the issue to vocal nationalist constituencies.[76] Nevertheless, there is no evidence that the conflicting claims over the islands undermined the political will to find a solution at any point in the negotiations. Chinese and Japanese negotiators met informally in April and August 1996, despite the ongoing crisis over the Senkaku/Diaoyu Islands. Officials met formally in December 1996 and February 1997, and they hosted eight rounds of official consultation and two subsequent informal rounds before signature.[77] Indeed, in an effort to defuse tensions, MOFA press officials disclosed that during talks on August 28 and 29, the Chinese and Japanese negotiators had formally agreed to extend the 1975 fisheries agreement on the basis of the EEZ regime.[78] Bilateral relations improved on November 13, 1996, when Japanese foreign minister Ikeda Yukihiko conceded that Tokyo would not include the controversial lighthouse (see chapter 2) in official navigational charts.[79] In April 1997, the two parties agreed to shelve the territorial dispute in the new agreement, thereby nullifying an impediment to cooperation.[80]

Beyond the territorial issue, the most serious challenge was how to define a zone of shared fisheries jurisdiction in an area of overlapping EEZs, without recognizing the validity of the basis for the other party's claim. Japan initially proposed a median line that bisected the East China Sea, the limit of Japan's 1977 EFZ, as the basis for the new fisheries agreement.[81] China's priority was to find a mechanism to avoid recognition of Japan's median line, whereas Japan sought to exercise jurisdiction far from its coasts to protect its coastal fisheries. To sidestep the delimitation issue, the two parties designated a large Provisional Measures Zone (PMZ) in the middle of the East China Sea for joint fisheries management. In a reflection of both sides' preferences, the PMZ is located in the middle of the East China Sea, and it does not use Japan's median line as a basis for its location (see map 3.1). Waters within the PMZ are managed by a joint

MAP 3.1
The Provisional Measures Zone

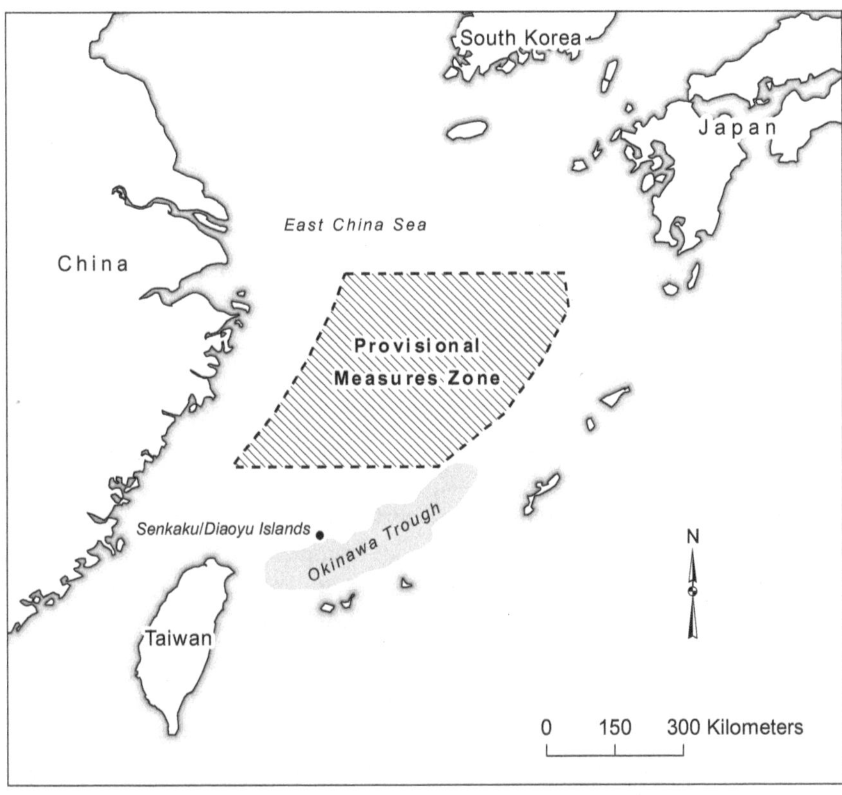

Note: This map does not display all the zones outlined by the 1997 China–Japan Fisheries Agreement. It merely shows the location of the PMZ to illustrate the area in which China and Japan have compromised on their jurisdiction over fisheries.
Source: Spatial Information System Laboratory, Flinders University.

fisheries authority. Fisheries in the area between each state's baselines and the seaward margin of the PMZ are under coastal state jurisdiction.

Determining the size of the PMZ, however, was complex because each party's preference was determined by their conflicting attitudes toward ocean enclosure. Japan—with a vocal and politically powerful fisheries lobby that sought maximum protection for its fishing grounds—wanted a small PMZ. This would mean that a larger share of the East China Sea would be governed as a Japanese EEZ, in which Japan could regulate the fishing activities of all vessels, including the Chinese vessels that fished this area. Conversely, China wanted a large PMZ. Given the nearly barren state of the Chinese coastal waters, a larger PMZ would give China greater access to waters closer to Japan, which were not yet overfished and which would be managed by the joint fisheries authority rather than Japan. Japan initially suggested a PMZ with margins 100 nautical miles from the two countries' respective coasts, and China suggested 24 nautical miles; the final compromise distance was 52 nautical miles.[82]

Negotiations were undoubtedly supported by the two countries' cooperative track record on fisheries issues. Despite a rising sense of food insecurity and more frequent fisheries disputes, China and Japan nonetheless had more than fifty years of generally positive interaction on fisheries issues before the commencement of negotiations toward the new agreement in 1996. Indeed, though some analysts argue that Northeast Asian fishery relations have been more conflict prone than cooperative, the Sino-Japanese relationship could be considered an exception.[83] Due to the geopolitical realities of the Cold War, the earliest fisheries agreements were nongovernmental and were reached between fisheries organizations from both countries.[84] The 1955 China–Japan Fishery Agreement that was signed between the Japan–China Fisheries Council and the China Fisheries Association was the result of recognition by both countries that fishing in the waters between the two states needed to be regulated. The Chinese were displeased to see so many Japanese fishing boats off their coast, and they thus adopted several protective measures to prevent Japanese fishing.[85] In their efforts to enforce the unilaterally drawn "Mao Zedong Line," the Chinese authorities detained 158 Japanese boats between 1950 and 1954.[86]

Subsequently, between 1955 and 1975 three fisheries agreements were signed between the Japan–China Fisheries Council and the China Fisheries Association.[87] Japan was not able to convince the Chinese to move the location of the Mao line until 1963, but they nevertheless negotiated continued access to Chinese coastal waters.[88] According to Sun Pyo Kim, even during periods when agreements were not renewed, stability prevailed because Japanese vessels generally followed the terms of the last agreement that was in force.[89] These agreements designated fishery zones, determined how many vessels from each state were permitted to operate in these zones, and outlined procedures for emergency port access, as well as communication protocols.[90] With diplomatic recognition in 1972, it became possible to negotiate a governmental fishery agreement. Signed on August 15, 1975, the thirty-year anniversary of Japanese surrender, the China–Japan Fisheries Agreement was largely identical to previous nongovernmental agreements, save for stricter conservation measures, including six conservation zones and seven closed zones in the East China Sea and Yellow Sea.

This track record also facilitated the two countries' efforts to deal with contentious issues like the Senkaku/Diaoyu Islands. The islands were sidestepped by the first agreement in 1955, and subsequent agreements maintained the same parameters. The first bilateral agreement reached in 1955 covered the sea areas north of 27N latitude.[91] The area south of 27N was viewed to be an area where neither party will interfere with the other's fishery activities and remained the southernmost point throughout subsequent agreements. However, ignoring the islands in 1996 proved difficult for Tokyo. In an effort to sidestep the territorial issue, early Japanese drafts of its EEZ legislation omitted the area west of 135 degrees longitude, where the islands are located. This was opposed by several cabinet-level politicians on the grounds that it could damage Japan's claim to the islands.[92] Nevertheless, Japan did not draw baselines around the islands with its EEZ claim.[93] In doing so, Japanese leaders allowed the existing fisheries order south of 27N to endure. The 1997 fisheries agreement merely called for the status quo in the area around the Senkaku/Diaoyu Islands. After reaching the agreement, China and Japan exchanged notes pledging not to apply one another's fishery laws to each other's vessels in the area surrounding the islands.[94] That the 27N line had been contained in previous agreements certainly helped to depoliticize this process. This was in no small part due to the depth of past interactions over fisheries issues.

Like its predecessor, the 1997 agreement was signed as part of a wider set of agreements on a symbolic date in the bilateral relationship—November 11, 1997—as part of the celebration of twenty-five years of diplomatic recognition between China and Japan. Subsequent discussions ahead of implementation on June 1, 2000, centered on the nature of authority in the PMZ and the catch quotas that would apply within it, but these talks were unaffected by the subsequent developments in bilateral relations.[95] For instance, Jiang Zemin's disastrous visit to Japan in late November 1998 did not derail the negotiations.[96] Combined with the fact that the seeds of cooperation were planted during a period of bilateral tension, in mid-1996, this indicates that policymakers on both sides remained committed to cooperation.

As the new fisheries agreement was designed to reflect UNCLOS and the new EEZ regime, the primary difference between the 1975 and 1997 agreements pertained to jurisdictional competence for resource management in the area covered by the agreement. The 1975 agreement, signed before the conclusion of UNCLOS, relied on flag-state jurisdiction over resource management. The 1997 agreement placed this authority with the coastal state, which is consistent with the EEZ regime. Japanese authorities could now regulate the behavior of Chinese vessels operating offshore, thereby closing the loophole in the 1975 agreement. The PMZ was created to avoid delimiting a boundary in the East China Sea, within which authority rests with the Joint Fisheries Committee. This panel is tasked with regulating catch limits, determining which species are exploitable, and determining the respective catch weights by the other party in the PMZ and other conservation mechanisms. Within the PMZ, flag-state responsibility applies rather than coastal state responsibility as is the case in the EEZ. If a Chinese authority witnesses a breach by a Japanese vessel, it can advise the Japanese authorities, but it cannot act itself, and vice versa. This procedure was designed to reduce the number of incidents between fishermen and was a priority for Japanese negotiators from the outset.[97]

Leaders in Beijing and Tokyo have been willing to enforce, as best they can, the terms of the fisheries agreement. Indeed, both parties have incurred domestic costs to do so. Japan has reduced its excess fishing capacity and policed illegal coastal fishing, while trying to maintain a critical mass of employment in the fisheries industry.[98] China has been less successful. Although it has reduced employment in its coastal fisheries industry, policing illegal fishing has been difficult. One scholar has noted that Chinese laws still do not adequately regulate foreign fishing in China's EEZ; nor do they prevent Chinese fishermen from fishing illegally off the coasts of neighboring states or without proper licenses off China.[99] Recent investments in China's Fisheries Law Enforcement Command should be understood in this light. Nevertheless, Beijing did take the relatively painful step of dramatically reducing fisheries capacity in Zhejiang Province. The agreement put 170,000 Chinese fishermen out of work and had secondary effects throughout the fish-processing industry in China's coastal provinces.[100] Beijing has subsequently attempted to reduce its fisheries capacity by scrapping vessels and cracking down on illegal fishing by Chinese fishermen.[101]

The Durability of Cooperation

Cooperation over bilateral fisheries issues appears to have endured. Meetings of the Joint Fisheries Committee are closed, but two inferences can be made based on open sources. First, although Chinese sources lament the fact that the bilateral fisheries agreements have cut off access to traditional Chinese fisheries areas, the very existence of this hardship is indicative of some degree of compliance.[102] According to one scholar, the loss of traditional fishing grounds due to the implementation of the bilateral fisheries agreements with South Korea, Japan, and Vietnam has partly driven the expansion of China's DWF industry.[103] Second, despite the escalation of tensions in the East China Sea since 2010, fisheries disputes between China and Japan are generally well managed and thus do not lead to the deterioration of their already-tense maritime relationship. This is likely because, although they are reported more widely, these incidents typically occur in undisputed Japanese waters, giving China little recourse to escalate tensions.[104] This stands in stark contrast to the Sino–South Korean fisheries relationship, which erupted in violence in 2010 and 2011.[105]

Nevertheless, despite the reciprocal nature of fisheries cooperation, it should be noted that two serious challenges remain. First, illegal fishing remains a problem due to the unemployment created by the agreement's conservation mechanisms. The Chinese fishing industry was particularly hurt by the agreement because it reduced the number of Chinese boats permitted to operate in Japanese waters at a time when China had a massive excess in fishing capacity.[106] This explains why Beijing delayed publicizing the final agreement, reached on February 27, 2000, until March 23. In 2000, only 900 of 4,000 requested permits were granted to Chinese vessels to fish in Japanese coastal waters, and the number of boats was limited to 600 at any one time.[107] Consequently, with no other skills and few employment alternatives, some Chinese fishermen continue to fish both Chinese and Japanese waters illegally, despite efforts by the Chinese Ministry of Agriculture to educate fishermen about the terms of the agreement and the environmental costs of unregulated fishing.[108] The JCG is far better organized and equipped to police Japanese waters than the Chinese authorities are to police their own waters.[109]

Shortly after the agreement was implemented in June 2000, Japanese authorities seized Chinese vessels in Japanese waters for a variety of offenses—such as catching the wrong species of fish, using too small a mesh in their nets, and incorrectly stating their boat's tonnage.[110] However, rather than representing a limit of cooperative will, these challenges represent a problem of adjustment to the new order and expose the limits of China's marine-policing capabilities. Nevertheless, the bilateral fisheries relationship remains troubled; discussions on fishing in the other party's

EEZ are tense and often do not end in an agreement. For example, there was no agreement on EEZ fishing quotas for 2001.[111]

Second, at the regional level, the conclusion of a host of overlapping bilateral fisheries agreements between China, Japan, and South Korea has not created a coherent multilateral strategy for fisheries conservation in Northeast Asia.[112] These states have resisted a trilateral approach to fishery stock management that, given the migratory nature of many species, is essential to prevent the collapse of fish stocks.[113] In light of China's emergence as a major seafood importer, the depletion of the Northeast Asian fisheries is likely to continue.[114]

The 1997 China–Japan fisheries agreement should be viewed as a successful attempt to share jurisdiction in contested waters, in light of China's and Japan's goals for the disputed space outlined in the MVM. Although Japan's fish catch continued to decline, the loophole created by the 1975 agreement was closed. The 1997 agreement also contained unparalleled conservation measures by Northeast Asian standards. If it is properly enforced, the agreement could ensure sustainable access to fish protein in the East China Sea. From the perspective of territorial dispute management, the agreement has reduced the number of confrontations between fishermen, although it arguably has increased the number of illegal fishing operations. Chinese and Japanese policymakers committed their fishermen to serious measures aimed at conserving marine resources; the weakness in conservation measures is the result of the trend toward bilateralism in Northeast Asia, along with the presence of highly migratory fish stocks, and not to a lack of resolve by policymakers to share jurisdiction in contested space.[115]

Both sides recognize that they have a shared interest in sustainable fisheries management in the East China Sea. This was manifested in a desire to arrive at an agreement that maximized a state's ability to access the disputed resource, in this case fish and seafood products. Further evidence of the limits of cooperation is the stagnant state of negotiations toward maritime delimitation. Chinese and Japanese leaders stayed true to bilateral discussions throughout the political turmoil of 1996, and they remained committed until the agreement was reached in February 2000. Although the PMZ is an innovative way to sidestep delimitation issues, it also leaves them unresolved. To protect future delimitation claims, the 1997 fisheries agreement notes that nothing in the agreement will prejudice either party's claims to the EEZ or the continental shelf.[116] Of particular importance, some scholars argue that despite these official statements to the contrary, the PMZ has implications for subsequent boundary delimitation. By assigning a distance from each party's baseline of 52 nautical miles, Japan and China have effectively indicated two areas of the East China Sea that are not in dispute: the area between each party's coastal baselines and the nearest boundary of the PMZ.[117] This could mean that China has recognized Japan's EEZ claim to a distance of 52 nautical miles offshore, as opposed to the outer limits of the continental shelf.

Despite this hedging, Chinese and Japanese leaders continued to meet bilaterally to discuss delimitation and other issues related to the Law of the Sea.[118] Bilateral fisheries talks were supplanted in August 1998 by consultations on delimitation, which underwent six rounds of talks until December 2003.[119] Nevertheless, China and Japan made little headway on delimitation issues. Subsequent chapters argue that this stalemate is driven by a growing awareness among Japanese and Chinese policymakers of new uses for ocean areas that make delimitation unappealing.

Conclusion

The 1997 China–Japan fisheries agreement is an example of explicit, formal, reciprocal cooperation that is durable. Japanese leaders were the driving forces of cooperation because China's rise as a fisheries power challenged their interpretation of the fisheries status quo between China and Japan. Tokyo required prodding by domestic constituencies to overcome decades of policy inertia on its stance toward ocean enclosure. Japan pursued cooperation to prevent further erosion of the fisheries order in East Asia. China, by contrast, reciprocated Japan's offer in order to enshrine some degree of its emerging strength and to pursue delimitation negotiations that could lead to recognition of its enormous maritime claims. Cooperation over the economic dimension of maritime space was relatively straightforward, provided that the contested-symbolic issue of the Senkaku/Diaoyu Islands—then the source of a political crisis—did not undermine cooperation.

The fact that the agreement was a renegotiation of an existing accord undoubtedly contributed to the cooperative outcome, not least because it provided a way to sidestep the contentious issue of the Senkaku/Diaoyu Islands that could be defended to domestic constituencies as being consistent with previous agreements. This point should not be overstated, however, because the EEZ regime presented new challenges that did not reflect the 1975 agreement. The negotiations over the size of the PMZ reveal that Chinese and Japanese leaders were motivated by both jurisdictional constraints and the desire to achieve an outcome that was best for the interests outlined in the MVM.

The signing of a new fishery agreement was a fitting accomplishment on the occasion of the twenty-fifth anniversary of China–Japan diplomatic recognition. It was made all the more significant by the fact that it came on the heels of a particularly bad period in the Sino-Japanese relationship, and was not derailed by subsequent developments. The agreement stands as an example of Sino-Japanese cooperation over scarce resources in an area of contested jurisdiction. As the fishery agreement was being implemented in June 2000, a new challenge emerged in the East China Sea dispute: How would China and Japan interpret the activities of the other in a body of water they just recognized that they shared? This is the subject of chapter 4.

Notes

1. The delay was due to complexities arising from overlaps with the 1998 Japan–Korea fisheries agreement.
2. See Akaha, *Japan in Global Ocean Politics,* chap. 7.
3. Kanehara and Arima, "Japan's New Agreement on Fisheries," 5.
4. Wang and Zhan, "Marine Fishery Resource Management in PR China," 198–99.
5. These data are from FAO, "Fishery and Aquaculture Country Profile: China."
6. Wang and Zhan, "Marine Fishery Resource Management in PR China," 199.
7. "Zhejiang Rejuvenates Fishery Industry," Xinhua News, October 24, 1997.
8. Song, "China's Ocean Policy," 998.
9. Liu, "Exploitation and Management of the Fishery Resources and Regional Cooperation," 53.
10. Valencia, *Maritime Regime for North-East Asia,* 245.
11. Zou, *Law of the Sea in East* Asia, 89.
12. Park, *East Asia and the Law of the Sea,* 56.
13. Swartz, "Global Maps of the Growth of Japanese Marine Fisheries and Fish Consumption," 12; Akaha, "Muddling through Successfully," 172.
14. Swartz, "Global Maps of the Growth of Japanese Marine Fisheries and Fish Consumption," 13.
15. Minister's Secretariat Statistics Department, MAFF, "Fishery Production."
16. Valencia and Amae, "Regime Building in the East China Sea," 193.
17. Hayashi, *Japan Fishery Products Annual Report,* 4

18. These data are from Office of International Policy Planning Division, MAFF, "Abstract of Statistics on Agriculture, Forestry and Fisheries in Japan."

19. Xue, *China and International Fisheries Law,* 90–100.

20. Ibid., 136–38.

21. Author's calculations based on FAO, "Fisheries and Aquaculture Information and Statistics Service." This increase was also driven by rising production of China's inland freshwater fish.

22. This is based on Xue, *China and International Fisheries Law,* 136–38.

23. Xue, "China's Distant Water Fisheries," 653.

24. Paik, "Fisheries Regime in Northeast Asia," 76.

25. Liu, "Exploitation and Management of the Fishery Resources and Regional Cooperation," 52.

26. Clive Schofield, cited by Dupont, *East Asia Imperiled,* 108n119.

27. Smith, "Japan's High Seas Fisheries in the North Pacific Ocean," 82–83.

28. These were particularly prevalent between squid and sea bream fishermen. See "Gov't Welcomes Japan-China Agreement on Fisheries Pact," Kyodo News, March 6, 2000.

29. Zou, *Law of the Sea in East Asia,* 92; Kanehara and Arima, "Japan's New Agreement on Fisheries," 8n21.

30. Valencia and Amae, "Regime Building in the East China Sea," 193.

31. Akaha, "Fishery Relations in Northeast Asia," 149–55.

32. Kang, "United Nations Convention on the Law of the Sea and Fishery Relations," 113.

33. On the link between the fisheries lobby, MAFF, and political factions in the ruling coalition in Japan, see Ludwig and Valencia, "Building North-East Asian Maritime Regimes," 91–95.

34. Indeed, this was a long-standing concern for MAFF dating back to the Soviet EFZ declaration in 1977. See Akaha, *Japan in Global Ocean Politics,* 131.

35. Song, "China's Ocean Policy," 986–87.

36. Fukui, "How Japan Handled UNCLOS Issues," 44.

37. Some argue that the ocean enclosure movement only partly explains the decline of Japan's DWF industry. E.g., Stokke argues that higher labor and fuel costs as well as excess capacity explain the decline of Japanese DWF fisheries in northern waters. Haward and Bergin argue that these concerns also had a damaging impact on Japanese distant water tuna fisheries. Nevertheless, these ancillary issues were sector specific and exacerbated the problem created by the enclosure movement, which had an impact across the entire fisheries industry. See Stokke, "Transnational Fishing," 231–43; and Haward and Bergin, "Political Economy of Japanese Distant Water Tuna Fisheries," 91–101.

38. Kwon, *Law of the Sea and Northeast* Asia, 49–51.

39. Akaha, *Japan in Global Ocean Politics,* 57.

40. Whether this threat was real or imagined, Japanese policymakers and people have long been hypersensitive to threats to food security. Food security concerns stemmed from the experience of food shortages during World War II, the US soybean embargo in 1972, and the impact of the first oil crisis on Japanese agriculture. According to some, food security concerns were so severe in Japan as to

increase the real cost of consuming food in Japan. See Chapman, "Energy and Food Security," 182–217; Yamada, "Problem of Food Security in Japan," 217–37; and Gorham, "Japan's Policy of Food Security," 31–45.

41. Chisholm and Tyers, "Food Security," 5. Some have argued that all Northeast Asian states have food security concerns, most acutely in the area of fisheries which account for the bulk of protein consumption yet are increasingly scarce. Dupont, *East Asia Imperiled*, 106–9.

42. Akaha, *Japan in Global Ocean Politics*, 42.

43. Niimi, "Problem of Food Security," 183–85.

44. Smith, "Japan's High Seas Fisheries in the North Pacific Ocean," 85; Fisheries Agency, *FY 2005 Trend in Fisheries*, 34.

45. Ludwig and Valencia note that the Japanese fishing lobby is not monolithic. The primary division is between the powerful DWF lobby, the Japan Fisheries Association (JFA), and the less influential National Federation of Fisheries Cooperatives (NFFC), which represents small coastal fisheries. See Ludwig and Valencia, "Building North-East Asian Maritime Regimes," 94.

46. Akaha, *Japan in Global Ocean Politics*, 135–36.

47. Ibid., 131.

48. This characterization is from Akaha, "Cybernetic Analysis of Japan's Fishery Policy Process," 179.

49. This was before the emergence of the international straits and innocent passage concepts. See Akaha, *Japan in Global Ocean Politics*, 117–18.

50. Fukui, "How Japan Handled UNCLOS Issues," 26.

51. The legal uncertainties associated with this were the topic of much academic debate before UNCLOS came into effect. See Lee, "Trouble under the Water," 585–611.

52. This reluctance to embrace the new ocean regime for fear of aggravating existing territorial disputes was widely shared across the Northeast Asian states at the time. Jin-Hyun Paik cites several reasons why the East Asian states were reluctant to declare EEZs, including the reduction of navigational freedoms, the implications for the litany of territorial disputes in the region, and the technical difficulties associated with delimitation. See Paik, "Exclusive Economic Zones and Maritime Boundary Delimitations," 177–81. On the technical difficulties associated with ocean boundary delimitation, see Johnston, *Theory and History of Ocean Boundary-Making.*

53. See Paik, "Exploitation of Natural Resources," 171–84; and Bailey, "States, Stocks and Sovereignty," 215–34.

54. State Council of the People's Republic of China, "Law on the Territorial Sea and the Contiguous Zone," February 25, 1992.

55. "Island Row Might Hamper Ratification of Sea Convention," Japan Economic Newswire, December 16, 1995; Dzurek, "Effect of the Diaoyu/Senkaku Islands on Maritime Delimitation," 412.

56. Akaha, "Cybernetic Analysis of Japan's Fishery Policy Process," 191–92.

57. Ludwig and Valencia, "Building North-East Asian Maritime Regimes," 94. With the decline of the DWF fisheries, the smaller lobbies were able to exert greater pressure on the government to declare an EEZ to protect the coastal fishery

grounds, given that the DWF fisheries objections were rendered moot as early as 1985 with the widespread acceptance of ocean enclosure and the parallel rise of Chinese DWF.

58. Noboru Azami, quoted in "Japanese Fishermen Assail Agreements with Korea, China," *Wall Street Journal*, April 3, 1997.

59. DWF lobbying efforts were now focused on securing compensation from the government. See Haward and Bergin, "Political Economy of Japanese Distant Water Tuna Fisheries," 94–95; and Fukui, "How Japan Handled UNCLOS Issues," 47.

60. "Fishing Industry Unions to Vote for 200-Mile Zone," Japan Economic Newswire, November 21, 1995.

61. "Fishermen Seek Early Establishment of Exclusive Zone," Japan Economic Newswire, February 28, 1996; Bong, "Flashpoints at Sea?" 63.

62. Akira Sugawara, quoted in "Fishery Leader Urges Talks to Be Completed within 1 Year," Japan Economic Newswire, February 20, 1996.

63. Government of Japan, *Law on the Exclusive Economic Zone and the Continental Shelf*, article 3(1); Hayashi, "Japan: New Law of the Sea Legislation," 577.

64. Greenfield, *China's Practice in the Law of the Sea*, 86.

65. Ibid., 100–101.

66. Xue, *China and International Fisheries Law*, 127. This is the area of China's claim; it is disputed by coastal states in the East and South China Seas.

67. Hayashi, "Regional Fisheries Management in the East China Sea," 221.

68. Kanehara and Arima, "Japan's New Agreement on Fisheries," 21; Zou, *Law of the Sea in East Asia*, 105.

69. This is a difficult assertion to make due to the opacity of the Chinese policymaking process. However, given the nature of China's stance at the UNCLOS III negotiations, its prompt signature of the document in 1982, as well as its behavior with regard of ocean jurisdiction issues since, there is little doubt that the expansion of Chinese control over East China Sea waters was widely supported across the government. Some sources allude to pressure from within China to renegotiate the fisheries agreement, but others argue there was no concerted push from any Chinese fisheries organizations. See, respectively, Zou, *Law of the Sea in East Asia*, 92; and Xue, *China and International Fisheries Law*, 98.

70. "PRC Declaration on Sea Baselines for Paracel Islands," *People's Daily*, May 16, 1996. This declaration also included baselines in the Paracel islands.

71. "PRC UNCLOS Ratification Statement," www.un.org/Depts/los/convention_agreements/convention_declarations.htm.

72. "Status of the Convention and Its Implementing Agreements," www.un.org/Dept/los/Legislationandtreaties/asia/htm.

73. Government of Japan, *Law on the Exclusive Economic Zone and the Continental Shelf* (Law No. 74 of 1996), article 1(2). Japan altered this stance in 2004 following its discovery of the Chunxiao project. Japanese officials now assert that Japan claims an EEZ 200 nautical miles from its baselines. Some interpret this as a hardening of Japan's position. See Drifte, "Politics of the East China Sea Gas Dispute," 15.

74. Zou, "China's Exclusive Economic Zone and Continental Shelf," 77.

75. Kim, *Maritime Delimitation and Interim Arrangements*, 27.

76. Chung, "Diaoyu/Tiaoyutai/Senkaku Islands Dispute," 135–64.

77. The dates relating to fishery talks are from Drifte, *Japanese–Chinese Territorial Disputes in the East China Sea,* table 2.

78. Chung, *Domestic Politics,* 48.

79. Ibid., 52.

80. "Japan, China Make Progress toward New Fishery Accord," Kyodo News, April 22, 1997.

81. Zou, "Sino-Japanese Joint Fishery Management in the East China Sea," 134.

82. "Japan, China to Ink New Fisheries Pact Soon," Japan Economic Newswire, September 3, 1997; Zou, "Sino-Japanese Joint Fishery Management," 135.

83. Valencia, *Maritime Regime for North-East Asia,* 264.

84. Tsuneo Akaha argues that agreements were able to be concluded because the issue of fisheries cut across the ideological divide of the Cold War. Akaha, "Fishery Relations in Northeast Asia," 144–45.

85. On early Sino-Japanese fishery relations, see Park, *East Asia and the Law of the Sea,* 70–84.

86. Zou, *Law of the Sea in East Asia,* 90.

87. The only period fisheries were not regulated by these agreements was between June 1958 and November 1963. The 1955 agreement was not renewed by China in 1958, which accused the Japanese of repeated infringements, and a new one was not negotiated until November 1963. See Greenfield, *China's Practice in the Law of the Sea,* 95. Others believe that the agreement was not renewed due to the Nagasaki Incident of 1958, which caused considerable diplomatic strain at the time. See Miyoshi, "New Japan-China Fishery Agreement," 32.

88. Kim, "UN Convention of the Law of the Sea and New Fisheries Agreements," 106.

89. Ibid., 106n27.

90. For the details, see Greenfield, *China's Practice in the Law of the Sea,* 95–102; and Park, *East Asia and the Law of the Sea,* 70–79.

91. Greenfield, *China's Practice in the Law of the Sea,* 91. Taiwan and the Senkaku/Diaoyu Islands are located south of this line.

92. Bong, "Flashpoints at Sea?" 63.

93. Roach, "China's Straight Baseline Claim," 1.

94. Xue, *China and International Fisheries Law,* 275–76.

95. Although catch limits are negotiated annually, generally speaking, China receives three times the catch limit of Japan. See Kim, "UN Convention of the Law of the Sea," 106; and Valencia and Amae, "Regime Building in the East China Sea," 193. The delay was also related to a raft of differences including how to handle the northern part of the PMZ, which overlaps South Korea's EEZ claim. See Zou, *Law of the Sea in East Asia,* 101–2; Hayashi, "Regional Fisheries Management in the East China Sea," 223. For the South Korean perspective on this issue, see Pak, "Resettlement of the Fisheries Order in Northeast Asia," 614–16.

96. "Question of Meaning: China's State Visit to Japan Leaves Relations Strained," *The Economist,* December 5, 1998; "Japan, China Hope to Resolve Fishing Dispute Next Week," Kyodo News, November 4, 1999.

97. Zou, "Sino-Japanese Joint Fishery Management," 134; "Japan, China to Continue Informal Fishery Talks Wednesday," Kyodo News, April 9, 1996.

98. See MAFF, *FY 2005 Trend in Fisheries*, 11.

99. Zou, "China's Exclusive Economic Zone and Continental Shelf," 75.

100. Valencia and Amae, "Regime Building in the East China Sea," 195; Zou, "Sino-Japanese Joint Fishery Management," 137.

101. For the details, see Yu and Yu, "Fishing Capacity Management in China," 351–59.

102. Yan, Su, and Zhang, "Concern about the Metamorphosis of Fishery Boundaries."

103. Mallory, "China's Distant Water Fishing Industry," 101–2.

104. See, e.g., "Chinese Skipper Nabbed of Nagasaki after Chase," *Japan Times*, November 8, 2011; "China Pressed for Skipper's Release," Kyodo News, November 27, 2011; and "Japan Arrests China Boat Captain for Illegal Fishing," Reuters, December 20, 2011.

105. See, e.g., Moon, "Chinese Sailors Admit Ramming Coast Guard Ship"; "Conflict at Sea with Chinese Vessel," *Joongang Daily*, March 5, 2011; and "South Korean Coastguard Killed by Chinese Fisherman," Reuters, December 12, 2011.

106. Indeed, in an effort to cushion its fishery industry from the blow of the 1997 agreement, China sought continued access to traditional Chinese squid fisheries in the Sea of Japan and the North Pacific for an additional five years at 1996 levels. See Xue, *China and International Fisheries Law*, 189.

107. "China Prepares for Implementation of Sino-Japan Fishing Pact," Japan Economic Newswire, March 23, 2000.

108. Chen, "Use of Oceans Faces Legal Restrictions."

109. On Chinese efforts to police illegal fishing by Chinese flagged vessels, see Zou, "Sino-Japanese Joint Fishery Management," 136–37.

110. Valencia and Amae, "Regime Building in the East China Sea," 196. On this and other inadequacies of the Northeast Asian fisheries agreements, see Xue, "Bilateral Fisheries Agreements for the Cooperative Management of the Shared Resources," 363–74.

111. Van Dyke, "North-East Asian Seas," 411.

112. See Pak, "Resettlement of the Fisheries Order in Northeast Asia," 587–622; and Kim, "UN Convention of the Law of the Sea and New Fisheries Agreements," 97–109.

113. On these issues, see, in particular, Valencia, *Maritime Regime for North-East Asia*, chap. 6. See also Paik, "Exploitation of Natural Resources," 171–84.

114. Lindkvist, Trondsen, and Xie, "Restructuring the Chinese Seafood Industry," 432–41.

115. Xue, "Bilateral Fisheries Agreements," 363–74; Zou, "Sino-Japanese Joint Fishery Management," 138.

116. See "Fishery Agreement between China and Japan," article 12, appendix I; and Zou, *Law of the Sea in East Asia*, 179.

117. Zou, *Law of the Sea in East Asia*, 105.

118. Chinese Ministry of Foreign Affairs, "China's Maritime Demarcation and Bilateral Fishery Affairs."

119. Drifte, "Japanese-Chinese Territorial Disputes in the East China Sea," 32.

CHAPTER FOUR

Cooperation on Marine Research Activities, 2000–2001

THE SECOND INSTANCE of Sino-Japanese cooperation over the East China Sea dispute occurred in February 2001, when the two sides exchanged a *note verbale* promising to notify the other when they undertook marine surveys in disputed waters. Once again, the conflict of interest stemmed from an unresolved dimension of maritime jurisdiction in the East China Sea brought to light by China's rise as a maritime power. Throughout the middle and late 1990s, Chinese naval and marine research vessels were seen more frequently in Japan's claimed EEZ. Following a number of diplomatic protests in 1999 and 2000, Tokyo attempted to coerce Chinese cooperation by suspending an official development assistance (ODA) loan in September 2000. The loan was released in October 2000, after Chinese foreign minister Tang Jiaxuan agreed in principle to hold talks toward a notification agreement. Unlike the fisheries agreement, the notification agreement failed to curtail Chinese survey activities, however. Tokyo accused Beijing of violating the consensus in July 2001, and this behavior has not subsided. Further, no subsequent diplomatic agreement on the marine survey issue has been negotiated.

Viewed through the MVM, the marine research issue is larger than simply a debate about who can do what and where in the East China Sea; it has implications for how Chinese and Japanese vessels of all description will coexist in the waters between the two states. Both parties viewed the legality of marine surveys in the context of the wider strategic implications for their freedom of action in disputed waters. Policymakers in Tokyo viewed Chinese intrusions into its EEZ as a strategic threat to its national security. China valued its survey activities as an economic issue; as a source of important scientific data and intelligence; and as a strategic issue, a source of operational experience for the PLAN. Given the countries' competing jurisdictional claims to the East China Sea, China was reluctant to curtail or to notify Japan of its activities in contested waters.

It thus comes as no surprise that cooperation was pursued coercively by a reactive Japan. Once again, the central policymaking apparatus in Tokyo was pressured from outside actors, particularly the defense establishment, to assert itself on the marine survey issue. Following several failed diplomatic overtures, Japan used ODA pressure to coerce a change in China's posture in the summer of 2000.[1] The depth of cooperation reflects the theoretical expectations derived from these conditions. Given the strategic nature of the issues at hand, there were few rounds of negotiations and it appeared that any agreement would be weak from the outset. The durability of cooperation was limited by two phenomena: a Chinese reluctance to abide by the agreement, and Japan's inability to attach meaningful costs to deviant Chinese behavior.

The Value of Marine Surveys in the East China Sea

States are entitled to conduct a variety of research activities on or below ocean waters. These entitlements are complicated by unclear regimes for different kinds of research, which are subject to different laws in different maritime zones, which in turn are interpreted differently by states. This is further complicated by disputed maritime boundaries. The root of the problem in the case of the East China Sea is the increase in Chinese marine research activity combined with its nonrecognition of Japan's EEZ claim.[2] As is illustrated below, Japan's own domestic and institutional shortcomings prevented a more robust response to this challenge from China. In short, how could Chinese and Japanese authorities enforce their jurisdiction over marine research in an area both claimed as their own?

In addition to illegal fishing activities, maritime incidents—such as vessels being boarded or fired upon—have been a feature of Sino-Japanese maritime relations in the early post–Cold War period.[3] Following a peak of seventy-two incidents between March 1991 and July 1993, Chinese and Japanese policymakers held talks to reduce the number of maritime incidents with mixed results.[4] The Japanese MSA first detected Chinese marine research vessels in Japanese waters in 1994.[5] Although the MSA recorded four Chinese research vessels operating in Japanese waters in 1997, this number jumped to twenty-three vessels detected on fifteen occasions the following year.[6] Chinese survey activity grew both in frequency and in size of expedition.

These intrusions became more unsettling as Chinese naval vessels were also spotted in Japanese waters. In May and July 1999, PLAN flotillas consisting, respectively, of twelve and ten vessels were detected in the Japanese EEZ north of the Senkaku/Diaoyu Islands.[7] This was the first recorded incident of Chinese warships in Japanese waters.[8] In the first half of 2000, Chinese naval vessels were spotted in groups of three to five vessels in March, April, and June.[9] In late May 2000, the MSDF destroyer monitored the *Yanbing* icebreaker as it traversed the Tsugaru Strait.[10] Although the strait is a high seas corridor, it was the first time a Chinese warship had traversed the strait from the Sea of Japan.[11] Furthermore, although no such activity was detected on this occasion, the *Yanbing* is capable of conducting intelligence-gathering operations. Indeed, it was subsequently detected again sailing repeatedly—three times by one estimate—through the Tsugaru Strait between May and June 2000 as part of its circumnavigation of Japan.[12] In June and July 2000, the *Dongdiao 232* research ship was observed operating in the Japanese EEZ, despite Chinese assurances in June to address the intrusions issue. Simultaneously, a second ship, the *Da Yang 1*, was spotted 170 kilometers off Fukue Island.[13] Finally, it was later revealed that 2000 was in fact the most active year to date for PLAN submarine operations, with a total of six patrol excursions recorded.[14]

The Economic Value of Marine Surveys to China

Chinese leaders value marine survey activity because of a growing demand for the data gathered, which are necessary for China's national development and security. Specifically, these purposes are the exploitation of maritime resources, safe navigation through the sea as a secure medium of trade, and the use of the sea as a medium over which to project power and achieve national security objectives. These uses of the sea are recognized as legitimate by all states, including by Japan. For instance, reports from the Japanese Defense Agency (JDA) have recognized that certain Chinese survey activities are legal in Japanese-claimed waters, but they have also drawn attention to those that have infringed on Japan's EEZ jurisdiction.[15] They are thus classified by the MVM as "economic" salience.

Hydrographic survey data contribute to safe navigation for ships. Because this information is provided in open sources, and contributes to the safety of all who use the area, these activities are not inherently politically contentious. The growth in Chinese survey capabilities reflects this interest in survey data. According to Bernard Cole, by the late 1990s China's research fleet was made up of forty-seven multipurpose ships capable of conducting marine scientific research (MSR), resource surveys, hydrographic surveys, and intelligence-gathering activities, while an additional eighty fishing trawlers could be used for offshore surveillance. This research fleet is operated by several bureaucratic departments, including the Academy of Sciences, the Ministry of Communications, the Hydrographic Department, and the PLAN.[16] Each bureaucratic arm has overlapping and competing requirements for the data. For example, the Kexue-class oceanographic research vessel, though ostensibly used for MSR activities, is also capable of conducting electronic intelligence-gathering operations.[17] Furthermore, there is some evidence that the ship is operated not only by the PLAN but also by the Institute of Oceanology of the Chinese Academy of Sciences.[18]

The Strategic Value of Surveys to China

There are also two relational aspects to Chinese survey activities, salience to Beijing that cannot be appreciated by Japan. First, though hydrographic data are purportedly for public dissemination, many of the survey data are also gathered for military purposes, which Japan views as antithetical to its interests. These data are classified as strategic because they are produced as a material object that can be divided or shared, but the legitimacy of these data in particular—the way they were gathered and their purpose—is not recognized by the other claimant. The Chinese use these data to meet the operational requirements of their more active navy. Safe navigation and accurate underwater topography are integral to advanced PLAN training operations, which have been prioritized to improve its operational prowess.[19] For example, submarine operations, such as blockade or area denial missions used in a Taiwan Strait conflict, cannot be successful without up-to-date knowledge of the ocean floor.[20]

Furthermore, the very act of conducting naval intelligence-gathering and research operations provides the navy with a pretext to gain valuable operational experience.[21] In the Japanese view, Chinese naval battle groups have transited the international straits that pass through Japan under the guise of conducting marine research, but have conducted military research instead. For instance, the circumnavigation of Japan by the *Yanbing* icebreaker in 2000 was significant not only because it symbolized China's expanding reach at sea but also because of what China was able to do with this reach. Although the *Yanbing* is listed as a research vessel, and appeared to conduct several research activities such as collecting data on tides and wave patterns, there were also concerns that the vessel may have gathered electronic intelligence on nearby air defense installations.[22]

The second strategic aspect of the survey activity is that Beijing views its survey activities as a legal extension of China's maritime claims and its nonrecognition of Japan's maritime claims. Because the Chinese claim the waters in which they are operating, they argue they do not need to seek Japanese permission for their resource or MSR surveys, both of which are regulated by the coastal state as part of its EEZ entitlements under part V of UNCLOS, or are permitted on the high seas. For example, in 1997, the MSA asked a Chinese exploration vessel to leave waters 75 nautical miles west of Okinawa. In reply to repeated requests, the captain of the Chinese vessels said: "We are on the high seas so there should be no problem. . . . We are not required to answer your questions."[23] However, this behavior is contrary to article 241 of UNCLOS: "Marine scientific research activities shall not constitute the legal basis for any claim to any part of the marine environment or its resources."[24] Nevertheless, Chinese behavior suggests that officials recognize the importance of state practice in supporting jurisdictional claims to maritime space.

The Strategic Value of Chinese Survey Activities to Japan

From the Japanese perspective, China's survey activities in Japanese-claimed waters cause apprehension about future Chinese behavior in East Asia. However benign the purpose of the data collection may be, China's lack of transparency regarding this purpose and its insistence on the legality of its approach places these activities in the strategic category. That Japan does not recognize the legitimacy of China's behavior is further illustrated by its opposition to China's maritime boundary claims and by its opposition to these activities in areas where they are nominally permitted, such as the straits that pass through Japan and the high seas areas that make up the waters south of the main Japanese islands. In Tokyo's view, the survey activities are part of a larger pattern of Chinese nonrecognition of Japan's maritime claims and a strategic-level concern about the nature of China's maritime expansion.

This perspective is based on the increasingly widespread view among Japanese security analysts that Chinese naval activities in the East China Sea are part of a strategy to legally and physically expand Chinese de facto control over a given contested area.[25] Left unchecked, this process could create a status quo in the East China Sea that is favorable to China, particularly in light of shifts in the regional balance of power.[26] This incremental process includes marine survey activities, resource exploitation, legal declarations of Chinese jurisdiction or sovereignty, naval patrols, as well as actual military operations. Japanese strategists tend to view these activities in the same light because of the difficulties of distinguishing between them.[27] According to Fumio Ota, then at the National Defense Academy of Japan, the motivations for Chinese survey activities depend on their location. Those conducted between Japan's median line and the Okinawa Trough are aimed at resource exploitation, while those conducted "east of Japan's Southwest islands" are aimed to gather data for military and resource purposes.[28] Furthermore, the probability that the survey data are used to make Japanese-claimed waters safer for Chinese submarines indicates that eventually "they [Chinese submarines] will pass through the (Bashi) Channel between Taiwan and the Philippines and make inroads into Japan's Pacific water zone."[29] For Japanese strategists, these training exercises are Liu Huaqing's naval strategy in practice—to assert control to the first island chain—which threatens Japan's national security interests.

Proponents of this view identify the Chinese expansion into the South China Sea in 1974, when it took the Paracel Islands chain from Vietnam by force, as indicative of this process.[30] This strategic apprehension was a minority view in the early 1990s because Chinese maritime activity seemed relatively benign. Suspicions were first aroused by the 1992 LTC and by strategic developments in China's naval posture. Subsequently, Tokyo became concerned about the large number of survey vessels that operate in the vicinity of the Senkaku/Diaoyu Islands and about significant improvements in Chinese naval and air military capabilities.[31] China's stated naval ambitions, to shift from coastal to an "offshore defense strategy" with an extended defense perimeter to beyond the "first island chain," reinforced these threat perceptions.[32] Furthermore, some Chinese strategists defined "offshore" as the area containing the EEZ and the continental shelf, which was particularly worrying for Japanese strategists because it implies an inevitable conflict between the two countries as Japan contests the Chinese entitlement to the full extent of these claims.[33]

Furthermore, subsequent articulations of China's maritime posture suggested that China's primary maritime interests lie within the first island chain, which contributes to Japan's perception that China's emergence as a regional maritime power will occur at the expense of Japanese national security. According to *China's National Defense in 2002*, the navy's primary missions are "to guard against enemy invasion from the sea, defend the state's sovereignty over its territorial waters, and safeguard the state's maritime rights and interests."[34] These interests include securing offshore islands and territorial waters, which may possess hydrocarbon or other resources that other states may claim as their own; the protection of the SLOCs through which China's trade passes; coastal defense to protect the coastal industrial bases upon which China's continued economic growth is predicated; and the deterrence of invasion of the mainland.[35] Simultaneously, US assessments of China's military strategy emphasized that the PLAN's central mission was area denial operations as part of a Taiwan Strait contingency.[36] Though reassuring to Washington, this assessment is quite a cause of concern for Japan because these area denial strategies operate close to its waters.[37] Even the most limited conceptions of Chinese seapower envision control over the East China Sea.[38] Chinese marine survey activity is clearly a concern to Japan because it is regarded as part of a wider expansionist exercise.

These values indicate that Chinese and Japanese territorial objectives on the survey issue were mutually exclusive in many respects. China had several reasons to continue its survey activities, but ensuring that Chinese vessels were not engaging in activities prejudicial to Japanese security became an increasingly important objective for Japan's security community. The importance the claimants placed on Chinese marine surveys in the East China Sea is summarized in the next subsection.

Marine Surveys and the Shifting Status Quo

In addition to the limited commonality of interest indicated in figure 4.1, the survey issue is further complicated by legal uncertainties surrounding its regulation. UNCLOS distinguishes between three types of marine research activities: MSR, resource-related research, and hydrographic research. The first two require coastal state permission in the EEZ; the third does not. The EEZ regime is a union between two separate, preexisting definitions of ocean space: "high seas," where flag-state laws apply; and "territorial waters," where coastal states have near-absolute sovereignty,

FIGURE 4.1
Maritime Value Matrix, 2000

Economic:	**Strategic:**
• Data gained from surveys	• PLAN operational experience (China) • Chinese maritime expansion (Japan) • Exercise jurisdiction in claimed waters
Shared-symbolic:	**Contested-symbolic:**
• Null	• Null

with the exception of innocent passage. The EEZ regime is a compromise between states that enjoyed the freedom of the seas, such as the United States and Japan, and coastal states that sought to maximize control over expanded ocean areas. This divided states that favored free access to waters for scientific purposes from states that were concerned about the security implications of foreign vessels operating near their shores.[39] The consensus reached in UNCLOS favored the latter; MSR activity in the territorial sea is subject to the express consent of coastal states. Within the EEZ, the coastal state is expected to consent to MSR, but it may deny permission if the research violates its EEZ entitlements such as resource exploitation or the construction of islands.[40]

The rules governing the legalities of survey activities in the EEZ are complicated by poorly defined concepts in UNCLOS. There is an explicit effort to define the rights and responsibilities surrounding MSR under part XIII of UNCLOS, but not to define it as separate from other scientific activities that occur at sea.[41] Thus the concept of MSR does not cover all manner of possible survey activities. As Hayashi notes, article 19(2) refers to research *or* survey activities (thereby drawing a distinction), and articles 21(1) and 40 distinguish between MSR and hydrographic surveys.[42] This implies that hydrographic surveys lie outside the restrictions outlined in part XIII, although UNCLOS does not explicitly outline regulations for hydrographic research.[43] According to one legal opinion, "It is foremost of all the function of the platform that determines whether part III on marine scientific research applies. Only where a *scientific research* activity is pursued the platform has to conform to its rules" (emphasis in the original).[44] As is described below, Chinese vessels are not forthcoming about the type of activity in which they are engaged; nor is it easy to identify a particular type of research visually.

States that favor free use of the sea, such as the United States, use this ambiguity to argue that some research activities—such as military research—do not require the consent of the coastal state as they are outside the definition of MSR. The legal regime surrounding research activity depends on the type and intent of the survey conducted.[45] Surveys that take place in an EEZ that are aimed at resource exploitation require coastal state permission under part V; they are part of coastal state jurisdiction over resource exploitation in the EEZ and include exploratory surveys. Drawing a further distinction, the United States and others argue that military intelligence-gathering activities are not subject to coastal state jurisdiction because, unlike scientific research, the information gathered is not publicly disseminated and because military intelligence-gathering activities are consistent with the norm of freedom of navigation and overflight through an EEZ.[46]

These definitional issues yield a very complicated operational environment. Chinese survey activities in Japanese waters are often performed by vessels capable of multiple types of survey, including military vessels. Thus it is difficult to ascertain in real time the type and intent of survey being conducted. For this reason, as one Japanese author has noted, a military vessel engaged in nonmilitary research in the EEZ exists in something of a "legal gap" as far as enforcement measures for the coastal state are concerned.[47] Thus it is not known which surveys at a given time require Japanese permission and which do not. In practice there are four types of possible survey activities in the Japanese-claimed EEZ: resources (requiring coastal state permission), MSR (requiring coastal state permission), hydrographic surveys (not requiring permission), and military intelligence gathering (not requiring permission).[48] These definitional issues are further complicated when two states claim EEZ jurisdiction over the same sea area because either may sanction the first two types of survey activities as an expression of their maritime jurisdiction.

The appearance of Chinese naval and survey vessels in the waters around Japan was a development that challenged Japan's reference point in its maritime environment. The salience of the issues outlined in figure 4.1 translated into competing Chinese and Japanese goals for marine research activities in the waters surrounding Japan. Tokyo desired a mechanism to regulate these activities consistent with its EEZ jurisdiction; Beijing opposed such a move based on its own claims. The challenge for Japanese leaders, therefore, was to identify the activity in which a given Chinese vessel was engaged and whether that activity was legal under international and Japanese law. Consistent with its interpretation of its entitlements under the Law of the Sea, China maintained that its activities were legal and resisted attempts to regulate its behavior. As in the previous case, it took pressure by actors outside the central policymaking apparatus in Tokyo to pressure Japanese leaders to take action.

Deciding to Cooperate

As in the case of fisheries, central policymakers in Tokyo were slow to recognize the nature of the Chinese challenge. A concerted lobbying effort by the defense establishment succeeded in pushing Tokyo to recognize the challenge to its reference point. By 1999, Japanese leaders viewed the Chinese research activities as violations of Japan's claimed EEZ, a pressing national security issue. Prime Minister Obuchi Keizo raised the issue with Premier Zhu Rongji during his first official visit to China in July 1999.[49] This change emerged from shifts in Japan's policy environment as Chinese intrusions became more frequent and more militarized. However, Japanese leaders were highly constrained by the legal uncertainties described above, which made it impossible to determine which laws, Japanese or international, were being broken. In light of China's reluctance to cooperate, Japan used diplomatic protest and ODA pressure to coerce Chinese cooperation.

Japan Pursues Cooperation While China Delays

Central policymakers in Tokyo have traditionally been reluctant to assert themselves against China unless the issue at hand presents a clear threat to Japan's national security, such as during the 1995–96 Taiwan Strait crisis, or offends Japanese sensibilities, as in the case of China's 1995 nuclear weapons test. Consequently, Japanese leaders had a fairly benign view of the growth in Chinese naval activities. By contrast, the defense establishment, reinforced by conservative politicians, held a dramatically different view of China's military expansion. These groups lobbied for a more assertive posture on the intrusions issue. That these security concerns were articulated in publicly available defense publications is particularly telling for two reasons. First, Japanese defense publications are among the most transparent in the world due to the comprehensive degree of civilian control over the military. Thus, when these publications mention a concern, it is a reflection of defense thinking.[50] Second, Japan is generally very sensitive to the concerns of neighboring states regarding its military posture. Any shift toward defense "normalcy" has traditionally invited condemnation from China and South Korea. Consequently, Japanese defense sources do not name names lightly. Although the security bureaucracy is typically regarded as the least influential government department in Japan, it nevertheless publicized its concerns about the intrusions issue.[51]

Thus, when publications first noted the intrusions as a defense concern in 1998, and mentioned China by name, it attested to the degree of concern in defense circles. The MSA's "Annual Report on Maritime Safety 1998" noted that "activities of foreign marine research vessels have been identified in the East China Sea. In particular, . . . Chinese marine research vessels have frequently been identified."[52] The *Defense of Japan 1997* referred to China's ambitions for a blue-water navy and its ambitions for disputed territory across Asia, including the Japanese occupied Senkaku/Diaoyu Islands. In 1998, the report went further and noted that China's increase in survey activity around the islands was connected to the sovereignty dispute.[53] This link was strengthened in the 1999 edition, which drew attention to the circumnavigation of Japan by PLAN vessels that year.[54] It is noteworthy that the intrusions issue was perceived in the context of China's maritime and territorial ambitions from the outset. The link between the disputed islands, China's military modernization, and Chinese survey activity is clear in the Japanese mindset.

Similarly, annual assessments of Japan's security environment published by the JDA's think tank, the National Institute of Defense Studies, were increasingly candid about the threat posed by Chinese maritime expansion, evidenced by the intrusions into Japanese waters. Chinese "naval activities" were listed as a growing security concern for Japanese security planners on the grounds that these were on the rise and seemed to be primarily located in the East China Sea.[55] A comprehensive analysis of the issue, including maps indicating the location of Chinese intrusions, was included in the 2001 volume. This volume argued that Chinese research activities were "designed to make such activities a fait accompli that China can use to its advantage in defining a boundary of its own EEZ and its continental shelf."[56] These reports indicate a reversal of Japanese policy not to confirm reports of Chinese naval incursions for fear of upsetting the bilateral relationship.[57]

These publications were in turn picked up by the Japanese media, which in turn affected public perception. Although conservative media publications like *Sankei Shimbun* covered the intrusions from the outset, it was not until 2000 that more centrist and liberal media picked up the story and voiced their concerns through editorials.[58] For instance, JDA reports on increased Chinese naval activity in fiscal 1999 were carried by the major news outlets.[59] By mid-2000, there was a high degree of editorial consensus across the spectrum of Japanese newspapers. Ahead of Foreign Minister Kono Yohei's visit to Beijing in late August, *Yomiuri Shimbun* warned that China's insensitivity toward Japan's concerns regarding the naval incursions exacerbated feelings of mistrust on the part of Japanese people.[60] Similarly, the liberal *Asahi Shimbun* viewed China's attitude toward Japan's concerns as "insincere and detrimental to its trustful relations with Japan."[61] In the wake of Kono's visit, a *Sankei Shimbun* editorial criticized the visit, arguing that "Japan is being too lenient toward the PRC if it interprets from such detached utterances that the PRC has decided to exercise self-restraint over the operations by its naval vessels."[62] In this climate, survey data from the Roper Center indicate that the Japanese people continued to view China as potential military adversary through 2000.[63]

Some experts question the link between media, public opinion, and Japanese foreign policy choices.[64] However, contrary to the pacifist assumptions made by many scholars about Japanese public opinion, recent research indicates that Japanese newspaper editorials are important shapers of public opinion on security matters.[65] Indeed, as Michael Green notes, the media plays a role in as much as it often inflates the nature of threats to Japan.[66] As noted above, there is evidence that Japanese people became more concerned about the implications of China's rise throughout the 1990s, and in some cases pressured Tokyo to apply ODA sanctions in response to perceived deviant Chinese foreign policy behavior. Indeed, as Rousseau finds, Japanese public opinion becomes less sanguine about China following perceived "deviant" behavior such as the nuclear tests or the Taiwan Strait missile exercises.[67] Moreover, others argue that by 2000, Japanese China policy was increasingly being influenced by the LDP and public opinion, rather than by MOFA's Asia bureau.[68] Thus, given the consensus among the range of newspapers noted above, conservative, central and liberal, it is reasonable to assume that public opinion at the time reflected this consensus in the media. As Mike Mochizuki notes, public opinion might not contribute to "concrete policy choices," but "public opinion can constrain policy outcomes enough to have general strategic consequences."[69] In short, failure to act on the intrusions could have been politically damaging to the LDP, which was already reeling from electoral setbacks in the June 2000 Lower House elections.[70]

Indeed, media reporting only partly reflected the legal nuances of the survey issue and thus inflated the immediacy of the threat to Japan. Japanese government publications distinguish between two types of vessels, but do not speculate on the types of activity those vessels undertake. An MSDF report published in September 1999 stated that there had been thirty-one incidents of Chinese naval vessels entering Japan's EEZ in fiscal 1999, and twenty-three marine exploration ships during the same period.[71] The report stated that the former is not illegal, but that the latter infringes on Japanese UNCLOS entitlements. By contrast, media reports often confused the functions and affiliations of Chinese ships. Some refer to the *Yanbing* as an icebreaker, while others refer to it as an intelligence ship, or a research vessel.[72] This is likely because, like many Chinese support ships, it has multiple functions, not all military in nature. Many Chinese icebreakers double as electronic surveillance ships and tugboats, while the *Dongdiao 232* doubles as a missile tracking ship and an electronic intelligence ship.[73] The distinctions between vessels and their various functions are generally absent from media reports, which often emphasize the military affiliation of the vessel involved, thereby inflating the threat.[74]

As the intrusions issue became more prominent in the media, Japanese policymakers increased the frequency and level of their diplomatic protests. No longer limited to senior foreign affairs bureaucrats, Japanese diplomatic representations took several forms. At the elite level, Prime Minister Obuchi's remonstrations raised to Premier Zhu were rebuffed on the grounds that there was nothing wrong with Chinese activities.[75] At the party level, LDP general secretary Hiromu Nonaka raised intrusions issue with Zhao Qizheng, director of the CCP's Overseas Publicity Office, on June 11, 2000, in a meeting between the CCP and Japan's ruling coalition parties.[76] Japanese diplomats raised the issue with their Chinese counterparts at the Seventh Japan–China Security Dialogue, also in June. They argued that China's intentions for its research vessels were not clear, and that Japanese consent was required. Japanese foreign minister Kono met with Chinese foreign minister Tang in Bangkok in late July 2000 and raised the issue once again.[77] Chinese interlocutors repeatedly rebuffed Japanese concerns on two grounds—first, that the survey activities occurred within the Chinese EEZ and thus did not require Japanese permission; and second, that military survey activities were normal and legal, and hence did not require Japanese permission. During the security dialogue, China agreed to address the issue of MSR but stood by its assertion that its military activities were "normal."

In light of Chinese intransigence, pressure grew for a more assertive posture. Nevertheless, Japan could not unilaterally respond to China's marine surveys due to the difficulties of identifying violations of Japanese EEZ jurisdiction. Because China uses both military and civilian vessels to conduct hydrographic surveys, MSR, and military activities, it is difficult to determine for what purpose—civilian, military, or end; commercial or public good—the data will be used. Furthermore, reports indicate that Chinese vessels conduct multiple types of research on a single voyage. For example, on separate occasions the *Dongdiao 232* was observed cruising steadily through the international straits that pass through Japan, but was also seen stationary for up to one hour, as well as sailing back and forth along the coast.[78] According to Sam Bateman, being stationary for periods of time would permit a ship to take bottom samples as part of a MSR project or a military mapping operation. When a ship is conducting a hydrographic survey, it will be under way following a regular pattern, such as sailing back and forth along the coast.[79] Thus the *Dongdiao 232* appeared to conduct both legal and illegal surveys (under international law) in Japanese waters on this occasion. Even if the trained eye can determine what kind of survey is occurring at a given time by examining a ship's movement, it is impossible to know the purpose of the information being used, which is the criterion for determining whether or not a given activity violates a state's EEZ jurisdiction.

These uncertainties prevented Japan from policing its waters without Chinese cooperation. When the MSDF dispatched a destroyer to monitor the *Haibing 723* after it passed through the Tsugaru Strait in late May 2000, it could do little other than observe. Without evidence that Japanese laws are being broken, there is little recourse for action to board the vessel to determine the type of research being conducted, or to force the vessel from Japanese waters.[80] Furthermore, because China does not recognize the Japanese jurisdictional claim, it can claim that its vessels do not need to request Japanese permission, nor follow MSA requests when asked to leave. MSA reports indicate that when Chinese vessels are hailed, the explanation given is that they are conducting legal marine research activities.[81] Therefore, despite rising concern in the defense establishment, the media, and the public, Japan's ability to police Chinese activities in its EEZ was limited. Consequently, Tokyo used ODA pressure to coerce Chinese cooperation. It is unlikely that the Chinese were compelled to negotiate because of this pressure; it is more likely that the decision to use ODA pressure was received in Beijing as an indication of the importance Tokyo placed on the issue.

Japanese policymakers initially tied the intrusions to concerns that Japanese aid either directly or indirectly supported Chinese military modernization.[82] This perception was supported by both increased Chinese research activities in the EEZ and its growing naval presence in Japanese-claimed waters.[83] This point was conveyed on several occasions to the Chinese. In May 2000, Japanese foreign minister Kono Yohei told his Chinese counterpart, Tang Jiaxuan, that Japan would review its ODA policy in light of China's increased military spending.[84]

The decision to use ODA coercively was opposed by MOFA, which had repeatedly ignored requests from the defense sector to use ODA pressure.[85] In fact, rather than curtailing ODA, on August 2, 2000, MOFA announced the extension of a special yen loan package totaling 17.2 billion on the grounds that special yen loans were separate from the ODA packages subject to annual review.[86] Members of the LDP, who viewed ODA as a diplomatic tool that could be used to address the intrusions issue, took issue with this as did conservative media.[87] On August 8, the Foreign Affairs Committee of the LDP declared that the Chinese intrusions were a threat to Japanese sovereignty and asked Kono to convey these concerns to the Chinese during his upcoming visit. The committee reiterated these concerns on August 24 and postponed approval for the loan.[88] In essence, the LDP compelled MOFA to attach conditions to the approval of a set of special yen loans to China.[89] Kono was sent to Beijing to request meetings on the implementation of a scheme to address the intrusions issue. He stressed that public support for ODA in Japan was on the wane in light of China's increased defense spending and due to the intrusions into Japanese waters.[90] At the height of these exchanges, the JDA released its annual white paper, which contained some of the most forthright criticism of Chinese foreign and defense policy on record.[91]

In light of this pressure, and despite vocal protests from state media and the MFA, China softened its stance on the intrusions issue.[92] Zhu told

Kono, "We had no idea that the activities of the exploration ships were causing concern in Japan."[93] Regarding research vessels, Tang agreed in principle to establish a notification scheme, but one that did not affect the delimitation of the East China Sea.[94] On the issue of military vessels, whereas the Chinese had previously described the activities as normal, Tang replied that the circumstances causing Japanese concern no longer existed. MOFA interpreted this to indicate there would be no more activities by Chinese naval vessels for the time being.[95] Perhaps as a sign of good faith, a Chinese research ship that had been operating in Japanese-claimed waters at the time of the meeting left the area.[96] The ODA loan was released on October 10 ahead of Zhu's visit to Tokyo.

The Depth of Cooperation

As a product of the enforcement challenges noted above, Japan required Chinese cooperation to police Chinese research activities in the EEZ. Although Japan was able to coerce the Chinese to sit at the bargaining table, Japan had little leverage to force a robust, binding agreement. Negotiations were brief, and the resulting enforcement protocols were weak. Japanese leaders initially sought to curtail the Chinese surveys or at a minimum to develop a mechanism to clarify their purpose. The primary avenue through which Japanese leaders conveyed their displeasure was at the Consultations on the Law of the Sea that followed the conclusion of the fisheries agreement in 1997. These director-general-level talks began in August 1998 and provided a forum for Japanese policymakers to air their grievances on the intrusions issue to China, but with little success. Indeed, these meetings occurred only twice between the conclusion of the fisheries agreement and the commencement of the notification agreement talks, in August 1998 and January 2000.[97] As illustrated above, Japanese diplomatic protests yielded very little. In contrast to Sino-Japanese interactions on the fisheries issue, interactions on the survey issue were infrequent, tense, and generally mistrustful.

Following the Kono–Tang talks on August 28, 2000, and Tang's agreement in principle to negotiate, negotiators at the deputy director-general level from the foreign affairs ministries met on September 15 and on September 27–28 to discuss the details of the notification agreement.[98] Jurisdictional issues were the primary stumbling blocks. Once again, China stressed that the problem resulted from the lack of a delimitation line in the East China Sea, and thus wanted to begin delimitation negotiations; as in the case of the fisheries, Japan refused.[99] Consequently, both parties entered the negotiations concerned that any agreement would confer legitimacy on an interpretation of the delimitation question. Because neither party wanted the notification plan to prejudice future delimitation negotiations, it was particularly difficult to agree on an area in which notification would apply.[100] The geographic scope of the agreement was thus kept deliberately vague.

Second, there was disagreement over the degree of transparency required. To fully address the issues outlined above, Japan sought full disclosure of the details of a survey, such as the size, duration, authorizing body, and scope of the survey. Consistent with its interests, China sought to minimize the details exchanged.[101] As illustrated above, China's survey activities are conducted by a wide variety of vessels capable of conducting multiple types of surveys on a given voyage. Disclosure of these details may have undermined China's freedom of action by regulating some of these activities and not others. Timing was also an issue. Chinese negotiators offered one week's notice of a voyage, while the Japanese sought six months.[102] Longer notification would facilitate Japanese monitoring of a given vessel, while one week's notice limited Japan's possible interdiction of a vessel to airborne monitoring, rather than seaborne. The final compromise called for a two-month notification prior to any Chinese survey conducted in "waters near Japan and in which Japan takes an interest," while Japan would notify China prior to any survey in waters "near" China.[103] Notification would include the name of the organization conducting the research, the vessel's name and type, and details of the research project, such as its length and the geographic area concerned.[104] The *note verbale* was exchanged on February 11, 2001.

The depth of cooperation reveals numerous shortcomings. First, a *note verbale* is a highly informal diplomatic instrument, in contrast to treaties or other bilateral expressions of interest; it is simply designed to exchange points of view. Second, the agreement did not set up any bilateral authority to manage the issue on an ongoing basis. The fisheries agreement, for instance, delegated some state authority to a jointly administered body. But the notification agreement contains no provisos for the punishment of violations; nor does it set up a body through which parties can air grievances. Although a mechanism already existed through the bilateral Consultations on the Law of the Sea, past Japanese protests had not altered deviant behavior on the survey issue. As a result the responsibility for enforcement fell to the political will and the capacity of the parties involved.

Problematically, Japan had little capacity to enforce the agreement because it lacked the legal and constitutional mechanisms to police Chinese behavior. Before its ratification of UNCLOS in 1996, waters outside the Japanese 12-nautical-mile territorial sea were considered high seas for all purposes other than fisheries. Thus, foreign survey vessels could operate freely regardless of their activity. Following UNCLOS ratification Japanese policymakers were of the view that MSR in its EEZ should not be conducted without Japanese consent, but that it should be subject to as little regulation as possible. This position was adopted because the Japanese government viewed MSR activities as being beneficial for all mankind in principle.[105] According to article 3 of Japan's EEZ law, "The laws and regulations of Japan . . . shall apply with respect to . . . the protection and preservation of the marine environment and marine scientific research in the exclusive economic zone or on the continental shelf."[106] However, no specific domestic laws relating to MSR were adopted. In fact, legal amendments passed following the declaration merely extended *existing* Japanese laws to the EEZ and territorial sea.[107] No new laws were written. Rather, a set of guidelines was adopted and communicated to the UN. However, the guidelines "confer on the government no new . . . competence, have no regulatory effect and do not bind the conduct of the government legally."[108] Consequently, Japanese laws could only be applied to surveys by foreign vessels to the extent that they pertained to a jurisdictional entitlement, such as fisheries or seabed resource exploitation. Despite the absence of specific domestic laws, however, the MSA is entitled to ask foreign vessels to stop the activity or leave the EEZ under international law.[109] However, as noted above, there is no way for Japanese authorities to ascertain the legalities of a given survey without boarding the vessel, the legal recourse for which did not exist at the time.

Furthermore, Japanese defense laws and doctrine were not adequately prepared to enforce Japanese laws on MSR, had they existed. It was not until October 2001 that new guidelines on the use of force at sea were passed through the Diet, and it was not until December 2001 that these were exercised against the "suspicious" ship in the EEZ that was later revealed to be a North Korean spy vessel.[110] The importance of a legal basis for a militarized response to an intrusion is demonstrated by an incident on March 23–24, 1999. Japanese MSA and MSDF forces chased two suspicious vessels from Japanese waters, which were later revealed to be North

Korean espionage vessels. The MSDF was not allowed to disable the fleeing vessels but was instead permitted only to fire warning shots from pursuing vessels and patrol planes.[111] The vessels escaped Japanese waters resulting in heavy criticism of the operational limits on Japanese coast guard and military vessels. The legal basis used for maritime security operations in this case was under fisheries and customs law, neither of which pertains to survey or military activities in the EEZ.[112] The problem is well articulated by JDA director-general Kazuo Torashima: "We need accurate information on their [Chinese vessels'] activity. We cannot say that we have no idea what they are doing. What we can do is to take actions that are allowed internationally. There are many ways to do that. One of the ways is to make complaints through diplomatic channels. . . . Japan's territorial waters fall under the jurisdiction of the Maritime Safety Agency and the Fisheries Agency. Therefore we all can collect information to make comprehensive decisions."[113]

Consequently, Japan was incapable of forcing Chinese vessels to share information about their activities and was incapable of expelling them from its EEZ. Despite Tokyo's view that conducting MSR activities in its EEZ without consent was forbidden, the Chinese survey activities did not violate any Japanese laws. Without a legal foundation upon which to base its opposition, a more assertive Japanese stance would at best have seemed unreasonable and at worst been illegal.

In the absence of robust enforcement mechanisms, violations of the agreement became routine. Chinese vessels typically violate the agreement by not offering prior notification, by conducting a different type of operation than that specified, or by operating in a different area of the sea than originally stated.[114] If these vessels operate under the official view that China's ocean "territory" extends to the continental margin, and that notification of research is required in areas "where Japan has an interest," they may not recognize the need to notify Japan of their research activities at all. For example, it is likely that the *Fendou 4*, which was twice detected in Japanese waters in 2001 and affiliated with the Ministry of Land and Natural Resources, was conducting resource based surveys of the seabed, as this function is part of the ministry's portfolio.[115] Consistent with China's view on its continental shelf claim, and the parameters of the notification agreement, notification of the *Fendou*'s operations was not offered.[116] Indeed, when contacted to explain their actions, the vessel's operators argued they were operating on the Chinese continental shelf.[117]

Furthermore, although Japan made diplomatic remonstrations to China over the continued presence of naval vessels in the EEZ in July 2001, there is no evidence that Beijing considered military activities to be covered by the agreement. For example, six naval vessels were seen in waters off Okinawa as early as February 2001, the time the notification agreement came into effect.[118] The *Defense of Japan 2001* reported that six sightings of Chinese warships had been made by May 2001.[119] The *Haibing 723* made two visits to the Japanese EEZ in July and November 2001, and was apparently conducting military research.[120] For some Japanese interviewees these events indicate that Chinese vessels violate the agreement deliberately.[121] In this view Chinese violations are part of China's position of nonrecognition of Japan's median line.[122] The nature of the violations of the agreement indicates this trend. Of the five cases of violation in 2001, three vessels were operating within 100 kilometers of the Senkaku/Diaoyu Islands.[123] In addition to being a politically sensitive area, these activities are consistent with the Chinese claim to the islands.

The Durability of Cooperation

The agreement functioned for a short period. China notified Japan of a marine resource survey that included drilling for hydrocarbons northeast of Okinawa and of a marine research study near Iwo Jima by the PLAN in July 2001.[124] Simultaneously, Japanese foreign minister Makiko Tanaka expressed her concerns that Chinese vessels were violating the agreement to Tang on the sidelines of the Association of Southeast Asian Nations (ASEAN) + 3 meeting in late July.[125] Clearly, as a function of the strategic value of the East China Sea, China had little reason to comply.

Interviews with Japanese strategists in 2008 suggested three possible reasons for the failure of the notification agreement to govern marine survey activity. Some expressed the view that the agreement has been misunderstood by both parties.[126] In this view the problems with defining exactly what constitutes marine research have led to misunderstanding about the conditions under which the agreement applies. Moreover, Tokyo expected that the notification agreement, combined with Japan's coastal state entitlements to regulate resource exploitation in its EEZ, meant that the Chinese would now seek consent for all surveys.[127] But the EEZ boundary, and as a result, the jurisdictional entitlements granted by the boundary, are under dispute, and thus Chinese research into resource exploitation sidesteps the agreement altogether. Ultimately, abiding by the agreement involves recognizing some aspect of where Japan's jurisdiction lies, despite the wording "waters of concern."

Others blame the agreement's weakness and place responsibility with bureaucratic politics within the Japanese foreign policy apparatus, specifically the "China School" in MOFA, which was in charge of negotiating the agreement.[128] The China School had been overruled by the LDP in the decision to link ODA with the intrusions issue in August, and watering down the resulting agreement with China could have been a way to regain lost face or a degree of control over China policy.[129] Evidence of a disconnect between MOFA and the security apparatus emerged when Foreign Minister Tanaka appeared to defend China's research activities at a Lower House Committee on Foreign Affairs meeting, saying that "there is no international law that prohibits conducting resources research in the EEZ."[130] Viewed against the backdrop of an internal battle for control over the power to make foreign policy, this view is plausible.[131] Certainly, the wording of the area governed by the agreement is sufficiently subjective so as to permit a Chinese vessel to disregard it completely.

A final reason cited by Japanese strategists is that bureaucratic misunderstanding has contributed to repeated violations of the agreement. This would explain the presence of a Chinese survey vessel in Japanese waters in early September 2000 after the Kono–Tang talks. Chinese officials dismissed the incident as an accident, and Japanese officials were reluctant to make a protest given the newly reached consensus on the survey issue.[132] As noted above, Chinese marine research is undertaken by a variety of bodies that are not responsible for relations with Japan; they are responsible for marine research.[133] For example, of the five violations of the agreement detected in 2001, some vessels were operating for the Chinese Academy of Sciences, while others were operating for the National Bureau of Oceanography or the Ministry of Land and Natural Resources.[134] One Japanese strategist expressed the view that the strength of certain bureaucratic arms, such as the PLAN, would permit them a degree of autonomy in their research activities.[135] Interviews with Chinese scholars partly corroborated this. One scholar noted that the MFA was not aware of the activities of the Han-class submarine that was detected in Japanese territorial waters in 2004.[136]

Ultimately, Chinese violations are likely combination of all three factors and reveal the strength of the strategic importance Beijing has placed on marine survey activities since the late 1990s. As one Japanese interviewee pointed out, bureaucratic mistakes happen, but they are not the norm.[137] In addition, Beijing may dispatch ships to undertake marine research for political purposes and politically powerful actors like the military may ignore central directives or only obey them for a short time. Thus the notification agreement could be viewed as a success from the Chinese perspective because it has retained a large degree of freedom of action regarding the behavior of its vessels in the disputed area of the East China Sea.

Conversely, the agreement is widely viewed as a failure in Japan because it has done little to curtail Chinese activities or its maritime expansion. Nevertheless, Japan has not sought a replacement, despite continued domestic pressure in light of recurring intrusions, as well as rising tensions over Chinese resource exploitation activities. Although the two sides continued dialogue on the survey issue at the Japan–China Security Dialogue in February 2004 and at issue-specific consultations on MSR activities in April 2004, these talks led nowhere.[138] This is likely due to a worsening diplomatic climate, particularly in the maritime realm.[139] In 2003, a Ming-class submarine transited the Osumi Strait, and the Han submarine incident in November 2004 marked the beginning of a significant downturn in bilateral relations.[140] However, as is detailed in subsequent chapters, Japanese strategic concerns about the expansion of Chinese maritime influence underwrote profound shifts in Japan's strategic posture.

Conclusion

The second case of Sino-Japanese maritime cooperation stands in stark contrast to the first. Unlike the fisheries agreement, Sino-Japanese interaction over marine surveys was colored by mistrust. As expected by the MVM, China and Japan were unable to coordinate their preferences because the salience of the issue translated into competing goals for disputed maritime space. Although Japan was able to coerce temporary Chinese cooperation through the use of ODA pressure, in all likelihood, the effectiveness of ODA pressure as a diplomatic tool was limited amidst talk of its eventual cessation accelerated at the time. Furthermore, the relative decline in the amount of aid reduced Chinese attachment to it.[141] Indeed, the use of ODA pressure in 2001 was likely only successful as a diplomatic symbol of the degree of Japanese concern, rather than as a tangible cost to deviant Chinese behavior. Combined with Japan's legal shortcomings, this made the

2001 notification agreement virtually unenforceable against China. The strategic importance of maintaining the strength of jurisdictional claims prevented the sharing of jurisdiction that was achieved by the PMZ outlined by the fisheries agreement.

Similar to the case of the fisheries agreement, domestic political pressure played an important role in pushing Japan from inaction to the pursuit of a cooperative solution. This pressure came from the security bureaucracy supported by media and public opinion, and it was aimed at Japanese politicians in response to a festering issue in the bilateral relationship. Although Japan succeeded in getting China to cooperate in principle, there were a number of problems with the notification agreement, both with its design and with the type of behavior it aimed to control. Whether by design or accident, the vague wording of the agreement has reduced its effectiveness in preventing unannounced Chinese research activities in Japanese waters. Furthermore, Japan remained incapable of enforcing its provisions unilaterally due to constitutional and legal restrictions on the exercise of Japan's EEZ jurisdiction.

However, these restrictions were modified following the first use of force by the Japanese military since World War II, on the North Korean spy vessel fleeing the Japanese EEZ in December 2001. In response to the Han submarine transiting Japan's territorial sea in November 2004, a "maritime security operation" was ordered, and MSDF vessels and planes tracked the submarine out of Japanese waters.[142] This is widely regarded as the highest level of alert the Japanese military has ever exercised, and only the second instance of a maritime security operation. Unlike previous instances, MSDF aircraft used sonar tracking to deliberately warn the submarine that it was being tracked.[143] Therefore, in response to this incident, Japan "clearly signaled to China that it is willing to flex military muscles of its own."[144] Regardless of these operational changes, domestic regulations on MSR in the EEZ have not been adopted, and Chinese vessels thus continue to operate outside the Japanese legal system. The analysis returns to these issues in chapter 6. In the interim, concerns over the survey issue abated because of the emergence of a new challenge to the status quo in the East Asian maritime order: China's efforts to develop hydrocarbons in the East China Sea. This is the subject of chapter 5.

Notes

1. I do not use the term "sanction," because the loan was never cut off; it was merely delayed. Further, the link between the ODA and the issue upon which Japan

sought a change in Chinese policy was more subtle that in previous instances of Japanese ODA sanctions. See Katada, "Why Did Japan Suspend Foreign Aid to China?" 39–58. Takamine defines sanctions broadly and views the 2000 delay as a sanction. See Takamine, "New Dynamism in Sino-Japanese Security Relations," 441.

2. Zou, "Governing Marine Scientific Research in China," 18.

3. This section draws from Hiramatsu, "China's Naval Advance," 130–32; and Graham, *Japan's Sea Lane Security*, 188–89. For an account of one such event, see "Japan Asks China to Investigate East China Sea Incident," Kyodo News, December 16, 1991.

4. Valencia, *Maritime Regime for North-East Asia*, 267.

5. MSA, "Annual Report on Maritime Safety 1998," 17.

6. Ibid., 34. "Number of Illegal Ships More Than Double," Kyodo News, September 20, 1999.

7. *East Asian Strategic Review 2000*, 209; JDA, *Defense of Japan 2002*, 63; "10 Chinese Navy Ships Seen in Waters near Senkaku Isles," Japan Economic Newswire, July 16, 1999.

8. JDA, *Defense of Japan 1999*, 38.

9. JDA, *Defense of Japan 2000*, 49.

10. Nishiyama, "Japanese Destroyer Tracks 'Suspected' Chinese Spy Ship Passing through Tsugaru-Kaikyo Strait."

11. Vessels transiting international straits may not carry out any research or survey activity without the prior consent of the coastal state because transit passage forbids transiting vessels to undertake activities which are not part of the act of transiting. See Churchill and Lowe, *Law of the Sea*, 405. However, the straits that pass through Japan are high seas corridors, so all research activities are permitted.

12. *East Asian Strategic Review 2001*, 202.

13. "Japan Vice Defense Minister: DA to Monitor PRC Vessel near Sea of Japan," *Sankei Shimbun*, July 18, 2000. *Dongtiao-232* is described by the JDA as a "missile range instrumentation ship." See *East Asian Strategic Review 2001*, 202; and JDA, *Defense of Japan 2002*, 63.

14. O'Rourke, *China Naval Modernization*, 12.

15. JDA, *Defense of Japan 2000*, 48–49.

16. Cole, *Great Wall at Sea*, 104. In addition, the National Marine Bureau, the National Land Resources Department, the State Education Department, and the China Marine Oil Company also operate civilian marine survey vessels. Saunders, *Jane's Fighting Ships 2008–2009*, 148.

17. Toppan, "World Navies Today: Chinese Scientific, Research and Experimental Vessels."

18. China Defence Today, "Type 625c Oceanographic Survey Ship."

19. State Council of the People's Republic of China, *China's National Defense in 2004*; Shambaugh, *Modernizing China's Military*, 101

20. Howarth, *China's Rising Sea Power*, 89–90. On the role of submarines in a Taiwan Strait scenario, see Goldstein and Murray, "Undersea Dragons," 161–96; and Glosny, "Strangulation from the Sea?" 125–60.

21. Valencia, "Maritime Confidence and Security Building in East Asia," 37.

22. "Chinese Spy Boat in Pacific Off Tokyo Last Month: Paper," Japan Economic Newswire, June 10, 2000.

23. "Chinese Vessel Leaves Okinawa Waters after Warnings," Agence France-Presse, May 2, 1997.

24. "United Nations Convention on the Law of the Sea," (UNCLOS), part XIII, article 246.

25. For this assessment as it relates to the East China Sea, see *East Asian Strategic Review 2001*, 200.

26. Author interview "C," February 4, 2008, Yokohama. This author was referring to a possible American withdrawal from the Asia-Pacific region.

27. Author interview "B."

28. Ota, "How Should Japan Respond to Chinese Maritime Expansion?"

29. Hiramatsu, "China Aims to Advance into the Pacific Ocean."

30. Hiramatsu, "China's Naval Advance," 118–32.

31. Samuels, *Securing* Japan, 140–43. The pursuit of hydrocarbon resources in the East China Sea was not a significant part of Japanese perceptions at the time, as Chinese efforts in this area were not yet significant.

32. Cole, *Great Wall at Sea*, 165–68.

33. See Huang, "Chinese Navy's Offshore Active Defense Strategy," 19, table 2, for these variations in definition. All definitions envision China exercising effective control of the East China Sea, the South China Sea, the Yellow Sea, and the Bohai Gulf. Others argue that only two divisions of waters exist in Chinese naval strategy, coastal and high seas. In this view the "high seas" can only be defended by blue water capabilities. See Herrmann, "Chinese Military Strategy and Its Maritime Aspects," 14–17.

34. State Council of the People's Republic of China, *China's National Defense in 2002*, chap. 3. Previous pronouncements placed the defense of "maritime rights and interests" on par with the defense of territorial integrity and national sovereignty. See State Council of the People's Republic of China, *China's National Defense in 2000.*

35. Ji and Xu, "In Search of Blue Water Power," 143; Ji, *The Armed Forces of China*, 161–63. The latter scenario is viewed to be particularly remote. See Li, "PLA's Evolving Warfighting Doctrine, Strategy and Tactics, 1985–9," 448; and Lewis and Xue, *China's Strategic Seapower*, 226. Others add using the PLAN as a diplomatic tool to this list of missions, although this is a relatively recent development. See Cole, *Great Wall at Sea*, 173. This includes port visits, military exchanges, and joint exercises.

36. US Department of Defense, *Annual Report to Congress*, i.

37. For a synopsis of China's sea denial strategy in a Taiwan Strait scenario, see Cole, "Beijing's Strategy of Sea Denial," 2–4. For a comprehensive analysis, see Cliff et al., *Entering the Dragon's Lair.*

38. Zhang, "Sea Power and China's Strategic Choices," 25.

39. Bateman, "Hydrographic Surveying in the EEZ," 165.

40. UNCLOS, part XIII. See also Kim, *Maritime Delimitation and Interim Arrangements*, 70.

41. MSR is loosely defined as a set of principles—e.g., it will be conducted exclusively for peaceful purposes, it will be conducted in ways consistent with the scientific methods compatible with the convention, it will not interfere with other legitimate uses of the sea outlined in the convention, and it will be conducted in ways consistent with the environmental protections outlined in the convention. See UNCLOS, part XIII, article 240. For a discussion of definitions from the Chinese perspective see Zhang, "Conflict between Jurisdiction of Coastal States," 317–31.

42. Hayashi, "Military and Intelligence-Gathering Activities in the EEZ," 130.

43. Some argue that hydrographic surveys should not require coastal state permission because the data collected are of universal benefit, do not prejudice the security of the coastal state, and are intended to provide safe navigation. See Churchill and Lowe, *Law of the Sea*, 405n3.

44. Wegelin, *Marine Scientific Research*, 356.

45. Bateman, "Hydrographic Surveying in the EEZ," 165.

46. Ibid., 167.

47. Document provided to the author by interview subject "A," not for citation.

48. For the purposes of this discussion, the term "survey activities" refers to all four of the typologies discussed; in other instances, the type of activity is specified.

49. Sasajima, "Japan's Domestic Politics and China Policymaking," 99–100.

50. On a related note, the degree of detail included in some media reports of Chinese intrusions suggests that such detail was made available by defense officials. These details include the location, bearing, speed, and duration of the journey of a given ship. See, e.g., "Japan DA Chief on PRC Navy Ships in Japanese Waters," *Sankei Shimbun*, July 15, 2000.

51. Takamine, "New Dynamism in Sino-Japanese Security Relations," 454; JDA, *Defense of Japan 2000*, 48–49. This assessment of the influence of the security bureaucracy is based on Calder, "Institutions of Japanese Foreign Policy," 4–6.

52. MSA, "Annual Report on Maritime Safety 1998," 17.

53. JDA, *Defense of Japan 1998*, 51; See also Kim, *Naval Strategy in Northeast Asia*, 173.

54. JDA, *Defense of Japan 1999*, 38.

55. *East Asian Strategic Review 2000*, 209.

56. *East Asian Strategic Review 2001*, 200.

57. This assessment is based on a variety of sources. Graham, in particular, notes that the Japanese government did not comment on media reports of Chinese submarine incursions in the mid-1990s. See Graham, *Japan's Sea Lane Security*, 213. This is reflected in Japan's generally softly-softly approach to China through the 1990s. See Green and Self, "Japan's Changing China Policy," 38–39. Others have called this the "Friendship Diplomacy Paradigm." See Mochizuki, "Japan's Shifting Strategy toward the Rise of China," 736–76.

58. Drifte, *Japan's Security Relations with* China, 57.

59. "Chinese Naval Ships on Rise near Japan," *Japan Times*, March 22, 2000; China Naval Visits in E. China Sea Cause for Concern: Sankei," Kyodo News, April 18, 2000.

60. "Japanese Editorial Excerpts," Kyodo News, August 28, 2000.

61. "Japanese Editorial Excerpts," Kyodo News, August 27, 2000.

62. "Japanese Daily Notes Kono's Visit to PRC Helped Promote Bilateral Relations," *Sankei Shimbun*, September 2, 2000.

63. See Shin Joho Center, "USIA #2000-I20012,"; and Shin Joho Center, "USIA Poll # 2000-I20045."

64. See Lehman, "Japanese Attitudes towards Foreign Policy," 123–41. One author makes this point with regard to public attitudes about the US alliance. See DiFilippo, "How Tokyo's Security Policies Discount Public Opinion," 23–48.

65. Shinoda, "Becoming More Realistic in the Post–Cold War," 171–90. On the pacifist assumption in public opinion research, see Miyashita, "Where Do Norms Come From?" 107.

66. Green, *Japan's Reluctant Realism*, 69.

67. Rousseau, *Identifying Threats and Threatening Identities*, 184.

68. Drifte, "Ending of Japan's ODA Loan Programme to China," 106. See also Takamine, "Domestic Determinants of Japan's China Aid Policy," 191–206.

69. Mochizuki, "Japan's Long Transition," 95–96. Discussions with observers of Japanese politics suggest the effect of public opinion on Japanese foreign policy, it pertains to a "realist" worldview as distinct from growing concerns about China, remains controversial. Author interview "L," June 15, 2011, Tokyo. See also Midford, *Rethinking Japanese Public Opinion and Security*.

70. See Beer and Watanabe, "Mori Continues to React, Not Lead after Election."

71. "China Naval Visits in E. China Sea Cause for Concern: Sankei," Kyodo News, April 18, 2000.

72. Strictly speaking, "*Yanbing*" refers to the class of this ship. As there is only one vessel of this class in operation, the name of the ship in question is *Haibing 723*. See China Defence Today, "Research & Survey Vessels."

73. Toppan, "World Navies Today: Chinese Scientific, Research and Experimental Vessels"; China Defence Today, "851 (Dongdiao 232) Electronic Intelligence Ship."

74. This assessment is based on the author's assessment of assorted media reports from Kyodo News, *Sankei Shimbun*, Agence France-Presse, and *Mainichi Daily News*. All have been referenced elsewhere.

75. Sasajima, "Japan's Domestic Politics and China Policymaking," 99–100.

76. "Nonaka Asks China to Address Maritime Intrusions," Kyodo News, June 12, 2000.

77. Masuda, "Japan's Changing ODA Policy towards China."

78. This information is gathered from "Japan DA Chief on PRC Navy Ships in Japanese Waters," *Sankei Shimbun*, July 15, 2000; and "Japan Vice Defense Minister: DA to Monitor PRC Vessel Near Sea of Japan," *Sankei Shimbun*, July 18, 2000.

79. Bateman, "Hydrographic Surveying in the EEZ," 168.

80. Nishiyama, "Japanese Destroyer Tracks 'Suspected' Chinese Spy Ship Passing through Tsugaru-Kaikyo Strait"; "Chinese Spy Boat in Pacific Off Tokyo Last Month: Paper," Japan Economic Newswire, June 10, 2000. This is notwithstanding the larger legal debate over whether it is ever acceptable for a coastal state to forcibly expel military or noncommercial vessels from the territorial sea. See Churchill and Lowe, *Law of the Sea*, 87–90.

81. "Beijing, Tokyo Scrapping over Territorial Sea Rights," *Mainichi Daily News*, June 10, 1999.

82. Kojima, "To Make China a Responsible Major Power," 38–45.

83. Ibid.; Drifte, "Ending of Japan's ODA Loan Programme to China," 105–7.

84. "ODA to China: Bold Review Based on Guidelines Necessary," *Sankei Shimbun*, May 12, 2000.

85. Takamine, "Domestic Determinants of Japan's China Aid Policy," 201.

86. Masuda, "Japan's Changing ODA Policy towards China."

87. "New Aid to China: The Incoherent Japanese Diplomacy without Strategies," *Sankei Shimbun*, August 18, 2000.

88. "LDP Delays China Loans over Encroaching Ships," Kyodo News, August 24, 2000.

89. Takamine, "New Dynamism in Sino-Japanese Security Relations," 455.

90. Ibid., 455.

91. "Editorial: A Defensive Report," *Mainichi Daily News*, August 4, 2000; JDA, *Defense of Japan 2000*, 45–49.

92. "Cancellation of Japan Loan Would Hurt Ties, Says China Paper," Kyodo News, August 28, 2000; "China Says Warship Operations Irrelevant to Loans from Japan," Kyodo News, August 25, 2000.

93. Zhu Ronji, quoted by Komori, "Latest Intrusion of PRC Vessels in Japanese EEZ to Have Serious Impact."

94. "Tang Jiaxuan, Kono Discuss Ties, Zhu's Visit, East China Sea Dispute," Xinhua Domestic Service, August 28, 2000.

95. MOFA, "Japan–China Foreign Ministers' Meeting."

96. "Chinese Ship Leaves Japan's Economic Waters off Kyushu," Kyodo News, August 29, 2000.

97. Drifte, "Japanese-Chinese Territorial Disputes in the East China Sea," table 3.

98. Takada, "Marine Scientific Research in the Exclusive Economic Zone," 138–40, 146–47. Reinhard Drifte has catalogued a total six rounds of formal meetings and one informal consultation between September 2000 and January 2001 en route to the exchange of a *note verbale* in February 2001. Drifte, "Japanese–Chinese Territorial Disputes in the East China Sea," table 1.

99. Valencia and Amae, "Regime Building in the East China Sea," 198.

100. The Chinese Foreign Ministry was quick to make this point. See "China Does Not Recognize Exclusive Economic Zone Unilaterally Announced by Japan," *Zhongguo Xinwen She*, September 14, 2000.

101. MOFA, "Press Conference 19 September 2000"; MOFA, "Press Conference 3 October 2000."

102. "Maritime Row Unlikely to Be Resolved before Zhu's Visit," Kyodo News, October 7, 2000.

103. Takada, "Marine Scientific Research in the Exclusive Economic Zone," 147–48.

104. "Japan, China Agree on 2-Month Maritime Notice System," Kyodo News, February 19, 2001.

105. Takada, "Marine Scientific Research in the Exclusive Economic Zone," 138–40.

106. Government of Japan, *Law on the Exclusive Economic Zone and the Continental Shelf* (Law No. 74 of 1996), article 3(1).

107. Hayashi, "Japan: New Law of the Sea Legislation," 572.

108. Takada, "Marine Scientific Research in the Exclusive Economic Zone," 141.

109. Ibid., 140.

110. JDA, *Defense of Japan 2002,* 128–31.

111. "Mysterious Ships Run for North Korean Waters," *Mainichi Daily News,* March 25, 1999.

112. This incident is detailed by JDA, *Defense of Japan 1999,* 208–14.

113. "Interview with New Cabinet Members: Defense Agency Director General Kazuo Torashima," *Sankei Shimbun,* July 17, 2000.

114. *East Asian Strategic Review 2002,* 213–15.

115. This affiliation is based on "Taiwan Threatens to Board Chinese Ship," *Daily Collection of Maritime Press Clippings,* 3.

116. This draws on the data from *East Asian Strategic Review 2002,* 214.

117. "Editorial Urges Tokyo to Limit PRC Vessel Access to Economic Zone," *Sankei Shimbun,* July 21, 2001.

118. JDA, *Defense of Japan 2002,* 63. According to Japan's National Institute of Defense Studies these vessels, which included four amphibious landing ships, were 470 kilometers off Okinawa outside the Japanese EEZ. *East Asian Strategic Review 2002,* 215.

119. JDA, *Defense of Japan 2001,* 54.

120. JDA, *Defense of Japan 2002,* 63.

121. Author interview "A," January 29, 2008, Tokyo. This is also the view of Hagstrom, *Japan's China Policy,* 150.

122. *East Asian Strategic Review 2002,* 214.

123. Ibid.

124. Valencia and Amae, "Regime Building in the East China Sea," 199.

125. MOFA, "Japan-China Foreign Minister's Meeting (Summary)."

126. Author interview "A"; Author interview "H," January 30, 2008, Tokyo.

127. Takada, "Marine Scientific Research in the Exclusive Economic Zone," 149.

128. Author interview "B." For details on the China School as a foreign policy actor, see Sasajima, "Japan's Domestic Politics and China Policymaking," 83–86; and Koji, "Domestic Sources of Japanese Policy towards China," 37–49.

129. The China School has traditionally been viewed as pro-China. E.g., it opposed ODA sanctions against China in response to the 1995 nuclear tests. See Katada, "Why Did Japan Suspend Foreign Aid to China?" 55.

130. "Japan Foreign Minister Defends PRC Marine Survey in EEZ," *Sankei Shimbun,* June 21, 2001.

131. On the battle between MOFA and the LDP for control over China policy and the decline of the China School, see Lam, "Mediating Geopolitics, Markets

and Regionalism," 172; Koji, "Domestic Sources of Japanese Policy towards China," 44–45; and Takamine, *Japan's Development Aid to China*, chap. 4.

132. Komori, "Latest Intrusion of PRC Vessels in Japanese EEZ to Have Serious Impact"; "China Should Give Notice of Maritime Research: Kono," *Japan Times*, September 9, 2000.

133. This possibility was corroborated by Professor Ma Yingjeo, deputy director of the Institute of World Politics and Economics, during the author's presentation to the Chinese Academy of Social Sciences on January 21, 2008, as well as in another interview. Author interview "E," January 18, 2008, Beijing.

134. This is based on the list contained in *East Asian Strategic Review 2002*, 214 cross-referenced with the data available from Toppan, "World Navies Today" and China Defence Today, "Research & Survey Vessels."

135. Author interview "B"; Hagstrom, *Japan's China Policy*, 150.

136. Author interview "D," January 14, 2008, Beijing. Others were of the view that PLA only follows the directives of the central authorities. Author interview "F," January 25, 2008, Beijing.

137. Author interview "C."

138. JDA, *Defense of Japan 2004*, 62.

139. Author interview "A." Conservative media accused the government of ignoring the issue so as to avoid provoking China because of this downturn in relations. See "DA Pressured Not to Announce PRC Ships Activity near Japan Due to 'Delicate' Ties," *Sankei Shimbun*, July 14, 2001.

140. The details of the Han incident are discussed by Dutton, "International Law and the November 2004 'Han Incident,'" 87–101.

141. Drifte, "Ending of Japan's ODA Loan Programme to China," 94–117. ODA as a percentage of Chinese GDP declined from 1.9 percent in 1989–90 to 0.8 percent in 2000–2001. Arase, "Japanese ODA Policy toward China," 93.

142. "China: 'Peaceful Rise in Light and Shadow,'" in *East Asian Strategic Review 2005*, 105–6.

143. These warnings were ignored. Dutton, "International Law and the November 2004 'Han Incident,'" 87.

144. Ibid., 99.

CHAPTER FIVE

Resource Development in the East China Sea, 2005–2008

IN 2004 CHINA AND JAPAN became embroiled in a dispute over hydrocarbon resource development in the East China Sea. The Chunxiao gas field lies approximately 5 kilometers west of Japan's median line in China's claimed waters. It was discovered in 2001 and is operated by the China National Offshore Oil Company (CNOOC). In many ways the field is a symbol in China of its concerted effort to develop its offshore areas and a symbol in Japan of its failure to use its maritime space. Both sides claim the right to exploit the natural gas in the field, but the MVM reveals that the Chunxiao dispute is about much more than offshore resources.

As a function of their competing maritime claims, China and Japan disagree on the location of the "disputed area" in the East China Sea, and by extension the area subject to joint development. The Chinese argue that the disputed area in the East China Sea lies between the Japanese-claimed median line and the Okinawa Trough, the limit of the Chinese continental shelf claim. Furthermore, because the Chunxiao gas field lies west of the median line, even according to the Japanese interpretation of international law, the field is Chinese. Japan claims that the Chunxiao field—as well as the neighboring Tianwaitian, Duanqiao, and Longjing fields—extend onto the east side of the median line into its EEZ and that, consequently, Japan is entitled to a share of the resources produced. Further ambiguity exists as to whether or not Japan claims a full 200-nautical-mile EEZ, which would extend beyond the median line, and include claims to these fields. Tensions arose after Japan detected a Chinese drilling installation at the Chunxiao gas field in May 2004, and they escalated in 2005, when Tokyo commissioned surveys of the median-line area. In July 2005, Tokyo granted

Teikoku Oil the right to conduct exploratory drilling on the east side of the median line, which triggered a period of posturing by both sides between April and October 2005. Nevertheless, the two sides held eleven rounds of talks between 2004 and 2007, which led to the consensus on resource exploitation in the East China Sea announced on June 18, 2008.

This chapter traces the shift from the tense diplomatic climate in 2004–5 to the cooperative one in 2008. Consistent with the fisheries case, the chapter reveals that the consensus on resource exploitation fulfilled economic aspects of both parties' objectives; it provides a framework for cooperation on resource development, without prejudicing maritime claims. Consistent with the previous case, however, strategic issues remain unresolved. Furthermore, in addition to the growing awareness in both countries of the tangible importance of maritime space, the issue became enmeshed in the contested-symbolic aspects of the bilateral relationship. To date, the consensus on resource development has not been implemented.

The Value of East China Sea Resources

The discussion that follows reveals that despite the fact that China and Japan shared an interest in the exploitation of hydrocarbons in the East China, strategic and contested-symbolic issues militated against cooperation. These relational values fostered a climate in which cooperation with the other was not possible—precisely because of who the other was.

Economic Value: Proximate Energy Security

Both parties perceived the resources of the East China Sea to be salient for economic reasons. Contrary to the onset of the East China Sea dispute in 1969, both parties felt a heightened sense of energy insecurity in 2004. Persistent Chinese exploration throughout the 1990s, at times in partnership with Japanese firms, yielded little in the way of commercial resources until the late 1990s. China's offshore production quadrupled between mid-1994 and mid-1996, reaching 380,000 barrels per day, but a drop in oil prices led to exodus of foreign partners.[1] CNOOC is quite bullish in its estimates and thus claimed that the total reserve base of all the East China Sea fields in development was 363.9 billion cubic feet.[2] CNOOC claimed that the Xihu Trough Basin, the geological formation stretching across the seabed of the East China Sea, had estimated natural gas reserves of 17.5

trillion cubic feet. Estimates of unproven oil reserves in the East China Sea vary between 70 and 160 billion barrels, though natural gas is the primary resource currently being exploited in the East China Sea.

The exploitation of the East China Sea's natural gas is consistent with China's energy security strategy in two ways: the diversification of primary energy source away from coal and oil, and the diversification of oil import sources away from the Middle East.[3] In 2004, China was able to meet close to 90 percent of its energy requirements through domestic energy sources.[4] Under the Tenth Five-Year Plan (2001–5), natural gas consumption was projected to rise from 2 percent to between 8 and 10 percent by 2020.[5] However, there are several barriers to greater consumption, including domestic production shortfalls, inadequate infrastructure, high costs to consumers, and import restrictions.[6] Most domestic gas reserves are far from their intended markets, whereas imported liquefied natural gas (LNG) is only economical close to terminals. However, some experts argue that offshore natural gas fields in the East and South China seas are "welcome exceptions to this rule."[7] Consequently, if it lived up to its potential, the East China Sea could provide China with a source of oil and gas close to the center of its military power and its high-demand coastal energy markets.[8] As evidenced by table 5.1, natural gas demand is projected to grow twice as fast as any other primary energy source through 2035.

In light of these plans to increase demand, primarily in coastal areas, offshore natural gas resources could play an important role in Chinese energy security. Early expectations were that CNOOC's gas projects in the East China Sea could potentially fuel the economies of Shanghai, Zhejiang Province, and Hong Kong.[9] However, despite a promising start, low global oil prices and few commercial discoveries reduced the interest of independent oil companies.[10] By 1999, only one independent enterprise remained involved in the East China Sea.[11] As foreign investment dried up, discoveries in the East China Sea languished. Nevertheless, China used its national oil companies to persist with exploration activities in the East China Sea, which led to a partnership between CNOOC, Unocal, and Shell for the joint development of the Xihu Trough in 2003. CNOOC's primary commercial interest in the East China Sea is to bring as much gas as possible to markets in eastern China as part of its competition for the potentially lucrative Shanghai gas market with onshore giant China National Petroleum Corporation, which pipes gas to Shanghai via the West–East Pipeline.[12] According to one Japanese expert on China's energy security, East China Sea gas costs $4–5 per million British thermal units, while gas piped

TABLE 5.1

China's Primary Energy Consumption and Demand Projections (millions of tons of oil equivalent)

	Consumption (C) and Demand (D) Projections					
Energy Source	*C, 2010*	*C, 2020*	*C, 2035*	*D, 2010*	*D, 2035*	*D, 2010–35* [a]
Coal	514	564	478	1,602	1,968	80.80%
Oil	357	554	677	448	752	2.20%
Gas	57	161	269	91.4	451.8	6.60%
Electricity	300	544	736	315.4	357.5	3.60%
Heat	64	80	74	No data	No data	N/A
Renewables	213	198	168	284	483	2.10%
Total	1,506	2,099	2,402	2,416	3,872	1.90%

Note: Oil data are from 2011. All projections are based on the "New Policies Scenario."

[a] Compound average annual growth rate.

Source: International Energy Agency, *World Energy Outlook 2012*.

through the West–East Pipeline costs $8 per million British thermal units.[13] Thus, China has an economic interest in East China Sea resources to provide secure energy sources close to high-demand markets. The energy potential of the East China Sea includes precisely the type of energy source that China wants—natural gas—in an ideal geographic location.

Japan's long track record of hydrocarbon import dependency did not yield a substantive interest in the exploitation of offshore resources in the East China Sea until 2003. At the onset of the East China Sea dispute in 1970, Japan imported 3.3 million barrels per day, which was 99.8 percent of its oil consumption, and 70 percent of its total energy use.[14] Japan subsequently took steps toward exploratory drilling and surveys in the East China Sea, but not in the area surrounding the islands due to Chinese sensitivities. After China claimed the islands and seas surrounding them, Japanese companies were forbidden from conducting seismic surveys or exploratory drilling in contested areas, while government ships proceeded with extreme caution.[15] All told, few seismic studies were undertaken of the disputed area, and no wells were sunk near the Senkaku/Diaoyu Islands.[16]

Currently, Japanese energy security strategy prioritizes the diversification of import source and energy type, structural industrial adjustment, the creation of a strategic petroleum reserve, and the pursuit of "direct" or "equity" oil purchased from exporting governments.[17] As evidenced by table 5.2, natural gas is projected to compose a growing share of the Japanese energy mix, perhaps even more so as the country revisits the role of nuclear power following the triple disaster of March 11, 2011.

East China Sea resource development thus has a logical appeal for Japan. To begin with, it is consistent with Japan's strategy of primary energy source diversification. According to the Agency for Natural Resources and Energy's Energy Security Study Group, gas will increase to 18 percent of the primary energy mix in 2030 from 15 percent in 2005.[18] East China Sea resources may also alleviate some of the threats to Japan's energy security. According to the Energy Security Study Group, these include political conditions in the Middle East, incidental threats such as terrorism or natural disasters, a reduction of investments or market manipulation by supplying nations, demand trends in importing nations such as China and India, and mismanagement of the domestic energy industry. The exploitation of East China Sea hydrocarbons mitigates these threats in three ways. First, it is not subject to Middle East price volatility due to political circumstances or terrorist attacks. Second, due to its geographic proximity to Japan, resource production in the Xihu Trough avoids the SLOC chokepoints through

TABLE 5.2
Japan's Primary Energy Consumption and Demand Projections (millions of tons of oil equivalent)

	Consumption (C) and Demand (D) Projections					
Energy Source	*C, 2010*	*C, 2020*	*C, 2035*	*D, 2010*	*D, 2035*	*D, 2010–35*[a]
Coal	29	28	27	115	92	−0.90%
Oil	171	158	135	214	157	−1.40%
Gas	34	39	43	86.4	102.2	0.70%
Electricity	86	88	93	87.4	95.2	0.30%
Heat	1	1	1	No data	No data	N/A
Renewables	3	4	7	18	63	5.20%
Total	325	318	306	497	447	−0.40%

Note: Oil data are from 2011. All projections are based on the "New Policies Scenario."

[a] Compound average annual growth rate.

Source: International Energy Agency, *World Energy Outlook 2012.*

which Japan's imported oil and LNG pass. And third, the exploitation of natural gas supports Japan's energy diversification plans, thereby reducing its vulnerability to oil price shocks.

This appeal is strengthened when considered in the context of the wider Sino-Japanese energy relationship.[19] Japan has embarked on an aggressive equity oil strategy to meet the target of 40 percent of Japan's oil imports coming from Japanese overseas concessions by 2030, up from the current 15 percent.[20] However, success has been limited, and these setbacks are perceived as gains for China.[21] For example, some analysts view Japan's decision to pursue the Azadegan project as driven by growing energy competition with China for Middle Eastern energy sources.[22] Problematically, Japan's stake was reduced to 10 percent from 75 percent due to Japanese foot-dragging and complications due to the Iranian nuclear issue.[23] Furthermore, early reports indicated a Chinese interest in filling the void left by Inpex at Azadegan.[24] This competition has also been evident over Siberian resources, despite shared Sino-Japanese interest in oil and gas imports via pipeline.[25] This zero-sum perception of resource development reflects Japan's growing preoccupation with supply security, and in turn it may explain Tokyo's sudden interest in East China Sea resource development.[26] When Japan discovered Chinese drilling installations in May 2004, interest among political elites in resource exploitation exploded. Japan subsequently commissioned surveys of the median-line area to gauge the resource wealth and in 2005 METI's annual energy white paper labeled the East China Sea as an important potential source of natural gas.[27] Clearly, in 2004 and 2005, a perception persisted that East China Sea gas was important to Japan.

The Strategic Value of the East China Sea

Resource development at Chunxiao is consistent with China's strategic maritime ambitions. As Michael McDevitt argues, Beijing's commitment to costly PLAN development is underwritten by its view that the navy is responsible for safeguarding China's primary strategic interests. These interests—whether preventing invasion, securing seaborne trade, securing energy interests, or deterring Taiwanese independence—all occur at sea.[28] Although the full scope of China's maritime strategic objectives and naval capabilities is subject to some debate, particularly with regard to its current and future ability and intention to match the US Navy, there is little question that, in 2004–5, it was clear that China intended to extend its naval power through the East China Sea to the shores of Japan.[29] Some Chinese strategists observe that for "realist" constituencies like the military, the Chunxiao issue relates to the broader exercise of Chinese naval power in the East China Sea and provides a basis for an expanded mandate beyond the first island chain.[30]

The place of resource development in this agenda is illustrated by the tendency of Chinese military writings to view maritime space in territorial terms. In 1995, Chinese military writings regarded the ocean as China's "second national territory" due to the importance of the resources that lay beneath.[31] In 2002, Land and Resources Minister Tian Fengshan noted that the East China Sea would become the primary site of China's offshore gas development in an interview with a military magazine.[32] This is striking because the bulk of CNOOC's offshore operations occur in the Bohai Gulf and the Beibu Gulf.[33] The PLAN's role as protector of this domain was outlined by the 2000 edition of China's defense white paper, which charged the PLAN not only with safeguarding China's territorial seas but also its "maritime rights and interests"—a statement that has been reiterated in every biennial paper since.[34] As David Shambaugh notes, Chinese strategists have redefined China's strategic frontiers to include its maritime areas; these are viewed as more than merely areas of jurisdiction—they are areas of sovereignty.[35]

Simultaneously, military authors became increasingly candid about Japan's impact on China's maritime security. One article notes that Japan's straits, through which Chinese trade passes into the Pacific Ocean, function as a potential "plug."[36] In an article detailing the strategic value of Okinawa to US forces, two authors note that by controlling Okinawa, American forces sit between "China's East China Sea and the Pacific Ocean."[37] This view of the Japanese islands as a strategic barrier between Mainland China and the wider Pacific has become a recurring theme among state media as well.[38] As a reflection of these concerns, the Chinese marine presence around Japan in 2004 was the highest on record, with twenty-two recorded intrusions into Japanese waters by naval and research vessels.[39]

Furthermore, from the Chinese perspective, modifications to Japanese military doctrine appeared to be designed to prevent the fulfillment of these ambitions. Changes to the operational rules for JCG vessels in 2001 were denounced as resurgent Japanese militarism.[40] Chinese military leaders took heed of the potential for the MSDF and the JCG to act against Chinese vessels under these new laws. The addition of the defense of offshore islands from invasion to the list of Ground Self-Defense Force operations in the 2004 National Defense Program Outline was further noted in

China as evidence that Japan was trying to resist China's rightful maritime expansion.[41] In short, by the time of the onset of the Chunxiao dispute, the development of East China Sea resources was located squarely within the view that China, as a great power, needed and was entitled to project power across the East China Sea and into the Pacific.[42] It was thus a reason for Chinese policymakers to value resource development in the East China Sea in a strategic sense.

Likewise, resource development in the East China Sea had developed a strategic quality for Japanese leaders. This perception is based on the failure of the notification agreement to curtail Chinese research vessels operating in Japanese waters, the continued presence of Chinese military vessels in Japanese waters, and the existence of the Chunxiao project itself. The discovery of a "Chinese Navy survey vessel" 40 kilometers (21.6 nautical miles) from the Senkaku/Diaoyu Islands in July 2004, amid numerous violations of the notification agreement that year, led to renewed calls for a stronger response to China.[43] As violations of the notification agreement became more regular, increased Chinese naval activity was mirrored by greater air force activity. The Japanese Air SDF (ASDF) has recorded an eightfold increase in violations of Japan's Air Defense Identification Zone in fiscal 2005.[44] Furthermore, more than half of these airborne intrusions occurred over the East China Sea.[45] Japanese threat perceptions were further reinforced by two incidents of submarines being detected in its territorial waters. In March 2003, a Ming-class submarine was detected in the Osumi Strait; and on November 10, 2004, a Han-class submarine was detected sailing in Japan's territorial sea off the Sakishima Islands.

From the Japanese perspective, China's expansionist designs were revealed during the early negotiations on the Chunxiao project. In May 2005, during the second round of talks, the Chinese tabled their joint development proposal that outlined areas near the Senkaku/Diaoyu Islands for joint development, rather than near the Chunxiao field.[46] For some Japanese strategists this was evidence that the PLAN was attempting to realize Liu Huaqing's aim to have control of the first island chain, and thereby gain control of the SLOCs near and beyond Japan.[47] Another interviewee intimated that this made compromise with China more difficult because of the suspicion that China will seek "more and more" from Japan in the East China Sea.[48]

Consequently, by 2005, there was a perception in Tokyo that oceanographic research vessels, the submarine intrusions, and the Chunxiao development were part of a larger strategy of Chinese maritime expansion.

These perceptions, which at first were a minority view located in the defense establishment in 2000, had become more widespread. Japanese media reports drew a link between the Han incident and the East China Sea dispute, and other sources report other submarine sightings near Chunxiao during the same period.[49] The *Defense of Japan 2005* cites oceanographic research vessels, along with the Han incident, as evidence that "the Chinese navy aims to extend space for offshore defensive operations while integrated combat capabilities are enhanced in conducting offshore campaigns."[50] In the words of one Japanese strategist: "The ultimate objective of China's military expansion is to expel the US naval force from sea areas in Asia. But China's immediate goal is clear: It is to take control of the East China Sea."[51] The Japanese concern is well summarized by one interviewee, who argued that Chinese control of the East China Sea simply could not be permitted because of the threat it would pose to Japanese interests.[52]

Contested-Symbolic Value: National Identity and Maritime Space

The period 2001–2005 witnessed an unprecedented downturn in the Sino-Japanese relationship, driven in large part by the deteriorating relationship at sea. Popular perceptions of the other grew increasingly negative due to the political manipulation of sensitive issues such as history and territorial disputes. During the Koizumi period, people holding anti-Japanese sentiments in China became particularly vocal and politically active. Although these sentiments were cultivated by the CCP in the early 1990s, due to the spread of the internet in China, they enjoyed a degree of independence from central control by the early 2000s.[53] Consequently, Chinese leaders are faced with the challenge of balancing their nationalist credentials with China's overarching national development goals.[54] China's elites recognize that a degree of pragmatism is needed to manage the country's relationships with Japan and the United States, the objects of the assertive nationalist discourse, but are at pains to balance this with the maintenance of their nationalist credentials.[55] However, the recurrent tension over state action in disputed maritime areas made this difficult. As a result, the Chunxiao dispute developed a contested-symbolic quality for leaders in Beijing and Tokyo.

Because Japan occupies pride of place in the Chinese nationalist discourse, disputes with Tokyo pose a unique set of problems. First, although they recognize the importance of the economic relationship, Chinese policymakers have long been suspicious of Japan and harbored their own negative sentiments.[56] Second, the list of grievances between the two is so great that dispute management efforts can be undermined by competing national objectives or by independent action by secondary political actors.[57] One scholar has identified an active debate over Japan policy, informed by popular opinion, between academics and foreign affairs bureaucrats between 2002 and 2004.[58] The outcome of this debate, borne out in the years 2005–6, was a rejection of the moderate view that favored accommodation with Japan. Therefore, during the apex of tensions over the Chunxiao dispute in 2005, anti-Japanese sentiment was particularly pervasive at the policymaking level, which in turn constrained Beijing's ability to be flexible.

Chinese leaders valued resource development in the East China Sea in contested-symbolic terms because, in a dispute with Japan over contested territory, Beijing is vulnerable to pressure from nationalist constituencies in Chinese society or within the policymaking apparatus. Some of the most active Chinese popular nationalist groups derive their names from the disputed islands. For example, the Chinese Federation to Defend Diaoyutai was founded by Tong Zeng in 1996 following the crisis over the islands. This group organized rallies to protest a wide range of Chinese nationalist grievances. Based in Hong Kong, the Action Committee for Defending the Diaoyu Islands orchestrated the March 2004 landing and regularly protests aspects of the Sino-Japanese relationship.[59] Of course, Beijing is not completely beholden to the whim of popular nationalist groups, but it is sensitive about maintaining the nationalist credentials of the CCP, which limits its ability to be pragmatic.

Likewise, in Japan, the East China Sea dispute was prominent in a domestic political discourse that was increasingly concerned about the implications China's rise for Japanese security. Because Prime Minister Koizumi Junichiro himself viewed nationalism as a political tool, he was somewhat more beholden to this constituency than previous Japanese leaders.[60] For example, Koizumi's 2001 election pledge to visit the Yasukuni Shrine annually on August 15 was less a product of his own nationalist sympathies and more an attempt to outflank his rival Hashimoto Ryutaro, a card-carrying nationalist.[61] This also allowed Koizumi to assert himself on the making of China policy.[62] By 2005, therefore, the political climate in Tokyo was one that was highly receptive to conservative and nationalist perspectives, which were both heavily critical of Tokyo's response to Chinese drilling in the East China Sea.

Conservative critics argued that China had stolen a march on Japan in the East China Sea that allowed it to hand Japan a fait accompli.[63] Polemic newspaper editorials drew a link between East China Sea delimitation and the potential implications for the Senkaku/Diaoyu Islands dispute. The *Yomiuri Shimbun*'s Okubo Yoshio argued (incorrectly) that Japanese recognition of China's claim to the East China Sea necessarily implied the surrender of the Senkaku/Diaoyu Islands.[64] Even the generally balanced *Nihon Keizai Shimbun* argued that China's posture toward the gas issue "seems to echo a series of Chinese actions in recent years that appear to reflect the country's maritime ambitions, such as a major buildup of its naval forces and expansion of activities of its vessels."[65]

The prominence of this perspective mattered because the making of Japanese foreign policy was becoming more centralized and more responsive to public opinion, which had taken a decidedly anti-Chinese turn.[66] At the time public opinion was influential on China policy for two reasons. First, Koizumi had wrested control of China policy away from the Asian Affairs Bureau in MOFA, and Japanese politicians generally were more influenced by public opinion on security issues due to electoral reforms.[67] In late 2004, annual Cabinet Office surveys revealed that only 37.6 percent of Japanese people felt favorably disposed toward China, the lowest level since the surveys began.[68] A year later this figure reached a new low of 32.4 percent.[69] Second, Chinese maritime expansion into the East China Sea had become a mainstream concern that exacerbated ingrained suspicions of China. This convergence of anti-Chinese views with mainstream concerns about the expansion of Chinese maritime power made the Chunxiao gas dispute a key domestic political issue for Japanese policymakers in 2005. Thus, the correct handling of the Chunxiao dispute from a popular perspective was essential for Japanese leaders. Unlike the previous case, exercising maritime jurisdiction had taken on an intangible quality as the issue became wrapped up in broader debates of each party's relationship with the "other."

These values translated into competing territorial objectives for Beijing and Tokyo. Whether a function of its resource needs, its strategic apprehensions about Chinese military expansion, or the domestic pressure that arose from perceived weakness on territorial issues, Japan's goals for the disputed space were to gain access to the Chunxiao field, or at minimum delay Chinese development of the area, and to prevent a pretext for further Chinese expansion across the East China Sea. From China's perspective, granting Japan access to the Chunxiao project or independent

FIGURE 5.1
Maritime Value Matrix, 2005–8

Economic:	**Strategic:**
• Resource value of the Xihu Trough	• Exercising jurisdiction in contested areas (China) • China's maritime expansion (Japan)
Shared Symbolic:	**Contested Symbolic:**
• Void	• Asserting jurisdictional and territorial claims (both parties) • Compromise with the "other"

Japanese exploitation of the disputed area could weaken China's claim to the entire East China Sea. Furthermore, the issue served as a pretext to seek to further expand the reach of the PLAN. Beijing was aware that compromise on these issues would risk costly domestic political fallout, while the domestic climate in Japan was becoming less tolerant of Chinese provocations. By referring to the area between the median line and the Okinawa Trough as "disputed," Chinese leaders implicitly recognized the legitimacy of Japan's claim to that area. However, neither party recognized the legitimacy of the other's broader objectives for the disputed space.

As a result, both parties sought to exercise their maritime jurisdiction in 2005 and 2006. The Chinese Navy confronted Japanese survey vessels operating near the median line and targeted a passing P3-C patrol plane near Chunxiao in September 2005. Japan increased its patrol flights and threatened to drill in the disputed area, which, according to a Chinese MFA spokesperson, made conflict "inevitable."[70] The *Global Times* argued that Tokyo was looking for conflict because its own media outlets were warning that China would respond militarily if Japan proceeded.[71] The period of tension may be explained by the fact that the two sides had competing interpretations of the status quo with respect to resource exploitation in the East China Sea.

Challenges to Reference Points in the East China Sea

From China's perspective, Japan's strident response to China's offshore development marked a policy shift because Japan had abetted these efforts in the 1990s. The Japanese government did not protest China's opening of the East China Sea to foreign oil companies in 1994, despite repeated sightings of Chinese resource survey vessels near the Senkaku/Diaoyu Islands. Indeed, a Japanese consortium successfully bid for blocks on the Chinese side of the median line.[72] Tokyo also did not issue any protest over the development of the Pinghu gas field when production began, despite concerns from some conservatives. Hiramatsu Shigeo, for instance, viewed Beijing's agreement with Texaco to develop the Pinghu field as part of China's preparations to "extend its reach into the East China Sea."[73] Japanese policymakers considered objecting to the Pinghu development in 1998, but decided against doing this because the field was not considered close enough to the median line to risk alienating China.[74] This decision followed years of tacit Japanese acceptance of Chinese exploration activities in Japanese-claimed waters.

Indeed, the fact that Japanese leaders debated these issues and resolved to do nothing could have been interpreted in Beijing as condoning China's activities. Addressing the Diet in December 1995 Takemi Keizo, chairman of the LDP's Special Committee on Ocean Matters, drew a link between China's shift to oil-importer status, its growing exploration activities, and the PLAN's expanded operational scope—the same points raised by Hiramatsu. He stated: "I'm deeply concerned that China's continued ocean research may accumulate a number of irreversible advantages in its favor. I ask the government to take measures to prevent such a situation."[75]

Despite these calls, Japanese actions conflicted with this message. The Asian Development Bank (ADB) granted a $130 million loan to Shanghai Petroleum to develop a pipeline from the Pinghu gas field to Shanghai in February 1996.[76] Clearly, Tokyo does not directly control the ADB, but its influence is sufficient to be interpreted by Beijing as tacit acceptance of the legitimacy of its activities. This was embarrassingly revealed by the Japanese government in February 2005, as it made preparations to release the findings of its surveys of the median-line area.[77] According to one Chinese scholar, the inconsistency in Japan's diplomatic position, reflected by the ADB's decision, undermined the legitimacy of its protests in the eyes of Beijing.[78] Therefore, Beijing's reference point, after decades of Japanese acquiescence and complicity with its offshore production activities, was that Japan did not seek a slice of the pie in the East China Sea.

Japanese inaction toward China's resource development can be explained by its own interpretation of the status quo in the East China Sea. Japanese policymakers and public were preoccupied with the Senkaku/

Diaoyu Islands for much of the 1990s, rather than resource development issues. Linus Hagstrom has argued that Japan's stance toward the Senkaku/Diaoyu dispute was characterized generally by "strategic nonaction," particularly by denying the very existence of a territorial dispute. Japan responded to Chinese attempts to claim sovereignty over the islands by reiterating its claim to them and denying that this fact was in dispute. This policy was effective because it supported Japan's strategic aims of encouraging a responsible China and did not escalate the territorial dispute.[79] However, this "strategic nonaction" also failed to advance Tokyo's interests with regard to resource exploration. As the challenger to the territorial status quo, China had nothing to lose by conducting exploration activities in the East China Sea; indeed, exploration activities near the Senkaku/Diaoyu Islands support the Chinese nonrecognition of Japan's median line. Thus, despite Tokyo's preoccupation with Chinese exploration activities near the islands, it was not concerned with these activities in what would become its EEZ.[80] For instance, China's Donghai oil well, drilled in 1982, is located in the disputed zone.[81] The policy of nonaction with regard to the disputed islands did not adapt to the changing nature of Chinese behavior in the late 1990s, which in turn undermined Japan's ability to respond to more concerted Chinese exploration activities in the wider East China Sea. Therefore, Japanese elites' reference point for the East China Sea was one that tolerated cyclical tensions with China over the disputed islands but was not preoccupied with unilateral Chinese production of resources in the East China Sea.

This incompatibility of interpretation was illustrated as tensions rose in 2004. Japan's acceptance of China's resource exploration activities in the East China Sea throughout the 1990s contrasted sharply with its sudden reaction in 2004. Following CNOOC's signing of production-sharing contracts with Unocal and Shell in August 2003, MOFA and the Agency for Natural Resources and Energy (ANRE) issued repeated requests that Beijing share seismic data gathered on the Chunxiao field.[82] Tokyo issued formal diplomatic protests following the detection of a drilling platform under construction at the Chunxiao site in May 2004. This reaction reinforced the Chinese perception that the Japanese claim was unsubstantiated and opportunistic. As one Chinese interviewee pointed out, Japan did not protest the East China Sea developments until a commercially viable production site was found.[83]

Tokyo's stated concern was that due to the proximity of Chunxiao to the median line, the geological features containing the gas might extend onto the Japanese side of the line. If this were true, Tokyo could have a claim to a share of the resources produced.[84] Chinese policymakers consistently rejected the basis of Japan's position on three related grounds: that the Chunxiao development was in an undisputed section of the East China Sea; that this section was under Chinese jurisdiction; and that these claims and production activities were consistent with international law. From China's perspective, Japan's sudden infatuation with East China Sea resource wealth between May 2004 and April 2005 was an attempt to fabricate a legal claim to resources that belonged to China. Indeed, Chinese state media was highly vocal on the legal justification of China's position, frequently denouncing Japan's "unilateral" median line.[85] Thus, Beijing argued, there was nothing wrong with Chunxiao, even under the Japanese interpretation of international law.[86]

Japanese policymakers privately recognize that this is a legitimate point, and in the words of one strategist, the median-line policy, officially adopted in 1996 as part of Japan's EEZ legislation, was a mistake.[87] Indeed, MOFA officials lamented the median line for this reason.[88] In claiming jurisdiction as far as the median line, rather than the 200-nautical-mile limit, Japan effectively conceded ocean space to China. Beijing thus viewed the Japanese decision to conduct seismic surveys east of the median line as a change in the status quo that has existed since each side declared EEZs in 1996. Several Chinese interviewees blamed the Japanese media for being unclear about these details, in particular that Chunxiao lay on the Chinese side of Japan's median line.[89] According to one Chinese official, the Japanese claim, following twenty years of the Chinese development, was "unbelievable and unreasonable."[90] As a result, Chinese decision makers viewed Japan's policy shift as an assertive turn motivated by opportunism.

This is an important insight into how Chinese leaders perceived the costs associated with cooperation in 2005. Granting Japan access to its East China Sea operations could result in additional Japanese claims elsewhere. Accepting the Japanese argument, either by sharing seismic data or by accepting the Japanese entitlement to a share of Chunxiao resources, could set a negative precedent for future Chinese drilling operations in the East China Sea. Cooperation could have included the recognition of the Japanese claim to the entirety of the disputed area between the median line and the continental shelf (see map 5.1). By contrast, the salience of the disputed space translated into three interrelated policy objectives for Tokyo. First, Japanese leaders were attempting to forestall Chinese maritime expansion, which would achieve the second objective, to ensure

MAP 5.1
Disputed Area in the East China Sea

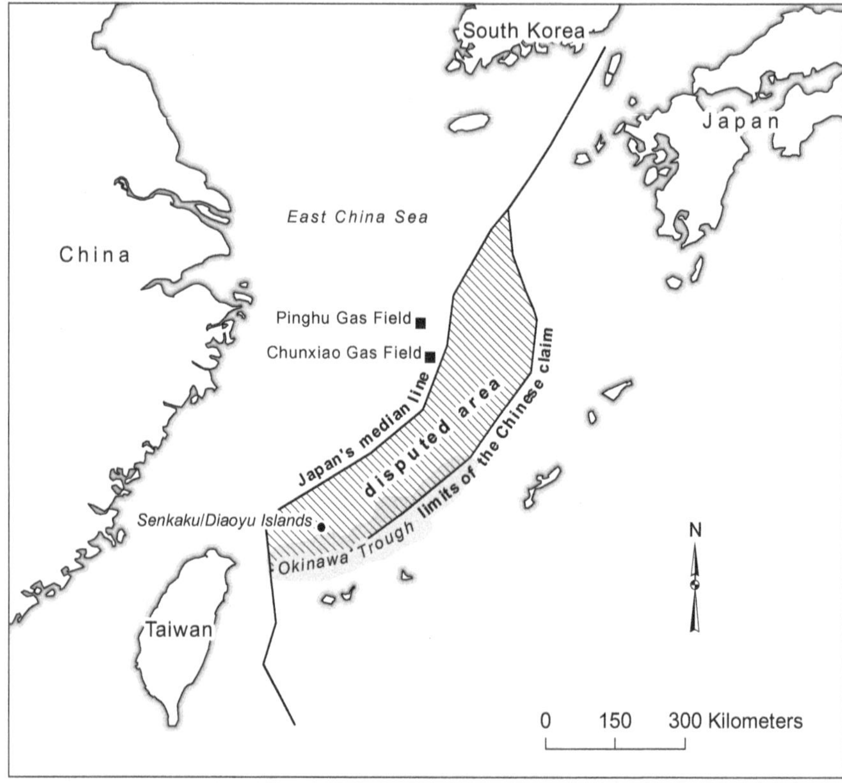

Note: It is important to state that Japan has not made public the coordinates of the median line. The one drawn here and in map 5.2 are based on existing open source maps and are an approximation.
Source: Spatial Information System Laboratory, Flinders University.

potential future access to East China Sea resources, and the third objective, to protect themselves from domestic accusations of apathy.

Deciding to Cooperate

Because neither party recognized the legitimacy of the other's territorial objectives, the two were at an impasse. As in the previous case, Japan attempted to coerce Chinese cooperation: It threatened to drill in the disputed area. Unlike previous cases, central leaders in Tokyo needed little prodding to act. In their view inaction could result in an increasingly favorable situation for China in maritime East Asia and would incur domestic criticism of being soft on China.[91] China, by contrast, was not to be coerced and instead began to view the resource issue as a pathway to improved relations with Japan in the post-Koizumi era. Furthermore, Japan's efforts to better enforce its maritime jurisdiction caused China to cooperate as a way to enshrine some element of its reference point into the new status quo in the East China Sea.

Japan's Coercive Cooperation

Following the discovery of the drilling platform, Japanese diplomatic protests were frequent and high profile. Japanese foreign minister Kawaguchi Yoriko raised the issue with her Chinese counterpart, Li Zhaoxing, at the Third Asia Cooperation Dialogue in Qingdao on June 21 and reiterated Japan's request for seismic data. In response, Li proposed that the delimitation issue be shelved and that the two sides focus on the joint development of the disputed area.[92] Similarly, METI minister Nakagawa Shoichi expressed his concerns to his Chinese counterpart, Zhang Guobao, vice minister of China's National Development and Reform Commission on the sidelines of the ASEAN +3 energy ministers meeting in Manila. He reportedly demonstrated to Zhang how resources could be siphoned across the median line using a cup and a straw.[93] Tokyo also lodged a diplomatic protest following reports that CNOOC was constructing a pipeline from Chunxiao to the Chinese coast.[94]

In light of perceived Chinese intransigence, Tokyo attempted to coerce a shift in Chinese behavior by pursuing the unilateral exploitation of resources in the disputed area (see map 5.1). Japan's strategy was intended to assert its jurisdictional entitlement to resource production in the East China Sea, while also procuring the data required to ascertain whether resources on the east side of the line were being accessed. By issuing protests, Japan avoided conferring legitimacy on Chinese developments in the disputed area. In a symbolic move, Nakagawa gave three of the fields at Chunxiao Japanese names: Shirakaba, Kusunoki, and Kikyo.[95] The decision to drill should be understood as an extension of this strategy. Drilling for hydrocarbon resources in the East China Sea is the ultimate expression of EEZ jurisdiction.

Japan's coercive policy was composed of two classic elements: capability and commitment. In the first instance, Tokyo commissioned the *Ramform Victory*, a Norwegian ocean survey vessel, to conduct a study of the median-line area between June 2004 and January 2005. Japanese policymakers initiated talks with Teikoku Oil and the Japan Petroleum Exploration Company to resuscitate concession blocs in the East China Sea from the 1970s after these companies acquired all the former stakeholders.[96] Tokyo also quadrupled funding for hydrocarbon exploration in the annual budget, from 3.8 billion to 12.9 billion yen.[97] In addition to building the capability to drill in the East China Sea, Japanese leaders also demonstrated their commitment to do so. Tokyo publicly announced that it was not dissuaded in its quest for East China Sea resources by the exit of Unocal and Shell from the Chunxiao project in September 2004.[98] As noted above, METI publications were sanguine on the prospects for offshore resource exploitation in 2005. This coercive policy shift witnessed some early success as China agreed to hold talks at the level of director-general in Beijing on October 25, 2004. However, the Chinese posture at the talks did little to encourage the Japanese of their good faith. The Chinese position conformed to its previous argument that its projects did not take place in a disputed area, and hence there was no need for Japan to be concerned.[99] METI minister Nakagawa was disgusted, reportedly saying "I don't know why these discussions were even held."[100]

The publication of the *Ramform Victory*'s survey findings on February 19, 2005, provided the justification for a more assertive posture. The report found a "high probability" that the Chunxiao gas field extended to the Japanese side and there was a possibility that CNOOC's drilling platform could extract resources from the Japanese side.[101] Nakagawa stated that Japan would prepare to grant drilling rights on its side of the median line unless China ceased its activities at the Chunxiao site.[102] On April 4, this message was carried directly to the Chinese Embassy by Sasae Kenichiro, director-general for Asian and Oceanic Affairs in MOFA and chief Japanese negotiator in the East China Sea talks. The Chinese condemned the decision and stated that Japan alone would be responsible for the costs.[103]

On April 14, 2005, Prime Minister Koizumi announced that Japan would "carry forward the procedures as planned" and open its side of the median line to bids for drilling concessions.[104] Beijing replied that such actions would be a "serious provocation" and that Japan would have to "take responsibility for the consequences."[105] Teikoku Oil was awarded the drilling contract in July 2005. The Chinese described the decision as a severe provocation and a violation of China's sovereign rights. Consistent with its jurisdictional claims, China's MFA denied Japan's right to drill in the disputed area.[106] Teikoku Oil supported Japan's coercive strategy by remaining vocally committed to the project, despite concerns about the economic viability of Japanese exploitation of resources on Japan's side of the median line.[107] Along with bullish assessments of the potential natural gas reserves, Teikoku executives released plans to build a pipeline to Okinawa and northern parts of Kyushu.[108] Furthermore, Teikoku president Masatoshi Sugioka expressed his willingness to "accept a bit of difficulty," a reference to possible Chinese interference with Teikoku's activities, provided Tokyo could assure the safety of the company's rig workers.[109] Finally, the Japanese government promised to fund the bulk of Teikoku's costs, thereby removing much of the risk to the company.[110]

These carrots were matched with sticks. Heading into the third round of talks, the expectation was that Tokyo would request Beijing to cease its activities or Japan would proceed with exploratory drilling.[111] However, at the meeting on October 1, 2005, Japanese officials downplayed their April ultimatum and proposed their first joint development plan to China.[112] The plan called for the joint development of four fields that straddled the median line, including the Chunxiao field. Tianwaitian and Duanqiao, two other fields near Chunxiao, were also included, as was Longjing, a field farther to the north.[113]

Beijing resisted every component of Japan's approach. Chinese officials had warned of unspecified "consequences" of the Japanese decision to explore in the East China Sea when it was announced.[114] Following Teikoku Oil's successful application for drilling rights, the *People's Daily* said that conflict was now "inevitable."[115] State-run current affairs publications argued that the Japanese decision was illegal and was evidence of Japan's "nonpeaceful" intentions toward China.[116] Furthermore, the Japanese media reported a Chinese show of force near the Chunxiao field on September 9 that reinforced Beijing's warnings to Tokyo—that a Chinese Sovremennyy destroyer had trained its guns on a passing Japanese patrol plane near the Chunxiao field, although it was reportedly not electronically targeted.[117] These revelations also coincided with the strongest Chinese rhetoric to date. Huang Xingyuan, chief spokesperson for the Chinese Embassy in Tokyo, said that any move by the Japanese to explore for oil or gas in the disputed area would be viewed by Beijing "as an invasion of Chinese territory and . . . a highly provocative act."[118] Koizumi's visit to the Yasukuni Shrine on October 17, 2005, triggered a six-month freeze in bilateral contact as China cancelled a subsequent round of talks scheduled for October 19.

China Reciprocates . . . Eventually

The MVM suggests that Beijing's overriding objective was to persist with the Chunxiao project over Japan's objections. Koizumi's threat to drill in the East China Sea coincided with the nadir of Sino-Japanese relations in April 2005. A steadily deteriorating relationship bottomed out with the outbreak of large anti-Japanese protests in major cities across China. Protesters raged against revisionist Japanese history textbooks, Japan's bid for a permanent seat on a reformed UN Security Council, and Japan's claims to the East China Sea. Official leadership visits had been frozen since October 2001 as a result of Koizumi's visits to the Yasukuni Shrine.[119] At the popular level, anti-Japanese sentiment in China was on the rise, evidenced by the hostile reception of the Japanese soccer team during the Asia Cup final in August 2004.[120] There is anecdotal evidence that conciliatory policies confront barriers in such a climate. Chinese interviewees intimated that it would be inadvisable to suggest pro-Japanese policies under such conditions. In some cases, proponents of these views have come under heavy criticism. This keeps moderate voices quiet during times of crisis.[121] There may also be a reluctance on the part of the Chinese policymaking apparatus to hear moderate advice if the bilateral relationship is poor. One strategist said that during the Koizumi era, writings on Japan needed to be critical before they could proceed with the crux of their argument.[122] In light of the contested-symbolic value of the East China Sea dispute at the time, Chinese elites would have found cooperation with Japan difficult to explain domestically.

China's rejection of Japan's strategy also supported the strategic dimension of its objectives. The presence of the *Ramform Victory* in China's claimed waters confirmed the pretext that a more active Chinese maritime enforcement presence was needed. The *Sankei Shimbun* reported that a PLAN vessel, disguised as a research ship, had made an "abnormal approach" on a Japanese survey ship during the seismic survey in July 2004.[123] A less ambiguous signal occurred in January 2005, when a flotilla of PLAN vessels was sighted near the Chunxiao installation.[124] On January 22, two Sovremennyy-class destroyers were seen sailing from Chunxiao toward the *Ramform Victory* as it was sailing close to the median line. This precipitated the dispatch of P-3C surveillance aircraft from Naha airbase, which observed the two destroyers alternately sailing in a zigzag pattern behind the survey ship before returning to Chinese waters.[125] In addition, the number of intrusions into Japan's Air Defense Identification Zone jumped eight times in 2005, causing a 60 percent jump in interceptions by the ASDF. In addition, Chinese aerial reconnaissance operations around the median line also increased.[126] The very existence of the gas fields created a pretext for more active Chinese military presence over the East China Sea.

China used bilateral talks as a forum to express its rejection of Japan's position. At the first round of talks in 2004, Beijing did not offer the data Japan sought and only made a vague offer of joint development. The second round of talks on the East China Sea proceeded as planned on May 31, 2005, despite Japan's ultimatum.[127] Although the two sides agreed to set up working groups on delimitation, China's joint development proposal served only to confirm Japanese suspicions. The proposal called for the joint development of the area between the median line and the Okinawa Trough, which further reinforced Japanese concerns about China's maritime expansion.[128] China appeared to accelerate the Chunxiao project in the wake of Japan's ultimatum. On August 10, 2005, Japan filed a protest through the Chinese Embassy following reports that pipes had been laid in preparation for production at the Chunxiao field.[129] On August 31, CNOOC chairman Fu Chengyu announced that production was slated to commence at the Chunxiao field within a month.[130] Finally, reports that a flare had been seen at the Tianwaitian field near Chunxiao—a common sight when production begins—resulted in Japanese protests on September 20.[131]

What factors, then, explain the shift from this intransigent posture to one that accepted Japanese terms for cooperation and, as is illustrated below, concluded an agreement that seems inconsistent with China's territorial objectives? Most scholars attribute this shift to China's interest in improving bilateral relations with Japan, and they view the June 2008 consensus as a logical outcome of this improved period.[132] In this view, Chinese leaders retain an interest in good relations with Japan, and started to look past Koizumi for a prime minister with whom they could work. From the Chinese standpoint, cooperation on an issue as sensitive as the East China Sea was impossible, given Koizumi's posture toward sensitive nationalist issues—specifically, the Yasukuni Shrine. As James Przystup notes, Chinese leaders deepened exchanges with Japanese elites in early 2006 with a view toward cultivating a relationship with the next Japanese leader.[133] Senior

Chinese leaders—such as Tang Jiaxuan, ambassador to Japan Wang Yi, and Dai Bingguo—reached out to senior Japanese leaders through established institutions of friendship like the Japan–China Parliamentarian Friendship Association. China also courted pro-Chinese leaders at the expense of perceived anti-Chinese ones. For instance, newly appointed pro-China METI minister Nikai Toshihiro was granted an audience with Wen Jiabao in the first cabinet-level contact since the October 17, 2005, Yasukuni Shrine visit. By contrast, former METI minster Nakagawa, a hardliner on Yasukuni and the East China Sea, was snubbed by senior Chinese leaders during his visit to Beijing.[134]

There is also evidence that cooperation on the East China Sea had a role to play in China's plan. Following an unofficial meeting between Sasae Kenichiro, the Japanese negotiator, and Cui Tiankai, his Chinese counterpart, in January 2006, a fourth round of talks was held in March. Although there was little progress, positive signs could be detected.[135] Both parties handled a Chinese sailing ban in the disputed area relatively smoothly, after a period of posturing. In April, the Chinese State Oceanic Administration website gave notice of a ban on ships operating near Chunxiao, and several Japanese fishermen were removed from the area. Because this was a violation of the Sino-Japanese fishing agreement, Japan issued a protest. Both sides dug in until Beijing declared that the location given for the ban was a mistake; it was intended to cover the Pinghu gas field, which was located well inside Chinese waters and was not contested by Japan.[136]

This marked the beginning of a more overtly cooperative atmosphere. Japan had reached out to China during the third round by dropping its preconditions for joint development discussions, and China reciprocated in April 2006 by softening on its shipping ban near the Chunxiao gas field. This embryonic cooperation led to a more institutionalized interaction after the first meeting between foreign ministers in more than a year occurred in Qatar on May 23, 2006. Foreign ministers Aso Taro and Li Zhaoxing pledged to accelerate talks, and positive interactions over the East China Sea resource issue became more regular. Talks on cooperation on resource development heralded an improvement in the overall tone of bilateral relations. This explanation seems plausible; but as the section below illustrates, the origins of the June 2008 agreement can best be understood as an effort by China to defend the emerging status quo in the East China Sea from Japan's promised drilling efforts.

The Depth of Cooperation

Despite the improved tone of the relationship, bargaining between China and Japan over resource exploitation in the East China Sea made few steps forward until a Chinese overture in late 2007. China's sudden change of heart in the latter part of 2007 was a function of Japan's efforts to make its threat to drill in the area more credible. After facilitating Teikoku's drilling license in 2005, Tokyo set about removing the legal barriers to the exercise of its jurisdiction in maritime space. Simultaneously, cooperative interactions became more frequent and substantive and elite exchanges deepened. Wen visited Japan in April 2007, and Prime Minister Yasuo Fukuda visited Beijing in December. Following Hu Jintao's visit to Japan in May 2008, the two sides announced a consensus on resource development on June 18, 2008. The key to the success of this bargaining phase was China's willingness to incorporate the median line into the final product.

Building Confidence amid Setbacks

Early discussions made little progress, other than efforts to construct confidence-building measures.[137] The sixth round of talks in early July 2006 established three technical working groups on legal matters, a hotline agreement and resource exploitation. Conservative Japanese media noted the decline of Chinese naval activities in the East China Sea, which was interpreted by some as an effort by Beijing to suppress anti-Japanese activities by bureaucratic constituencies within China.[138] Following the election of Abe Shinzo as Prime Minister in September 2006, and his stated commitment to repair the relationship with China by managing the Yasukuni issue, the confidence-building measures began to materialize.[139] The legal experts met in January 2007 and discussed the jurisdictional claims related to the East China Sea dispute. ANRE representatives met with their counterparts from the National Development and Reform Commission to discuss matters related to resource exploitation in April 2007. Finally, the JCG and the State Oceanic Administration met in July 2007 in an effort to establish a hotline between the two branches.[140] Although these developments occurred during an eighteen-month period and achieved little in the way of binding commitments, they are indicative of a departure from the confrontational rhetoric and military posturing that had marked the first phase of the dispute.

This progress was not without setbacks, however. In February 2007, the *Dongfangfong #2*, a research vessel, was spotted in Japanese waters 30 kilometers (16 nautical miles) northwest of Uotsuri/Diaoyu Island. Although Beijing had informed Tokyo of the operation, the vessel was not where the Chinese authorities claimed it would be.[141] Furthermore, in the seventh round of talks, which set the stage for Wen's visit to Japan in April 2007, the Chinese offered to share the seismic data on Chunxiao with Japan. Japanese negotiators described this move as "constructive."[142] However, the long-sought-after data were not provided at a subsequent April 2 meeting. Nevertheless, Wen and Abe's joint statement of April 11—to make the East China Sea a "sea of peace, cooperation and friendship"—reflected the desire on both sides to move on from the Koizumi era.[143]

Despite the rhetoric, substantive progress remained elusive. Rounds eight, nine, and ten of the talks—held between May and October 2007—yielded little progress other than rhetorical commitments to reach a solution as fast as possible. The major sticking point was how to manage delimitation issues in a joint development agreement. China maintained its stance that Chunxiao was in Chinese waters and therefore not privy to joint development. Under its proposal, fields located near the Senkaku/Diaoyu Islands should be jointly developed because they were in the disputed area. Chunxiao and Tianwaitian, located in Chinese waters and approaching the production stage, were off limits.[144] Japan, meanwhile, was reluctant to consider joint development of fields located inside the disputed area because its priority remained accessing fields that could potentially contain Japanese-claimed resources. Any agreement would establish some kind of precedent that, though not legally binding, could confer legitimacy on one party's interpretation. Neither party was interested in sacrificing its claim to the entire East China Sea as part of the agreement.

Japan's Coercive Cooperation

A breakthrough occurred on October 31, 2007, when Sasae told the LDP Special Committee on Ocean Affairs that Chinese negotiators had agreed in principle to joint development of fields in the median-line area, depending on how Japan dealt with the median-line issue.[145] This small concession indicated that Beijing was flexible on the location of joint development, but remained wary of the longer-term implications for its East China Sea claims. Anticipation grew amid improving relations and media speculation about reciprocal state visits between Prime Minister Fukuda Yasuo and

President Hu. Kyodo News reported that China had tabled a joint development proposal that included the median line at ministerial consultations ahead of Fukuda's visit to China in late December 2007. Speculation grew that an agreement would form part of a landmark Hu-Fukuda declaration on the state of the bilateral relationship. Although it did not, at the May 2008 summit in Tokyo both leaders were upbeat about the prospects for progress.[146] According to Hu, "Prospects for settling the dispute are already in view, and I'm happy about this."[147] The China–Japan Consensus on Resource Development was announced at separate press conferences on June 18, 2008.

Rather than being a gesture to improve relations, China accommodated the median line in order to prevent further Japanese efforts to drill in the disputed area. The Chinese concession in mid-2007 is a function of China's shifting reference point with regard to the status quo in the East China Sea. Although Japan remained committed to talks with China throughout the period 2004–6, this posture was balanced by a coercive edge. Japan had threatened to drill and made preparations to do so throughout 2005 based on the findings of its surveys of the median line. In 2006, this effort shifted to address the institutional barriers to Japanese exploitation of offshore resources. China interpreted this effort as an attempt to prepare to call China's bluff—that Japanese drilling would be tantamount to war—and conduct exploratory drilling of its own. To avoid such an eventuality, which carried with it the possibility of low-level conflict with Japan and the potential for escalation to war with the United States, China adopted a more conciliatory posture in negotiations after mid-2007.

Despite the bellicose rhetoric coming from Nakagawa and Koizumi in 2005, a number of institutional barriers prevented Japanese leaders from carrying out their threat to drill. For instance, at the time there were no Japanese laws governing offshore resource exploitation, or that defined which agency was responsible for the protection of offshore drilling installations. This situation presented a major challenge to Japan's threat to drill in the East China Sea. Recognizing this, in 2006 the LDP Special Committee on Maritime Interests released draft legislation to protect survey ships in the Japanese EEZ.[148] In 2005, the opposition Democratic Party of Japan (DPJ) announced its intention to submit legislation banning other countries from exploring for resources in the Japanese EEZ, which was subsequently matched by the LDP. Over the course of 2006, a working group was formed, in concert with the think tank community led by the Nippon Foundation, to draw up a more comprehensive body of laws that policed not only resource exploitation but also the entirety of Japan's claimed maritime space. According to a retired vice minister of defense who was intimately involved with drawing up this legislation, Japanese policymakers "realized that (in the context of the East China Sea issue) Japan's domestic law was not in sufficient conformity with UNCLOS and also that Japan lacked a comprehensive integrated ocean policy. Inevitably, this led to the establishment of the Basic Ocean Law."[149] The importance of China's maritime activities in this effort cannot be overstated. China's intransigence in the Chunxiao talks was integral to galvanizing the necessary political support for action by the Japanese government. Furthermore, Prime Minister Abe Shinzo accelerated debate on the Basic Ocean Law to ensure that it would be passed during Wen Jiabao's visit to Japan in April 2007.[150] The legislation passed the Diet, with bipartisan support and very little debate, on April 21, 2007.[151] The message to China was clear: Japan was preparing to assert itself in the East China Sea.[152]

The June 2008 agreement thus reflects a significant concession by China: a 2,700-square-kilometer joint development zone (JDZ) that straddles the median line.[153] The Chinese statement of June 18, 2008, refers to the common understanding reached between Wen and Abe in April 2007, as well as a "new" common understanding reached in December 2007. This appears to be a reference to the first time China proposed a development zone that incorporated the median line in some way. However, contrary to some analyses, this act does not imply Chinese formal recognition of the median line.[154] It does, however, imply flexibility by China.[155] Before this development, the negotiations had been stalemated on legal interpretations of this very issue for more than eighteen months. As one scholar has argued, the agreement reflects a degree of reciprocity from China.[156] Given the scale of overlap between the two claimed zones, the JDZ lies in an area closer to Japan's preferred location than China's, which called for a JDZ on the fringes of its claim near the Senkaku/Diaoyu Islands. By contrast, the JDZ lies on the fringes of Japan's 200 nautical mile EEZ claim. The agreement is thus impressive on the one hand for the concession made by China, yet disappointing on the other hand given that in the absence of a binding implementation mechanism, the agreement is only as strong as the political will for cooperation in Beijing and Tokyo.

The agreement is composed of three parts. The first part outlines a 2,700-square-kilometer JDZ south of the Longjing field that roughly bisects the median line (see map 5.2). Joint development of Longjing was part of Japan's joint development proposal tabled in October 2005. The fact that

MAP 5.2
The Sino-Japanese Joint Development Zone in the East China Sea

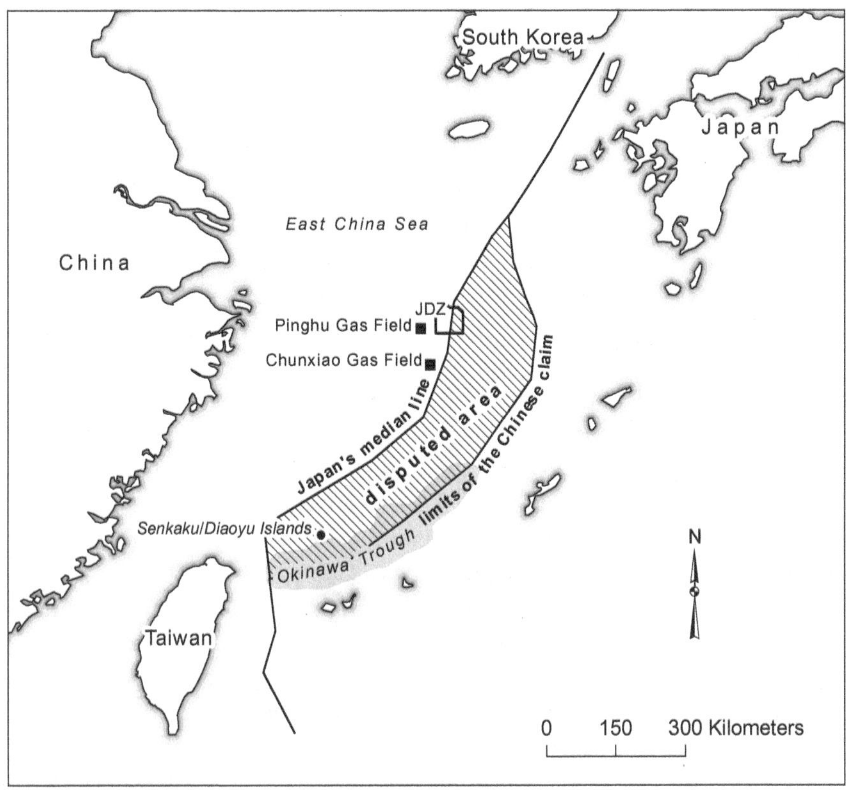

Source: Spatial Information System Laboratory, Flinders University.

the JDZ is south of Longjing most likely reflects Chinese concerns about the commercial viability of resources at the Longjing field.[157] Joint exploration of the zone will be conducted and developed "under the principle of mutual benefit."[158]

The second part of the "consensus" permits Japanese companies to invest in the Chunxiao field in a manner consistent with Chinese law. Under the Regulations Concerning the Exploitation of Offshore Petroleum Resources in Cooperation with Foreign Enterprises, foreign companies typically obtain up to a 50 percent stake in a concession bloc.[159] Japanese companies would play an identical role to that of Shell and Unocal before their exit from the Chunxiao project in September 2004.[160] The primary difference is that by 2008, the exploration work at the Chunxiao field was complete; the remaining task is to connect the field to pipelines to Mainland China. It remains to be seen how much gas or revenue Japanese entities would be entitled to, but it is likely to be less than 50 percent, as the costly exploration burden has already been borne by CNOOC and its partners. The third part of the "consensus" calls for a treaty to be signed to implement the agreement.

This arrangement also represents a compromise by Japan because it has effectively conceded jurisdiction over the Chunxiao field to China. However, its officials have been reluctant to admit this publicly.[161] Indeed, the consensus does not explicitly address the ownership of the Chunxiao field. Some commentators criticized China for reiterating its claim to the Chunxiao field following the agreement.[162] This statement was made in response to a comment by a Japanese official that Japan has not recognized Chinese sovereignty over Chunxiao.[163] Given this statement, however, it is unlikely that Japan will gain access to other fields near the median line in a capacity other than that alluded to in the June 2008 consensus—as a junior partner financing a Chinese-run operation. Retaining control of its Xihu Trough operations was of paramount importance to China.

The June consensus leaves a number of issues unresolved, two of which are significant. First, the delimitation of the East China Sea remains disputed. Some sources, including those within the Japanese government, have indicated that because the median line is used to determine which fields are "disputed," this implies de facto recognition of the line by China.[164] In the words of the *Yomiuri Shimbun*, "As the agreement included joint investment in and the development of a gas field that straddles the median line, it can be interpreted that China accepted Japan's proposals based on its median-line claim, even if it was in a limited manner."[165] This is unlikely, however, given that China routinely denies the existence of the line. Beijing reiterated this stance through its foreign minister, Yang Jiechi, in the days that followed the announcement.[166] Further, China continues to exploit the ambiguity of the notification agreement to continue naval intrusions into Japan's waters, much to Tokyo's displeasure.[167] Indeed, China's more active posture in Japanese-claimed waters since then could be explained by its perceived need to demonstrate its nonrecognition of the median line in the wake of the 2008 agreement, a phenomenon discussed in chapter 6.

A second unresolved issue is the joint development of other fields near the median line.[168] The announcement does not explicitly mention these fields—it merely notes that the two sides will continue consultations on joint development of the East China Sea. Nevertheless, Japanese media initially speculated that all fields straddling the median line will be jointly developed at a ratio of 50:50.[169] In January 2009, Japanese leaders protested what they claimed was unilateral Chinese development of the Tianwaitian gas field, located near the Chunxiao field. Citing defense sources, the *Sankei Shimbun* argued that China was beginning work on the Tianwaitian field. The *Sankei Shimbun* argued further that, in the absence of an agreement, the Japanese expected the Chinese to freeze development at Tianwaitian, Longjing, and Duanqiao.[170] The MFA replied that the June 2008 consensus included only development of the Chunxiao field and the JDZ.[171]

The agreement is also vague on the specifics of how resources are to be divided following a discovery in the JDZ, merely noting that the "specific matter will be decided by the two sides through consultation."[172] In the absence of enforcement mechanisms outlined in a binding treaty, the consensus has proven to be of limited durability as other dimensions of territorial value have limited the political will to implement it.

The Durability of Cooperation

Limited cooperation was achieved on the economic issue of resource exploitation. However, the implementation of the consensus has faltered due to territorial objectives informed by other dimensions of territorial value. From a contested-symbolic standpoint, the deal remained vulnerable to domestic criticism because it was seen to pose a threat to China's maritime claims, and also on the grounds that it was with Japan. It is widely speculated that nationalist elements in the Chinese government opposed the deal and condemned the concessions made to Japan.[173] Nationalists would have been critical because China allowed a joint development zone that straddled the median line.[174] In the days that followed the announcement, reports surfaced that Beijing had in fact suppressed some nationalist protests in cities in China.[175] Other reports indicate that China's vocal online nationalist community was critical of the agreement with Japan.[176] Indeed, Japanese officials close to the negotiations believe that nationalism in China prevents the conclusion of the implementation treaty.[177] One Japanese interviewee described the concession made by China as a "gift" to the Fukuda administration, and another agreed that Fukuda's popularity in China was vital to the talks.[178] His absence, therefore, may undermine further cooperation.

The strategic dimension of the East China Sea makes the deal unpopular with several constituencies within China. In light of the PLAN's interests in the strategic value of the East China Sea outlined above, and the related territorial objective of maintaining a presence in these waters, it is plausible that it would also have opposed cooperation with Japan in 2008. One Chinese interview subject pointed out that the PLAN's dominance of the East China Sea is integral to China's long-term energy security.[179] In this context senior PLAN officials would have found cooperation with Japan an unpalatable policy option. As Robert Sutter notes, "As Chinese-Japanese territorial conflicts grow in scope and intensity, they intrude ever more directly on these PLA priorities."[180] Consequently, the navy would support any policy that leads to the expansion of its mandate.[181] Given its past influence over China's territorial posture and the current perception that secure sea approaches are vital to China's future security, the PLAN's continued influence on territorial questions in 2008.[182] Similarly, CNOOC has continued to develop East China Sea resources at politically contentious fields including Tianwaitian and elsewhere in defiance of Japanese protests in an effort to double its overall oil and gas production to 100 million metric tons per year by 2020.[183]

Likewise, the contested-symbolic aspects of the Chunxiao dispute hardened Japanese government and popular attitudes toward maritime issues with China and Tokyo's response left a lasting impact on Japanese China policy. At several points between 2004 and 2008, it was clear to Japanese leaders that they were poorly equipped institutionally to resist China's expansion in the East China Sea. At the height of political tensions, the Japanese media were critical of the lack of policy coordination vis-à-vis Japan's maritime policy—specifically, of the perceived lack of coordination between MOFA, which is responsible for negotiations related to territorial disputes, and the ANRE in METI, which is responsible for regulating exploration for deep sea resources.[184] Indeed, this lack of policy coordination may explain the decision by the ADB to finance the Pinghu gas field pipeline in the late 1990s. The Ministry of Finance may have agreed to the ADB loan on the grounds that greater production of natural gas could help alleviate global prices for Japan, a natural gas importer. It would not consider the possible consequences for the boundary dispute, as would MOFA or the defense community. One reason for this lack of coordination may be that the issue of resource exploitation in a disputed area does not fit comfortably within the portfolio of any particular branch of the Japanese government. Accordingly, the Japanese government subsequently set up a multiministry panel to deal with the Chunxiao issue in 2004, because "it is not an issue to be handled by a single department or agency of the Government."[185]

As Japanese frustration with Chinese intransigence grew, pressure within Japan mounted for a more active posture that focused on the reform of the institutions of Japanese government. For instance, critics lamented not only the fact that the *Ramform Victory* was harassed by China, but also the slow response of Japanese military assets to Chinese advances.[186] One editorial in the *Yomiuri Shimbun* is worth quoting at length:

> For more than 40 years, the Japanese government has shelved private-sector applications for exploring rights in the disputed area, and refused to grant permission for initial surveying and development plans. Furthermore, Japan remained inactive with regard to the matter even after the mid-1990s when China started full-fledged oceanic surveys in waters off its coast.
>
> Such attitudes have reflected excessive consideration by the Foreign Ministry and other government entities toward China. For example, the Japanese government reluctantly started collecting data on seabed resources in the area in July—only after the Chunxiao gas project came to light—because of a spate of criticisms within Japan over the government's inaction.[187]

Japan's threat to drill in the East China Sea, the hallmark of its coercive approach, was widely celebrated in Japanese newspapers. The *Yomiuri Shimbun* decried the past "ostrich" policies toward China and celebrated the demonstration of "firm resolve to protect [Japan's] maritime resources."[188] The *Asahi Shimbun* and the *Nihon Keizai Shimbun* were more circumspect; they supported the government's decision but counseled against inadvertent escalation in light of the tense political relationship.[189] This sentiment was reflected in public opinion polls conducted by the *Yomiuri Shimbun* in October 2005. A total of 70 percent of Japanese surveyed believed that China should cease its survey activities in the East China Sea, and 65 percent believed that Japan should proceed with its own drilling operations if China did not stop.[190]

Japan's coercive approach also had widespread bipartisan support. For instance, in mid-April 2005 fourteen Diet members from the LDP, its coalition partner New Komeito, and the DPJ flew over the disputed area to inspect Chinese drilling installations.[191] Surveys of Japanese politicians and bureaucrats revealed frustration with China's "competitive" behavior in the East China Sea and support for an assertive policy.[192]

The importance of the strategic and contested symbolic aspects of the East China Sea to Japan is illustrated by the political nature of Japan's threat to drill in the disputed area. According to a number of experts in Japan's resources sector, the East China Sea's natural gas is in fact of very little use to Japan, notwithstanding public statements by Japanese officials. The Xihu Trough itself is a relatively shallow geological formation, which makes offshore resource exploitation more cost-effective than in deeper waters elsewhere. However, the Okinawa Trough provides a geological barrier that dramatically increases the costs of transporting gas by pipeline to Japan. Indeed, one Japanese energy expert admitted being skeptical in 2005 that drilling by Teikoku was feasible in absence of the government assistance that the Koizumi government pledged.[193] Natural gas cannot be liquefied at sea and must travel by undersea pipeline to the Japanese coast to be consumed. An undersea pipeline would be nearly impossible due to the long distance and the depth of the Okinawa Trough, which descends beyond 2,000 meters.[194] In the absence of a lengthy detour, or a technological breakthrough, a pipeline transporting gas from the East China Sea to the Japanese mainland would be very expensive and arguably impossible.[195] More generally, the construction of offshore pipelines in Japan is further hamstrung by the issue of compensation for fisheries groups that may be adversely affected.[196]

Furthermore, conversations with energy experts in Japan indicate a profound pessimism about the prospects for commercial discoveries east of the median line.[197] According to officials at a relevant Japanese ministry, these barriers mean East China Sea gas is not commercially viable to a Japanese company.[198] The presence of the organic matter that creates the conditions for the formation of oil and gas resources becomes less concentrated the farther offshore one drills. Japanese drilling would thus occur in a deeper and relatively nonprospective area of the East China Sea. Given the transportation barriers noted above, the most economically feasible option would be to pipe gas to China. However, due to the competitive nature of the two states' energy security policies, this arrangement would likely require a dramatically different bilateral political climate than that which has existed since 2005. Indeed, if Tokyo were prepared to ship its Xihu Trough natural gas to China for reexport to Japan, then more affordable options, such as swaps for natural gas imported to China from elsewhere, would also be considered.[199] Ultimately, East China Sea gas remains less economical than LNG imported from Australia or Indonesia.[200]

Therefore, Japan's threat to drill was likely a bargaining tactic designed to resist Chinese advancement across the East China Sea. It is unclear how widely known the geological barriers to unilateral Japanese drilling are in policy circles. These barriers are rarely mentioned in media reports critical of drilling prospects; these are generally skeptical of the total size of the resource base.[201] If the barriers are mentioned, it is only in passing, indicating that the full implications of this situation may not be fully understood.[202] According to one interview subject, Japanese government officials and the media are aware of this issue but do not discuss it publicly.[203] ANRE publications do not mention anything resembling barriers to Japan's development of the East China Sea's resources.[204]

It is possible that Chinese officials are also aware of these problems, but may have perceived the chances of escalation as sufficiently elevated that it would be preferable to freeze the resources question with a generous agreement that could then be ignored. The agreement could be seen as a victory for Japan's coercive strategy on the grounds that it provides a framework for joint development and has kept Chinese drilling operations from crossing the median line. However, China's subsequent reluctance to enter into meaningful joint development may indicate that Beijing is confident that Japan will not drill unilaterally. Although the strategy proved adequate to elicit a cooperative gesture from China, it was insufficient to elicit lasting cooperation on the question of resource exploitation. However, by agreeing to a framework for cooperative resource development that included Chinese-claimed space, Japanese officials were able to meet their territorial objectives and limit the Chinese challenge to their reference point. They had a framework to access disputed resources and had forestalled China's maritime expansion.

However, China's maritime rise would move to other issue areas, which would force Japan to make a more robust institutional response. Therefore, by the time the consensus on resource development was announced in June 2008, the stage was set for a more lasting confrontation between Japan and China in the East China Sea. An assertive Japanese posture was politically popular as government anxiety across the political spectrum grew in light of China's maritime activities. Of particular importance, despite the logical appeal of East China Sea resources to Japan, outlined at the beginning of this chapter, considerable structural impediments suggest that Japan's assertive turn was less about a genuine effort to access the economic value of the disputed area, than the strategic motivation of resisting China's maritime expansion. As illustrated in chapter 6, Japan's maritime policy and its China policy were becoming more proactive as Japanese policymakers understood the importance of exercising Japan's claimed jurisdiction in contested areas. Likewise, constituencies in China ensured that talks to implement the consensus on resource development were held hostage to subsequent crises in the relationship, including the September 2010 collision between a Chinese fishing trawler and a JCG vessel.

Conclusion

The third case of cooperation between China and Japan on maritime jurisdiction in the East China Sea is more successful relative to the notification agreement, but less so compared with the fisheries agreement. The 2008 consensus provides a framework to exploit resources in the East China Sea and meets aspects of both states' territorial objectives. Leaders in Japan had been heavily criticized for their inability to prevent the "theft" of Japanese resources. The agreement silences these critics because it addresses the concern that resources on the Japanese side of the line may be tapped. The location of the JDZ is consistent with Japan's concerns about China's maritime expansion because there is no new recourse for Chinese entities to operate near the Senkaku/Diaoyu Islands, as there would have been if the JDZ had been located nearby. It also provides a precedent for future cooperation at other Chunxiao fields that were not included in the agreement, including Can Xue and Duanqiao. CNOOC and Beijing have rejected Japanese investment in the Tianwaitian field because this field is already producing gas, and the commercial focus has shifted to recouping sunk costs. Nevertheless, Japanese leaders could argue for a time that they were able to defend Japan's entitlement to disputed maritime space while creating a framework for cooperative resource exploitation. Although the East China Sea's gas remains of marginal importance to Japan's energy security—despite increases in natural gas consumption after the March 2011 disaster—Japanese leaders were able to use the issue to take a popular stand against China.

China used the Chunxiao dispute to enshrine some sense of its reference point into the new maritime status quo, lest Japan attempt to alter it to something less favorable to China. It compromised its territorial preferences, subject to conditions.[205] China accepted a JDZ that straddled the median line because it perceived a Japanese threat to its reference point in the East China Sea, one under which China was able to exploit resources without Japanese interference. Despite its compromise, China's objectives remain intact, particularly because it has been reluctant to proceed with joint development. The agreement allows China considerable freedom of action while reinforcing its entitlement to produce resources on its side of the median line. Japan did not get access to any of the other fields at Chunxiao. Both Tianwaitian and Duanqiao may straddle the median line and were part of previous Japanese proposals, but remain out of reach.[206] Although the June 2008 consensus does not limit China's resource efforts west of the median line, it does limit future unilateral Chinese efforts to develop resources east of the median line. Japan would view this as particularly provocative behavior. Ultimately, the consensus on resource development reflects a great deal of potential and very little follow-through. Chapter 6 considers the future of this relationship in the context of the emerging challenge of the conduct of state vessels operating within disputed maritime space.

Notes

1. Anonymous, "China's Upstream Programs Advance Onshore and Offshore," 31; EIA, "Privatization and the Globalization of Energy Markets," 34.
2. EIA, "East China Sea." An updated (2012) version of this report indicates that some Chinese sources suggest reserves of 250 trillion cubic feet in undiscovered gas.
3. On China's energy security strategy, see Calder, "Coping with Energy Insecurity," 49–66.
4. Downs, "China," 1.
5. Cole, "Oil for the Lamps of China," 27.
6. Fridley, "Natural Gas in China," 5–65.
7. Andrews-Speed, *Energy Policy and Regulation*, 132.
8. Yuan, "China's Offshore Oil Development," 107–26.
9. Anonymous, "China Expects Offshore Production to Buttress Overall Output Target," 64.
10. For the details of China's more productive offshore areas at the time, see IEA, *Global Offshore Oil Prospects to 2000*, 118–20.
11. Petzet, "Exploration, Production Futures Bright for East China Sea," 80–81. Primeline Petroleum Corporation discovered a commercially viable gas field, Vicky-1, in 1997. Renamed Lishui, the field has proven reserves of 292 billion cubic feet of gas, and negotiations are ongoing to bring the gas to market in Wenzhou in Zhejiang Province. Primeline Petroleum Corporation, "Lishui 36–1 (Vicky) Discovery."
12. "Rivals Race Petrochina to Shanghai," *Petroleum Intelligence Weekly*, August 27, 2003; Fridley, "Natural Gas in China," 44.
13. Author interview "Z," July 28, 2011, Tokyo.

14. Tanner and Kennett, "Petroleum Developments in Far East in 1971," 1828; Akao, "Resources and Japan's Security," 16.

15. Harrison, *China, Oil, and Asia,* 174.

16. Woodard, *International Energy Relations of China,* 172.

17. MOFA, "Strategy and Approaches of Japan's Energy Diplomacy"; Koike, Moji, and Albedaiwi, "Overseas Oil-Development Policy of Resource-Poor Countries," 1764–75.

18. ESSG, "Interim Report," 23.

19. For an analysis of the competitive dimensions of this relationship, see Vivoda and Manicom, "Oil Import Diversification in Northeast Asia," 223–54.

20. ANRE, *New National Energy Strategy,* 14.

21. Corcoran and Hosoe, "Japan Gov't to Assume More Aggressive Energy Role."

22. Shaoul, "An Evaluation of Japan's Current Energy Policy," 411–37. See also Calabrese, "In the Shadow of Uncertainty," 81–101.

23. Forster, "Japan Seeks Oil Security in Iraq, Indonesia after Iran Setback."

24. Penn, "Battle of Azadegan."

25. Goldstein and Kozyrev, "China, Japan and the Scramble for Siberia," 163–78.

26. Anonymous, "Japanese Energy Policy Focuses on Supply Security," 33. For a pessimistic account of Japan's energy future and the implications for supply security, see Yokobori, "Japan," 305–28.

27. "Energy White Paper States for First Time Gas Fields Issue 'Important,'" *Sankei Shimbun,* May 19, 2005.

28. McDevitt, "Strategic and Operational Context Driving PLA Navy Building," 481–522.

29. For those that argue that the US Navy is vulnerable to the Chinese navy's sea denial strategy, see Yoshihara and Holmes, "Command of the Sea with Chinese Characteristics," 677–94; and McVadon, "China's Maturing Navy," 90–107. For the argument that China's navy remains vulnerable, see Beier, "Bear Facts and Dragon Boats," 287–316; and Cole, "Right-Sizing the Navy," 523–56.

30. Author interview "D."

31. Chang and Chen, "Nationalist Ideology of the Chinese Military," 59.

32. Yu, "PRC Land and Resources Minister Interviewed on Security of Oil Resources."

33. "News Briefs International: China," *Platt's Oilgram,* April 20, 2006.

34. State Council of the People's Republic of China, *China's National Defense in 2000,* chap. 3, section V.

35. Shambaugh, *Modernizing China's Military,* 67.

36. Liu and Feng, "Going Global: Dialogue Spanning 600 Years."

37. Lu and Guo, "Okinawa: 'Hub' of the Pacific."

38. Liu, "China's 21st-Century Navy Prospects."

39. Przystup, "Japan–China Relations: Trying to Get Beyond Yasukuni," 116.

40. Bin, "Japan Steps up Military Expansion at Sea."

41. "Impact on China–Japan Ties," *Zhongguo Tongxun She,* September 22, 2004.

42. Collins et al., *China's Energy Strategy.*

43. "Anger Builds over EEZ Violations," *Japan Times*, July 22, 2004.

44. Author's calculations based on data from Arase, "Japan, the Active State?" 579.

45. Document provided to the author by interview subject "A," not for citation.

46. "China Bringing Okinawa 'within Range': What Underlies Oilfield Development in the East China Sea," *Sentaku*, January 2006.

47. Author interview "H."

48. Author interview "A."

49. "Gov't Hastens to Identify Mystery Sub / Presumed Chinese Vessel May Be Linked to Gas Field Development," *Yomiuri Shimbun*, November 11, 2004; Harrison, "Seabed Petroleum in Northeast Asia," 4.

50. JDA, *Defense of Japan 2005*, 14.

51. Kitamura, "US Military's Perception of Japan and National Strategies That Japan Should Have."

52. Author interview "B."

53. Esteban, "Management of Nationalism during the Jiang Era (1994–2002)," 181–214; Dickson, "Dilemmas of Party Adaptation," 141–58.

54. See Gries, *China's New Nationalism*, chap. 7.

55. See Downs and Saunders, "Legitimacy and the Limits of Nationalism," 114–46.

56. Shih, "Defining Japan," 539–63; Zheng, "National Humiliation, History Education, and the Politics of Historical Memory," 783–806.

57. Allen Whiting hypotheses that Chinese surveys near the disputed islands in the mid-1990s were less about antagonizing Japan and more about ensuring access to oil reserves. See Whiting, "China's Japan Policy and Domestic Politics," 17. For the second point, see Chang and Chen, "Nationalist Ideology of the Chinese Military," 44–64.

58. Gries, "China's 'New Thinking' on Japan," 831–50. This hard-line turn in Chinese foreign policy was also reflected by the demise of the "peaceful rise" rhetoric. See Suettinger, "Rise and Descent of 'Peaceful Rise,'" 1–10.

59. Zhang, "Influence of Chinese Nationalism on Sino-Japanese Relations," 15–34.

60. Nationalism has become more politically salient in Japan as a result of the economic stagnation of the 1990s and due to generational changes. On the emergence of this dynamic, see Inoguchi, "National Identity and Adapting to Integration," 216–33; and Saseda, "Youth and Nationalism in Japan," 109–22.

61. Mochizuki, "Japan's Long Transition," 105.

62. Hughes and Krauss, "Japan's New Security Agenda," 163.

63. Murayama and Noguchi, "Japan–China Boundary Issue."

64. Okubo, "Political Pulse."

65. "Editorial: Japan, China Should Negotiate Gas Development Deal," *Nihon Keizai Shimbun*, October 22, 2004.

66. This trend in public opinion is reported by Kotler, Sugawara, and Yamada, "Chinese and Japanese Public Opinion," 93–125; and Takahara, "Japanese Perspective on China's Rise," 218–37.

67. See Shinoda, *Koizumi Diplomacy*; and Pekkanen and Kraus, "Japan's 'Coalition of the Willing,'" 429–44.

68. "More Japanese View China Unfavorably," *Yomiuri Shimbun*, December 19, 2004.

69. "Fewer Japanese Feel Friendly toward China," *Yomiuri Shimbun*, December 25, 2005.

70. "Japan's Move in the East China Sea Makes Conflict 'Inevitable': Report," *People's Daily*, July 16, 2005.

71. "Japan's Provocation in East China Sea Very Dangerous," *Renmin Ribao*, July 21, 2005.

72. "Japanese Consortium Wins Blocks 41/17 and 42/03 in East China Sea," *Petroleum Economist*, January 19, 1994.

73. Hiramatsu, "China's Naval Advance: Objectives and Capabilities," 132.

74. "Government Aims at Fresh Start in Negotiations on Gas Field Development, Fears China Creating Fait Accompli," *Sankei Shimbun*, November 10, 2004.

75. Takemi Keizo, quoted in "Planning National Strategies-Resources and Energy / China Warnings Went Unheeded," *Yomiuri Shimbun*, April 28, 2005.

76. "Asian Development Bank Approves Loan to Develop Ping Hu Oil/Gasfield in East China Sea," *Petroleum Economist*, February 28, 1996.

77. "Gov't-Funded Pipeline for China," *Yomiuri Shimbun*, February 25, 2005.

78. Zha, "Calming Troubled Waters."

79. Hagstrom, "Quiet Power," 168.

80. "Spokesperson: Vessel Leaves Disputed Area near Diaoyutai Islands," Agence France-Presse, February 15, 1996; "Drillship Enters Senkaku Area," *Petroleum Economist*, March 1, 1996.

81. Johnston and Valencia, *Pacific Ocean Boundary Problems*, 105. This drilling period also led to discovery of Longjing 1 and 2 and Pinghu 1.

82. Nakazawa, "Gov't Slow to Wake up to Potential of EEZ."

83. Author interview "I," January 15, 2008, Beijing.

84. MOFA, *Diplomatic Blue Book 2005*, 37.

85. See, e.g., Liao, "China Refuses to Accept the Idea of 'Middle Line' but Proposes 'Common Development.'"

86. See the statements by Chinese Foreign Ministry spokesperson Kong Quan quoted by Watkins, "Japan, China in Stalemate over Maritime Boundaries," 28.

87. Author interview "A." Tokyo has subsequently attempted to argue that it claims a 200-nautical-mile EEZ, which is addressed in chapter 6.

88. "Gov't Starts Survey of EEZ Riches," *Yomiuri Shimbun*, July 8, 2004.

89. Author interviews "F," "E," and "I."

90. Statement of Liu Jinsong, first secretary at the Chinese Embassy in Tokyo to the Foreign Correspondence Club of Japan. "Chinese Official Raps Japan's 'Provocative' Action over Gas Dispute," Kyodo News, June 7, 2006.

91. Discussions with multiple Japanese officials, June and July 2011.

92. MOFA, "Press Conference 22 June 2004."

93. "Oil Rivals See Value of Cooperation," *Nihon Keizai Shimbun*, July 5, 2004.

94. "Japan Eyes More Protest over China's Pipeline to Disputed Gas Fields," Kyodo News, August 27, 2004.

95. Przystup, "Japan–China Relations: Summer Calm," 119–20.

96. Watkins, "Japan, China Dispute Field," 30.

97. "Japan Moves to Drill in the East China Sea," *Japan Times*, January 17, 2005.

98. "Japan to Go on Exploring Gas Resources in E. China Sea," Kyodo News, September 30, 2004.

99. Jennings, "China Wants to Continue Gas Exploration Dispute with Japan."

100. Watkins, "Japan, China in Stalemate over Maritime Boundaries," 28.

101. Quoted by Harrison, "Seabed Petroleum in Northeast Asia," 4.

102. Negishi, "Japan Ready to Drill in Disputed Waters"; "Tokyo Rattling Drill Bits over Disputed Gas Fields," *Yomiuri Shimbun*, April 2, 2005.

103. Brooke, "For Japan and China, Strains from a Line in the Sea."

104. Junichiro Koizumi quoted by Suryanarayana, "Japan Raises Stake in East China Sea, Grants Rights for Drilling."

105. Quoted by Aoki, "China Accuses Japan of 'Provocation' Ahead of Machimura Visit."

106. Jennings, "China Protests Japan's Decision to Drill E. China Sea Gas."

107. Jennings, "Sea Area Disputed by China, Japan May Offer Little Oil or Gas." One energy security expert suggested that Teikoku Oil was never seriously interested in participation at the Chunxiao field. Author interview "V," Tokyo, July 8, 2011.

108. "Teikoku Oil Starts Gas-Drilling Preparations in the E. China Sea," *Nihon Keizai Shimbun*, September 6, 2005.

109. "Teikoku to Drill Despite Risk of China Action," *Japan Times*, August 27, 2005.

110. Negishi, "Japan Ready to Drill in Disputed Waters."

111. Tokyo to Talk Gas Extraction with Beijing," *Nihon Keizai Shimbun*, September 26, 2005.

112. Negishi, "Japan Proposes Joint Use of Deposits in East China Sea Fields."

113. "Nakagawa Reveals 4 Gas Fields Eyed for Joint Efforts," *Yomiuri Shimbun*, October 4, 2005.

114. Quoted in "PRC FM Spokesperson Warns Japan of 'Consequences' over Drilling Rights Decision," Agence France-Presse, April 14, 2005.

115. Reported in "Japan's Move in the East China Sea Makes Conflict 'Inevitable': Report," *People's Daily*, July 16, 2005.

116. Duan, "Review of Japanese Government's Granting of Test Exploitation Authorization."

117. "Chinese Warship Pointed Gun at Japanese Patrol Plane in Sept.," Kyodo News, October 2, 2005; "Oil and Gas in Troubled Waters; Japan and China," *The Economist*, October 8, 2005.

118. Faiola, "Japan–China Oil Dispute Escalates."

119. Sutter, "China and Japan: Trouble Ahead?" 37–49.

120. Przystup, "Japan–China Relations: Not the Best of Times," 120–21.

121. Author interview "J," January 24, 2008, Beijing.

122. Author interview "D."

123. "China Interferes with Survey of Natural Resource in East China Sea; Transmits Sound Waves and Makes Abnormal Approach," *Sankei Shimbun*, March 28, 2005.

124. Harrison, "Seabed Petroleum in Northeast Asia," 4.

125. "Planning National Strategies-Resources and Energy / More Open China a Threat to Japan," *Yomiuri Shimbun*, April 13, 2005.

126. "ASDF Scrambles up 60 percent in '05; Chinese Intrusions Jump 8-Fold," *Yomiuri Shimbun*, April 22, 2006.

127. Aoki, "Japan, China Remain Apart on Gas but Proposal Tabled."

128. MOFA, *Diplomatic Blue Book 2006*, 42–43.

129. "Japan Protests China's Imminent Production at Chunxiao Field," Kyodo News, August 10, 2005.

130. "Japan Regrets China Move to Produce Gas in E. China Sea," Kyodo News, August 31, 2005.

131. "Japan Confirms China Pumps Gas or Oil in E. China Sea," Kyodo News, September 20, 2005.

132. Au, "East China Sea Issue," 223–41; Peterson, "Sino-Japanese Cooperation in the East China Sea," 441–74.

133. Przystup, "Japan–China Relations: Spring Thaw," 117.

134. Przystup, "Japan–China Relations: Looking beyond Koizumi," 125.

135. It could be argued that the replacement of Nakagawa with the pro-China Nikai Toshihiro as METI minister is evidence of Japan's willingness to move forward. See Pilling, "Japan Strikes Easier Tone on Gas Disputes."

136. For the details of this incident, see Przystup, "Japan–China Relations: Spring Thaw," 120–21.

137. This section draws on Manicom, "Sino-Japanese Cooperation in the East China Sea," 455–78.

138. "PRC Naval Vessels Activities in East China Sea 'Drop Sharply' in 2006," *Sankei Shimbun*, November 4, 2006. This decrease was not sufficient to be mentioned in the discussion of the Chinese maritime threat in the subsequent defense white paper. See Japan Ministry of Defense, *Defense of Japan 2007*, 59.

139. On the improvement of relations under Abe, see Jiang, "New Dynamics of Sino-Japanese Relations," 15–41.

140. MOFA, "Meeting between the Japan Coast Guard and the State Oceanic Administration of China."

141. "Chinese Research Ship Sighted near Senkaku Isles," *Yomiuri Shimbun*, February 5, 2007.

142. Kumagai, "Japan, China to Start East China Sea Talks."

143. Yoshida, "Fukuda, Hu Put Focus on Future."

144. Tianwaitian entered full production in April 2007. See EIA, "East China Sea."

145. "Japan–China Gas Field Talks Upgraded to Minister Level," *Yomiuri Shimbun*, November 13, 2007.

146. "Fukuda, Hu Agree to Boost Ties / Joint Statement Future-Oriented; Gas Issue 'Close to Resolution,'" *Yomiuri Shimbun*, May 8, 2008.

147. Hu Jintao quoted by Nakamoto and Dickie, "Japan and China near Gas Fields Accord."

148. Przystup, "Japan–China Relations: Yasukuni Stops Everything," 116.

149. Akiyama, "Use of Seas and Management of Ocean Space," 17.

150. Kawasaki and Hashimoto, "Maritime Law a Start to Securing Interests."

151. Only the Social Democratic Party opposed the bill. For an example of the supportive media tone, see Tanaka, "Planning National Strategies."

152. Japanese officials are reluctant to characterize this period as a "confront China in the East China Sea" policy. Rather, they characterize it as a confront China where it tries to interfere with Japanese policy. Author interview "S"; author interview "Q," June 28, 2011, Tokyo.

153. The only available English-language text of the agreement is from Chinese sources; an official Japanese translation is not available. This analysis relies on the text contained in "China, Japan Reach Principled Consensus on East China Sea Issue," Xinhua News, June 18, 2008. The only difference between the two relates to the title of the second section that deals with the Chunxiao gas field, which has different titles for the same text. One author argues this is likely because the Chinese version reinforces the Chinese claim to the Chunxiao field, which is not disputed in the Japanese version. See Drifte, "From 'Sea of Confrontation' to 'Sea of Peace, Cooperation and Friendship'?" *Japan Aktuell*, 43–44. The Japanese-language version is available at MOFA, "Japan–China Cooperation in the East China Sea."

154. Gupta, "An 'Early Summer': Sino-Japanese Cooperation in the East China Sea."

155. "Japan, China Strike Deal on Gas Project Areas in Disputed E. China Sea," Kyodo News, June 16, 2008; Cheong, "China–Japan Deal on East China Sea."

156. Zhang, "Why the 2008 Sino-Japanese Consensus on the East China Sea Has Stalled," 60–65.

157. "Gov't Offers Beijing New Gas Deal," *Yomiuri Shimbun*, February 6, 2008.

158. "China, Japan Reach Principled Consensus on East China Sea Issue," Xinhua News, June 18, 2008.

159. State Council of the People's Republic of China, "Regulations of the People's Republic of China concerning the Exploitation of Offshore Petroleum Resources in Cooperation with Foreign Enterprises."

160. "Shell, Unocal Exit East China Sea Project; CNOOC Says It Still Intends to Start Output in Mid-2005," *Platt's Oilgram*, September 30, 2004.

161. Discussions with multiple Japanese officials, Tokyo, June and July 2011.

162. French, "Sense of Community Elusive for East Asia."

163. Yang, "Q&A: Chinese FM on East China Sea Issue."

164. Kawakami, "Mutual Gas Benefit Stressed / East China Sea Exploration Pact Highlights Japan–China Ties."

165. "Gas Field Agreement Helps Japan-China Ties," *Yomiuri Shimbun*, June 19, 2008.

166. Chinese Ministry of Foreign Affairs, "Foreign Ministry Spokesperson Jiang Yu's Regular Press Conference on June 17, 2008."

167. See, e.g., "China: 'Peaceful Rise in Light and Shadow,'" in *East Asian Strategic Review 2005*, 105; JDA, *Defense of Japan 2006*, 48–49.

168. The Korean reaction to the agreement is also noteworthy, but is beyond the scope of this book. See "Korea Alarmed by China–Japan Deal on East China Sea," *Korea Herald*, June 23, 2008.

169. "Japan–China Gas Deal Leaves Key Issues Unresolved," *Nihon Keizai Shimbun,* June 19, 2008.

170. "China Breaks Accord, Conducts Drilling the 'Kashi' Gas Field in the East China Sea," *Sankei Shimbun,* January 4, 2009.

171. "Japan Protests China Gas Field Moves," *Asahi Shimbun,* January 6, 2009.

172. "China, Japan Reach Principled Consensus on East China Sea Issue," Xinhua News, June 18, 2008.

173. "Editorial: Joint Project with China," *Japan Times,* January 29, 2009.

174. Blanchard, "China's Peaceful Rise," 230–35; Dutton, "Carving Up the East China Sea," 64.

175. Chen, "Anti-Japanese Protesters Assail Beijing's Gas Pact."

176. Przystup, "Japan–China Relations: Progress in Building a Strategic Relationship," 8; Wu, "China Shelves Island Dispute, Yet Again."

177. Author interviews "S" and "Q."

178. Interview with experts at the Ocean Policy Research Foundation, May 13, 2010, Tokyo; author interview "S."

179. Author interview "D."

180. Sutter, "PLA, Japan's Defense Posture, and the Outlook for China–Japan Relations," 184.

181. Although the consensus is that Chinese policymaking is becoming more institutionalized and the PLA's influence on foreign policy is decreasing, two areas where it remains influential are issues relating to the Taiwan Strait and Japan. See Cheung, "Influence of the Gun," 61–90; and Swaine, "Chinese Decision Making Regarding Taiwan," 289–336.

182. See Fravel, "China's Search for Military Power," 125–41.

183. "Asia and Australasia," *Petroleum Economist,* February 7, 2013.

184. "Gov't Foot-Dragging on China Gas Rig Blamed on Ministry Sectionalism," *Yomiuri Shimbun,* June 20, 2004.

185. Press Secretary Hatsuhisa Takashima, quoted by MOFA, "Press Conference 18 June 2004."

186. See, e.g., "Planning National Strategies-Resources and Energy / China Warnings Went Unheeded," *Yomiuri Shimbun,* April 28, 2005.

187. "Japanese Editorial Excerpts," Kyodo News, October 27, 2004.

188. "Japanese Editorial Excerpts," Kyodo News, April 15, 2005.

189. See "Japan Should Tackle China Sea Gas Project Carefully," *Nihon Keizai Shimbun,* April 15, 2005; "Japanese Editorial Excerpts," Kyodo News, April 15, 2005.

190. Curtin, "Sea of Confrontation." Some have argued this favorable public opinion was government driven. However, this assumes a significant degree of policy coherence on the part of the Japanese that is not supported by the research in this book. See Jiang, "New Dynamics of Sino-Japanese Relations," 32.

191. "Lawmakers Inspect China's Gas Projects in the E. China Sea," Kyodo News, April 10, 2005.

192. Solis, "How Japan's Economic Class Views China and the Future of Asian Regionalism," 3–4.

193. Author interview "V."

194. This assessment is based on that given by Smil, *Energy at the Crossroads,* 47.

195. Guo, "Territorial Disputes and Seabed Petroleum Exploitation," 23–24.

196. Miyamoto, "Natural Gas in Japan," 150n61.

197. Indeed, recent estimates of the reserve base offer the more circumspect estimate of 1 to 2 trillion cubic feet of proved or probably natural gas. See EIA, "East China Sea," updated September 25, 2012.

198. Author interview "Z," July 28, 2011, Tokyo.

199. E.g., if Japan trusted China enough to assume noninterference in such an arrangement, then Japan could also trust China to swap said gas for ship-borne LNG headed to Japan from elsewhere in the world. This is a common practice in energy industries and is done when it is more cost-effective.

200. Author interview "V."

201. An example of the first is Jennings, "Sea Area Disputed by China, Japan May Offer Little Oil or Gas." One exception is Hiwatari, "Japan in 2005," 30, who notes that it would be cheaper to send gas to China than Japan.

202. Hall, "Japan–China Oil Slick."

203. Author interview "B." One Japanese interviewee expressed the view that because the resources were not cost-effective, the East China Sea dispute was more about "pride"; author interview "C." Another was not aware of these barriers despite having the view that Japan "owned" the resources in the East China Sea; author interview "G," January 29, 2008, Tokyo.

204. See ANRE, *Fiscal 2005 Annual Energy Report.*

205. China has used issue linkage strategies in the past. See Wiegand, "China's Strategy in the Diaoyu Islands Dispute," 170–93.

206. See Yoshida and Terada, "Japan, China Strike Deal on Gas Fields"; and Tsukamoto, "Japan, China Seal Deal on Gas Fields."

CHAPTER SIX

Managing Two Maritime Powers

AT THE DAWN of the twenty-first century, cooperation over contested jurisdiction in the East China Sea seems farfetched. In 2012, the contested-symbolic issue of the sovereignty of the disputed islands resurfaced after a secondary political actor, Tokyo governor Ishihara Shintaro, embarked on a campaign to buy three of the Senkaku/Diaoyu Islands. With the termination of the China–Japan consensus to manage nationalist provocations after September 2010, neither country could ignore Ishihara's efforts. This round of tension makes the cooperative track record presented in this book all the more compelling. The case studies reveal that Beijing and Tokyo have at times been able to prevent popular nationalist groups from triggering crises over the Senkaku/Diaoyu Islands; they have managed to reduce the number of confrontations between fishermen; and they have arrived at some understanding of the conditions under which resource exploitation in the East China Sea may occur. However, both view the exercise of their maritime jurisdiction in disputed areas of the East China Sea as a vital strategic interest. This is no better demonstrated than China's efforts to establish a "new normal" around the islands in light of a perceived shift in the status quo by Japan—a challenge to China's reference point—in the form of the Noda Yoshihiko government's nationalization of the islands on September 11, 2012. The near-continuous presence of Chinese patrol vessels in the islands' territorial sea reflects a broader effort to dramatically increase China's maritime presence in the East China Sea, which combined with Japan's understanding of the importance to resist this effort, has dramatically increased the number of confrontations between Chinese and Japanese vessels at sea.

In light of these developments, it is worth exploring contemporary dispute management efforts in the context of the shifting maritime environment between Japan and China. Neither party's reference point is satisfied with the status quo in the East China Sea. Placing this reference point in the context of the MVM reveals that both sides have conflated the symbolic and material aspects of contested space, which militates against cooperation. Nevertheless, the grounds for optimism rest on evidence that both sides seem committed to continued interactions on outstanding challenges in contested maritime space, which was also witnessed in previous cases. On this basis, the chapter first explores the shifting postures toward the dispute in China and Japan and concludes with a trade-off that exchanges China's economic interests in resource exploitation with Japan's strategic concerns about interaction with Chinese vessels at sea.

Assertive Japan?

The evidence indicates that Japan has been unable to stem China's maritime expansion because of limits on its ability to assert, use, and defend its maritime jurisdiction. The notification agreement failed in part because Japan lacked the capability to enforce its domestic laws on China; removing domestic restrictions in 2007 supported Japanese coercion of China. Japan's assertive turn attempts to address policy weaknesses in three areas: the legal authority to conduct an activity at sea, and by extension to prevent unauthorized actors from conducting that activity; limits on the use of force by the agencies that protect Japan's maritime domain; and the political will of Japanese political leaders.

As noted in chapter 5, concerns about China drove the reform of Japan's ocean policy, and by 2008, there was a consensus across government that Japan confronted a number of legal and institutional limitations that impeded a more proactive ocean policy. By one estimate, administration over Japan's maritime affairs is divided between more than ten government departments and agencies.[1] Centralizing this bureaucratic structure was one of the aims of Japan's ocean policy reform. Moreover, Japan's new ocean policy was crafted to signal China. The Basic Ocean Law was passed by the Diet on April 21, 2007, which coincided with Wen Jiabao's visit to Tokyo. The bill came into effect on July 20, Japan's Marine Day, which marks its ratification of UNCLOS in 1996, but is sponsored Japanese conservatives.[2] The bill is merely the beginning of an assertive shift in Japanese ocean policy.

The Basic Ocean Law created a new cabinet-level Headquarters of Ocean Policy, headed by the minister of the Ministry for Land, Infrastructure, Transport, and Tourism (MLIT), directly under the stewardship of the prime minister. The Headquarters of Ocean Policy is tasked with preparing domestic legislation to permit the exercise of Japan's jurisdiction over its ocean domain in the areas of EEZ management, environmental protection and preservation, resource development, and marine transportation.[3] It is staffed by approximately forty officials from various government agencies and departments, including defense, MLIT; MOFA; the Ministry of Agriculture, Forestry and Fisheries; and METI. However, it did not remove parallel functions from existing departments. Thus, METI is still in charge of offshore resource development; and MLIT—via the JCG—remains in control of security in Japanese waters.[4] Although these ministries provide staff to the ocean policy headquarters, some argue that it remains unclear whether vested bureaucratic interests will be overcome as barriers to sound policy development and implementation.[5] One official interviewed from the office suggested that bureaucratic rivalries remain active.[6]

Simultaneously, the Diet passed the Law on Establishing Safety Areas for Maritime Structures, which reinforced Japan's threat to drill in the disputed area in the East China Sea. With this threat came the realization that if Teikoku proceeded with exploratory drilling, exploration ships would need to be protected, which was then impossible under Japanese law. UNCLOS permits states to pass domestic laws outlining safety zones surrounding gas and oil platforms in their EEZ, but Japan's EEZ legislation merely asserted its rights to seabed resources; domestic laws were never modified to enable these rights to be asserted.[7] The law on safety zones in the EEZ outlines a 500-meter safety zone surrounding structures in the EEZ that passing vessels are forbidden from entering. It also provides the legal basis for the JCG to expel vessels that enter the safety zone.

Subsequent legislation supports the exercise of Japan's maritime jurisdiction. The Law on Navigation by Foreign Ships through the Territorial Sea was first tabled by the opposition DPJ in October 2005 and came into effect July 1, 2008. The law outlines violations of innocent passage by foreign ships. In 2012, modifications to the Coast Guard Act enabled the JCG to search suspicious ships; order them to leave the territorial sea; and board and arrest them if necessary, provided investigations yielded sufficient justification.[8] The Coast Guard Law had already been amended to allow the use of force to prevent maritime intrusions by suspicious vessels, and in certain circumstances the authority to do so rests with the captain of a JCG vessel.[9]

Japan updated its mining law in 2011 to facilitate its efforts to drill in offshore areas. Under the old law, passed in 1950, interested companies could win offshore bids without demonstrating any interest in near-term drilling. The result was that companies would bid for contracts to hold them for future use, preventing others from exploring in the meantime.[10] Although the reform of the law is long overdue, there are signs that concern over China motivated the timing. Currently, there is no punishment for conducting unauthorized drilling in Japanese waters, and there is some concern that this has emboldened Chinese survey operations in Japanese waters.[11] Indeed, calls for a law that explicitly bans exploration by other countries, particularly China, in the EEZ have existed for some time.[12] According to the 2008 Basic Plan on Ocean Policy,

> In order to ensure Japan's interests in its EEZ and continental shelves, it is also necessary to develop and strengthen a surveillance and crackdown system for appropriately exercising Japan's jurisdiction over exploration and development. For this purpose, patrol vessels, ships and aircraft should be properly replaced and repaired and necessary personnel should be secured. Coordination among related agencies should also be enhanced. Furthermore, regarding the problem that exploration of mineral resources has been managed and scientific researches by foreign vessels have been conducted in these zones without Japan's consent, the government should deliberate over institutional countermeasures to take appropriate actions.[13]

These changes to the mining law strengthen legal restrictions on unsanctioned exploration activity in offshore areas, which has been framed in the context of a burgeoning energy rivalry in the region. According to Akiyama Yoshio, executive councilor at Mitsubishi Materials Techno Corporation, "The current mining law is outdated. It's an issue of the nation's interest as China, Russia and South Korea are conducting their own exploration in parts of our exclusive economic zone."[14] The terms of the new law are a direct consequence of Japan's growing maritime awareness. According to one MOFA official, the old law did not distinguish between the land and the sea, and consequently it left offshore drilling unregulated. Under the new law, only Japanese companies are allowed to drill offshore, which means that foreign companies will need to incorporate a subsidiary in Japan and set up an office there.[15] There are also provisions to ensure that concessions are acted upon once they are procured, because under the old law companies were not obligated to commence exploration. During the past decade discontent has grown across the Japanese government that little offshore drilling was occurring in Japanese waters, even as new discoveries in minerals and gas hydrates were being made.[16] Japanese officials privately concede that the law alone is insufficient to enforce Japan's mining rights in its waters, but they are quick to add that the law itself was in dire need of change.[17]

These legal and institutional reforms reflect a wider consensus within the Japanese bureaucracy that China's maritime rise is something that cannot be ignored.[18] This sense is reflected in part by Japan's definition of its EEZ claim. As noted above, Japanese diplomats lamented the median-line claim because it extended Japan's claim to less than the maximum 200 nautical miles. Senior LDP leaders publicly toyed with the notion of changing Japan's EEZ claim from the median line to claim a full 200 nautical miles in 2005, and they have since downplayed its importance.[19] This modified claim places the Chunxiao field within disputed waters. Japanese officials close to the issue have suggested that the median line was always intended as a provisional boundary, a starting point for negotiation, and that Japan had never surrendered its right to a full 200-nautical-mile EEZ claim.[20] However, Japanese scholars recognize that this has not been well communicated, given that many analysts assume that Japan's EEZ claim extends only as far as the median line.[21] As part of this shift, Japanese leaders started protesting Chinese progress on all fields near the median line, not only the Chunxiao field but also at Tianwaitian. However, Japan's EEZ law has not been changed to reflect this reality; and the nature of its opposition to the Chunxiao field—that it extends on to the Japanese side of the median line—undermines this view.

It is difficult for states to alter their maritime claims over the course of a dispute. If Tokyo's opposition to the Chunxiao field had in fact been due to the location of the field relative to Japan's coast—that is, that it is within 200 nautical miles—it should have said so at the outset. Instead, Japan's stated concerns related to the proximity of the field to the median line. This problem is a result of the bureaucratic incoherence that has characterized Japanese policy. In 2005, there was some disagreement between various government agencies as to where the median line itself was located relative to the Chunxiao gas field. ANRE described the field as being 6 kilometers from the median line, whereas the JCG described it as being 2 kilometers.[22] Regardless, Foreign Minister Matsumoto Takeaki purportedly conveyed a 200-nautical-mile EEZ claim to Yang Jiechi during his visit to China in July 2011.[23] Despite Japan's legal reforms, therefore, its assertive shift is hamstrung by past policy errors.

A second way that Japan is shifting to a more assertive posture is by loosening restrictions on the agencies charged with its defense. China's maritime rise has overtly driven Japan's evolution toward a more active defense posture since 2004.[24] The report *Defense of Japan 2004* included "measures against suspicious vessels" as one of fourteen priority issues, which is a far cry from the attitude in the 1977 defense white paper, which noted that Japan was not capable of defending its maritime claims.[25] The 2005 National Defense Program Guidelines explicitly mentioned defeating an invasion of Japan's offshore islands and patrolling Japan's offshore areas and surrounding seas for the first time.[26] In response to three decades of territorial disputes and two decades of Chinese intrusions into its waters, Japan had finally added the defense of its offshore islands into its defense doctrine. The 2010 National Defense Program Guidelines listed an increase in territorial, sovereignty, and economic disputes as the first characteristic of the security environment around Japan and correspondingly called for the strengthening of forces in the Nansei region.[27]

From a force structure standpoint, Japan has slowly been shifting its military power southward. Of particular note are the relocation of F-15 fighter aircraft to Naha airbase on Okinawa and the construction of an electronic intelligence gathering station on Miyakojima to improve the ASDF's ability to track Chinese aircraft.[28] Reports of a blind spot in aerial surveillance of areas southwest of Miyakojima has led to a reorientation of surveillance aircraft from Aomori Prefecture to Naha airbase to extend the range of Japan's maritime domain awareness.[29] Furthermore, Japan is considering reinforcing the ASDF radar station on Miyakojima with Ground Self-Defense Force troops or placing troops further west on Ishigaki or Yonaguni Island to upgrade reconnaissance capabilities.[30] This effort mirrors China's expanding military presence even as it is couched in the language of disaster relief.[31] The 2005–9 Mid-Term Defense Program placed a premium on addressing the Chinese naval threat, increasing the submarine fleet from sixteen to twenty-two. It is clear that Japan's force posture is becoming more preoccupied with its maritime space, and specifically regarding China's actions in that space.[32]

However, this shift in force structure remains subject to Japan's constitutional constraints on the use of force. Although legislation is being considered to permit surface MSDF patrols of the EEZ, the mere fact that these patrols require emergency legislation eliminates military initiative.[33] Diet deliberations in 2004 to strengthen the MSDF's ability to interdict suspicious ships traveling through Japanese waters were limited by constitutional constraints. Although international law permits the use of warning shots and other coercive measures against suspicious vessels that ignore orders to heave to, because of article 9 restrictions, the final bill severely restricted the MSDF's right to use these measures.[34] As a result, the enforcement of Japan's maritime jurisdiction will continue to rest with the highly capable JCG.

However, the interpretation of article 9 has widened significantly since the early 1980s. Indeed, it is widely accepted that shifts in Japanese security policy, particularly in the maritime realm, are a function of the ad hoc threat-based evaluation of Japan's security situation by political and bureaucratic actors.[35] In light of the emerging bureaucratic consensus discussed above and Japan's legal reforms, the remaining barrier to a more assertive Japanese response to China's maritime expansion lies with the political will of Japan's political leaders, who remain reluctant to fully exploit the country's expanded jurisdictional competencies.

This reluctance may be attributed to the general political chaos that has characterized Japanese elite politics since Koizumi left office in September 2006. The subsequent merry-go-round of prime ministers, with an average term of one year, has made it difficult for leaders to drive a foreign policy agenda. This condition has been exacerbated by the domestic challenges presented by a stagnant economy and recovery from the massive earthquake and tsunami, and subsequent nuclear power plant disaster, that befell Japan on March 11, 2011. The lack of political will to assert Japan's jurisdictional claims is illustrated by Tokyo's response to the first intrusion by a Chinese government vessel into the territorial sea of the Senkaku/Diaoyu Islands in December 2008. On the spectrum of potential Chinese violations of Japan's jurisdiction, the entry of a Chinese state vessel into the territorial sea of the contested islands is possibly the most severe, just short of invasion. Nationalist protesters and fishermen are not agents of the Chinese state. However, the *Haijian 51* and *Haijian 46* of the China Maritime Surveillance (CMS) fleet are charged with policing China's EEZ and were detected 6 kilometers (3 nautical miles) from the Senkaku/Diaoyu Islands, well within the territorial sea.[36] The ships claimed that they were on patrol in Chinese waters when confronted by the JCG and refused to leave.[37] This was an unprecedented act by Chinese state actors in the dispute. JCG reports speculate that the vessels may have conducted some kind of survey activity while in the area.[38] Both acts are a flagrant violation of Japanese sovereignty, but one that is fully consistent with China's claim over the islands.

According to Richard Bush, a JCG patrol ship ordered the two ships to leave Japanese waters and threatened to move into a position to force the Chinese from the waters. The Chinese vessels responded, threatening a collision, and the Japanese vessel backed off.[39] Under Japan's Law on Foreign Vessels in the Territorial Sea, passed just six months earlier, the JCG was permitted to board and investigate the Chinese vessels. This would clearly be an escalatory step that in the minds of the Japanese leadership surely would have triggered a response from China. Furthermore, such a response may have been inadvisable because the JCG vessel on scene was outnumbered.[40] Japanese restraint kept tensions in check, arguably at the cost of maintaining its claim. In August 2011, vessels from the Fisheries Law Enforcement Command (FLEC) entered the islands' territorial sea, resulting in a diplomatic protest from Vice Foreign Minister Sasae Kenichiro to Cheng Yonghua, the Chinese ambassador to Japan.[41] Since the 2012 crisis ships from the CMS and China's new unified coast guard enter the territorial sea on routine basis.

This lack of political will has not been lost on a growing chorus of conservative voices, who stress the need for looser rules of engagement for Japanese ships to assert themselves against China.[42] Short of direct escalation, interviews with Japanese strategists indicate a number of alternative ways to assert Japan's claim to the East China Sea. Many suggested involving the self-defense forces to convey Japanese resolve. One interviewee suggested giving the duty for patrols of the EEZ to the MSDF rather than the coast guard, which would send the message to Beijing that Tokyo is prepared to meet Chinese encroachments with military force.[43] Another suggested that the MSDF patrol the area jointly with the US Navy.[44] Although Washington has been reluctant to become involved in the East China Sea dispute, both these strategists viewed the existence of the US alliance, combined with China's relative military weakness (to a united MSDF–US Seventh Fleet), as an opportunity for Japan to assert itself.[45]

Clearly, there is thinning patience in Japan for Chinese activities in its claimed waters, which has the potential to escalate disputes in the maritime relationship in two ways. First, because Chinese state vessels now regularly enter the territorial sea, they interact in close proximity with their Japanese counterparts. Thus far, neither side has physically asserted its contested jurisdiction against a state vessel from the other side. However, the risk of an incident, through an accident or poor or unprofessional seamanship, is high. Under the conditions noted above, Japanese leaders are unlikely to yield in such an event. Indeed, the application of Japan's authority to detain the fishing boat captain for violating Japan's territorial sea in September 2010 stands as an example, despite being a civilian vessel. This crisis could have been significantly more serious if a collision had occurred with a Chinese state vessel within Japan's territorial sea. There is also no evidence that China intends to reduce its naval presence around Japan. Aside from entering the islands' territorial sea, Chinese vessels now pass through the Miyako Strait and sail on to conduct training exercises in the Pacific Ocean several times per year. Indeed, some Japanese begrudge the fact that Chinese ships were sighted in Japanese waters during the 3/11 disaster and that a Chinese helicopter buzzed a Japanese destroyer less than two weeks after the disaster.[46]

The second way Japan's thinning patience could trigger an escalation is that it is unlikely that Japan will lose interest in offshore resource development. Despite industry suspicions about the prospects for oil and gas in the Xihu Trough, there is considerable interest in frontier seabed deposits, such as methane hydrates and deep sea minerals.[47] The Basic Ocean Policy was celebrated in some quarters as bringing Japan closer to drilling in the disputed area.[48] METI's $213 million acquisition of the *Ramform Victory* indicates that offshore resource exploration remains a policy priority.[49] However, as noted in chapter 5, China has made clear that any unilateral drilling by Japan in the disputed area would invoke a Chinese military response. Further, if Japan successfully set up drilling installations in the disputed part of the East China Sea, Chinese vessels may deliberately violate the safety zones as part of Beijing's nonrecognition of Japan's jurisdiction east of the median line. This in turn could invite a response from Japanese authorities.

The potential for escalation is in some ways contingent on political will from Tokyo. Early signs from the Abe administration, which was elected in late 2012, are that it has backed off some of the hawkish elements of its campaign platform.[50] Nevertheless, improvements in Japan's capability to exploit the East China Sea's resources and confront China may increase domestic pressure for it to do so. Because a constitutional change in Japan remains highly unlikely, despite the efforts of the Abe administration, it is worth asking why Japan is preparing to respond militarily to a Chinese threat, when it cannot take the military initiative nor develop the offensive weapons necessary to do so. It could certainly be argued that these are defensive measures intended to respond to Chinese encroachments on Japan's maritime rights. Perhaps Japanese leaders are again trying to coerce Chinese cooperation by appearing to strengthen their ability to react to perceived transgressions from China.

Since the events of September 2010 and 2012, crisis management may be becoming more difficult as both states loosen the restrictions on their increasingly numerous and capable enforcement vessels that patrol their disputed waters. Furthermore, though Tokyo has been at pains to make clear that a Chinese invasion of the Senkaku/Diaoyu Islands would trigger an American intervention under article 5 of the United States–Japan alliance, it is somewhat less clear whether spats between enforcement vessels in the East China Sea merit such involvement.[51] Given that Japanese naval and coast guard vessels are already more capable than their Chinese counterparts, the loosening of legal restrictions on Japanese enforcement vessels could be viewed as an attempt to increase the credibility component of Japanese deterrence vis-à-vis China. If this is the case, rather than leading to escalation, these efforts could again result in an effort to manage tensions in the East China Sea.

China's International Strength and Domestic Weakness

The second feature of the contemporary maritime environment between China and Japan is that Chinese foreign policy seems to be caught between international confidence and domestic insecurity.[52] Although China continues to eschew a global leadership role, many scholars have noted its growing confidence, which is illustrated by its more overt and unapologetic pursuit of its national interests since the December 2009 climate conference in Copenhagen.[53] This foreign policy approach is a striking contrast to its "Charm Offensive" of the early twenty-first century.[54] Paradoxically, this international projection of confidence is mirrored by a deep-seated sense of domestic insecurity. The CCP seems to fear its own people. This is illustrated not only by the unprecedented crackdown on Chinese dissidents since 2011, but also by Beijing's willingness to damage bilateral relations with its neighbors to assuage domestic nationalist sentiment.[55] This characteristic is illustrated by the continued and more forthright application of Chinese jurisdiction in contested waters throughout East Asia, and particularly by the fallout from Senkaku/Diaoyu crises in 2010 and 2012.

This book has illustrated that territorial and maritime disputes with Japan attract considerable nationalist sentiment in China, which can constrain the policy options available to Chinese leaders. Recent crises in Sino-Japanese relations bear out the geopolitical consequences. Following the collision near the Senkaku/Diaoyu Islands in September 2010, and again following Japan's nationalization of the islands in 2012, nationalist demonstrations raged across China.[56] China's response to the collision was particularly tough, possibly as part of an effort to avoid accusations of weakness by Chinese nationalists. Beijing's initial response was consistent with that of a challenger state trying to assert its claim; it defended the fishing boat captain's actions and denied Japan's right to detain him at all.[57] Although China's reaction in 2012 was more strident, the Chinese argument that it did not provoke the Japanese move has widened the range of options available to China. Specifically, the crisis created the pretext for China to dramatically increase its physical presence near the islands, which reinforces the domestic narrative that the CCP is protecting Chinese territory from resurgent Japanese "neomilitarism."[58]

Although nationalists are not a monolithic group and their direct impact on foreign policy is difficult to measure, it seems clear that Beijing will escalate disputes to avoid domestic criticism and then seek pragmatic solutions once domestic discontent has been suppressed through the CCP's media controls.[59] Although the CCP can control nationalism through police activity and media censorship, Chinese leaders judge that tolerating a period of nationalist fervor is wise to ensure its legitimacy.[60] Furthermore, both media and interview sources indicate that this is recognized by Japanese leaders. One source located in the Cabinet Office at the time of the collision in 2010 noted that much of the Japanese governments' concern at the time related to the CCP's ability to balance its nationalist credentials with its reluctance to escalate the dispute.[61]

However, this delicate balance could be upset by the state-driven interest in an expansionist maritime strategy and the concomitant emergence of domestic actors whose interests are served by this agenda.[62] These groups carry both a bureaucratic and nationalist interest in activities perceived as confrontational by Japan. For instance, despite its greater institutionalization, the military remains influential on Taiwan Strait and Japan policy.[63] Japanese policymakers have suggested that cooperative constituencies, such as the Chinese MFA, have been sidelined by bureaucratic constituencies that are able to argue that are they defending China's territorial integrity by resisting cooperation.[64] Indeed, the *Washington Post* reported that Japanese officials observed that unlike previous crises over the Senkaku/Diaoyu Islands, the military played a dominant role in the 2010 crisis, apparently drowning out the moderating influence of the Chinese MFA.[65]

China's naval strategy has moved away from the language of "island chains" into a distinction between near and far seas.[66] Chinese strategic thinkers express anxiety about the state of affairs within the near seas, which include the East and South China seas.[67] Island states allied with the United States are seen to "hem" China in, and jurisdictional disputes with Japan "are compressing and nibbling away at the buffer zone of Chinese territorial waters." On the whole, "China is being encircled by leading maritime powers in the Asia-Pacific region extending from the south all the way up to its northeast coast." The solution is to use China's growing naval power to "break through the encirclement."[68] Furthermore, there is a view that China's maritime periphery has become more threatening as a consequence of competing claims by China's maritime neighbors and their improving ties with the United States.[69] This is not to suggest that the entire strategic narrative is driven by threat. The noted Chinese foreign policy pundit Major-General Luo Yuan, of the China Society of Military Science, has noted that China cannot contribute to international peace and security, as it is often asked to, without moving beyond the near seas.[70]

Far from being only a nationalist or military preoccupation, however, maritime interests have shifted to the center of Chinese policymaking as these interests are now described under their own heading in China's five-year plans (FYPs). Resource exploitation is front and center in the Twelfth FYP, which calls for the development of the maritime oil and gas industries as well as the "rational" use of maritime resources.[71] Although this is similar to the Eleventh FYP, which contains a section titled "Protect and Develop Ocean Resources," the Twelfth FYP adopts the more holistic goal of the development of a maritime economy.[72] Some have attributed this to an effort to increase the share of China's economic growth generated by maritime industries.[73] According to the *China National Offshore Development Report 2011*, China's marine economy grew by 13.5 percent in 2010 and amounted to 9.6 percent of China's total gross domestic product.[74] Outgoing president Hu Jintao's call for China to become a maritime power in his final address during the Eighteenth Communist Party Congress should thus not come as a surprise.[75]

The development of a maritime economy requires a number of institutional reforms to better exercise maritime jurisdiction and has important implications for the Sino-Japanese maritime relationship. The Eleventh FYP called for the development of an official maritime strategy based on the five "presences" designed to reinforce Chinese claims to contested areas: public administration, laws and legislation, defense, public opinion, and economic affairs.[76] China's civilian agencies, particularly the Maritime Safety Administration under the Ministry of Transport), the CMS (under the State Oceanic Administration), and the FLEC (under the Ministry of Agriculture), are mandated to enforce aspects of China's jurisdiction. The Maritime Safety Administration is charged with policing commercial shipping and maintaining navigation aids, the CMS are charged with patrolling China's EEZ, and the FLEC is in charge of fisheries enforcement.[77] Moreover, recent work by the research arm of Japan's Ministry of Defense expresses the concern that the military is coordinating the activities of Chinese coast guards in waters near Japan.[78]

There is no doubt that each branch competes for a share of the budget allocated for maritime enforcement.[79] Under these circumstances, these institutions may operate under an incentive structure that does not reward moderation or that may not even integrate foreign policy consequences into the calculus. By the end of the Twelfth FYP period, the CMS—which currently boasts 10 aircraft and 300 patrol vessels—will grow to 16 aircraft and 350 patrol vessels.[80] In addition to increasing in number, Chinese civilian enforcement vessels are increasing in size. The FLEC, for instance, has more than 1,300 patrol ships, but only nine that displace more than 1,000 tons. Both the CMS and the FLEC have an important role in China's maritime disputes with Japan. The largest FLEC vessel, the 2,580-ton *Yuzheng 310*, was rushed to the Senkaku/Diaoyu Islands for its maiden voyage in November 2010.[81] The CMS pays regular visits to the Chunxiao gas field and are monitored by Japanese P3-C patrol planes.[82]

These factors—including Beijing's nationalist narrative, uncertain command-and-control structure, and bureaucratic rivalries—have complicated China's presence in disputed waters in the South China Sea and Yellow Sea.[83] Perhaps as a consequence of these internal weaknesses, Chinese leaders are projecting the image of a strong, united, increasingly powerful China, notwithstanding traditional statements that China remains a "developing country." This suggests that the CCP may be imprisoned in a cell of its own making. By tying its legitimacy to nationalist foreign policy agendas that favor a confrontational stance on issues of territorial integrity, particularly those with Japan, Beijing has left little room for compromise. Simultaneously, the pretext for a more active Chinese presence in contested waters is increasing as a function of its growing maritime agenda. This new confidence has been most acutely manifested in the maritime realm.[84] Problematically, these efforts come as Japan is removing the restrictions that have impeded it from taking the initiative in the past.

Conflating Values in the East China Sea

Clearly, both claimants are confronting rising disincentives for cooperation that stem from the "relational" aspects of disputed space. In China, cooperation with Japan carries potential domestic consequences for the CCP's legitimacy. In Japan, resisting China's maritime activities is increasingly popular in the government and among Japanese people. Both these developments relate to the contested-symbolic use of space. Concomitant with a rising interest in the material utility of maritime space, this has created a situation in which the maritime environment has taken on a strategic quality. Cooperation with the "other" is so unacceptable that both sides are directing resources to the exercise and enforcement of their maritime jurisdiction, lest they lose something of both tangible and intangible value: the ocean. Although the most successful agreements have been able to isolate economic aspects from other dimensions of maritime space, figure 6.1 indicates that economic issues have become complicated by strategic concerns.

For example, the June 2008 consensus partly fulfilled Japan's strategic objective of forestalling Chinese maritime expansion; the JDZ is located in the middle of the East China Sea, rather than near the Senkaku/Diaoyu Islands, as China had proposed. Beijing's continued reluctance to begin

FIGURE 6.1
Maritime Value Matrix, 2010–12

Intrinsic-tangible: Economic	**Relational-tangible: Strategic**
• Void	• Exercising jurisdiction • China's maritime expansion (Japan) • Resource value of the Xihu Trough (China)
Intrinsic-intangible: Shared-symbolic • Void	**Relational-intangible: Contested-symbolic** • Asserting jurisdictional and territorial claims • Compromise with the "other"

implementation talks relates to both concerns about the effect on China's claims and domestic resistance from within Beijing. Since the June 2008 consensus, China has become a much more active player in the maritime areas surrounding Japan; and the potential consequences of full implementation of the consensus—with its implicit recognition of the Japanese-claimed median line—could threaten the strategic importance Beijing places on the East China Sea. The question of resource development has therefore taken on a strategic dimension for China, whereas exploitation of oil and gas in the disputed area is economically unimportant for Japan.

Current China–Japan maritime relations are hamstrung by continued discord over the implementation of the June 2008 consensus and the issue of state interaction on the sea. Some have argued that the June 2008 consensus was not negotiated in good faith and was deliberately cast aside by China as a barrier to its maritime expansion.[85] By contrast, a Japanese official close to the negotiations believes that China negotiated the agreement in good faith but that domestic political machinations and bureaucratic politics have impeded further talks.[86] Japan's efforts to implement the treaty have been hamstrung by competing interpretations, specifically whether the treaty included an understanding that drilling would cease at other fields until such time as rules for exploitation had been established.[87] In January 2009, Japan protested Chinese upgrades to the Tianwaitian gas field on this basis. China, by contrast, argued that because Tianwaitian was outside the scope of the consensus, it was perfectly acceptable to proceed with development.[88] After winning power in September 2009, the DPJ government accused China of violating the agreement after MSDF patrols flights reported that it appeared that the Chunxiao field was producing gas in December 2009.[89] Japanese foreign minister Okada Katsuya subsequently stated that Japan would take "appropriate measures" if China continued to exploit gas at Chunxiao.[90] The Chinese replied that they had not yet received any expressions of interest from Japanese companies.[91] Chinese activity at Chunxiao was condemned by Chief Cabinet Secretary Edano Yukio in March 2011, and Japan again protested the detection of a flare at the installation in early 2012.[92]

In an effort to clarify the terms of the agreement, Foreign Minister Yang Jiechi argued that Japanese entities were entitled to cooperatively develop the Chunxiao field with China and that this was distinct from the principle of joint development applied to the JDZ.[93] The cause of this confusion rests squarely with Japan because it has refused to recognize Chinese sovereignty over the Chunxiao field—despite the fact that the first clause of the 2008 consensus, which permits Japanese entities to participate at Chunxiao under Chinese laws, implicitly recognizes Chinese sovereignty over the Chunxiao gas field. According to one Chinese official, many observers in China interpreted these protests as an attempt by Japan to change the terms of the June 2008 consensus.[94] One Japanese official privately conceded that Japan has accepted Chinese sovereignty over the Chunxiao field, but that publicly Japan seeks to treat the delimitation separately from Chunxiao. Japan's reluctance to clarify its maritime claims has complicated signaling to China that Japan recognizes that Beijing made a concession to achieve the 2008 consensus.[95] These complications aside, however, implementation is hamstrung by the perceived costs that the CCP would incur to its leadership credentials, a function of the contested-symbolic nature of the East China Sea issue. Japanese officials have been told by their Chinese counterparts that "the environment is not right," a statement that some find bewildering. They point out that in the absence of the festering Yasukuni Shrine issue, the environment could not be better.[96]

Implementation of the stagnant resource agreement is further complicated by the growing activity by Chinese and Japanese vessels in contested maritime space. Chinese civilian enforcement vessels enforce China's maritime rights in disputed waters. Chinese survey and military vessels that operate in the East China Sea, including near the disputed Senkaku/ Diaoyu Islands, argue that they are in Chinese waters and are entitled to do so. Since the 2012 nationalization of the islands, Chinese vessels have routinely entered the islands' territorial sea, contributing to a growing sense in Japan that China is attempting to exercise de facto jurisdiction over waters, and perhaps eventually territories, claimed by Japan. The growth of these patrols since the first intrusion in 2008 reflects a pattern familiar to Japanese strategists. Chinese activity near the islands and in the wider maritime area has become progressively more frequent and forthright in the application of Chinese jurisdictional authority, which fits with the slow but steady expansion of the geographic scope of China's maritime activities since the mid-1990s.

Consistent with this pattern, since September 2010, Chinese authorities have formally announced their intention to patrol disputed areas with greater regularity, with both aerial and surface assets.[97] Although it is unclear whether this announcement is politically motivated, Beijing has at times used these patrols to send political signals to Japan. Shortly after the September 2010 crisis, the FLEC dispatched fisheries patrol vessels to the islands and, in a perceived provocation to Japan, entered the contiguous zone upon their arrival.[98] Subsequently, Chinese vessels were spotted near the islands on thirteen occasions between the 2010 crisis and the 2012 nationalization. They would typically venture to the fringe of the 12-nautical-mile territorial sea and circumnavigate the islands.[99] Chinese ships entered the territorial sea on three occasions during this period, which were likely to send a political signal. On August 24, 2011, two FLEC vessels entered the territorial sea on the eve of the expected resignation of Japanese prime minister Kan Naoto.[100] CMS vessels entered the territorial sea on March 16, 2012, purportedly as part of a propaganda effort to publicize growth of China's presence near the islands.[101] Three FLEC vessels entered the territorial sea on July 12 in an effort to dissuade the Noda government from preempting Ishihara's effort to purchase three of the islands.[102] That vessels did not enter the territorial sea on every occasion, on "usual patrols," is a sign of escalation management by Beijing.[103]

In the wake of the Noda administration's nationalization of the Senkaku/Diaoyu Islands on September 11, 2012, the behavior of China's enforcement vessels has changed. CMS vessels were dispatched to the islands the day the nationalization occurred, arriving September 14. Chinese vessels have since maintained a near-constant presence near the islands, patrolled in groups of two or more, and regularly entered the territorial sea. Another important difference is that rather than either ignoring or refusing JCG requests to leave, Chinese vessels have begun to demand that the JCG leave the territorial sea, which is then reported in the state media.[104] Furthermore, on December 13, 2012, a CMS plane flew over the islands, in the first Chinese violation of Japanese-claimed airspace. Japanese fighters were scrambled from Naha, which prompted a protest by Beijing for entering Chinese airspace over the islands. Given that Beijing made the decision to increase aerial patrols in January 2012, but waited almost twelve months to carry out a patrol, the flight could be read as a Chinese provocation, as it came on the heels of an increasingly frequent Chinese presence near the Senkaku/Diaoyu Islands.[105] Finally, the PLAN has conducted exercises in the waters near the islands, including—according to one Japanese report—within the islands' contiguous zone.[106]

These incidents amount to an explicit Chinese effort to exploit the opportunity created by Japan's nationalization to remake the status quo around the islands to one that closer approximates its preferences. Defending the patrols, Chinese MFA spokesman Hong Lei stated that "the Japanese side should face up to the reality that the situation over the Diaoyu Islands has undergone fundamental changes."[107] According to the *Global Times*, "Japan's 'actual control' over the islands has gone."[108] JCG vessels now need to remain on station near the islands, which is straining resources.[109] By the end of 2012, Japanese sources suggested that Chinese vessels entered the territorial sea nineteen times since the nationalization.[110]

China's explicit effort to change the status quo near the islands is mirrored by efforts to do the same in the East China Sea, as it relates to the exercise of maritime jurisdiction. On May 3, 2010, the JCG marine survey vessel *Shoyo* was confronted and pursued by a CMS vessel when it was operating near Amami Oshima, 40 kilometers (22 nautical miles) east of Japan's claimed median line in the East China Sea. The *Haijian 51* shadowed the *Shoyo* for four hours and communicated that the JCG vessel was in Chinese waters and ordered it to cease its activities.[111] Foreign Minister Okada Katsuya lodged a protest with the Chinese Embassy in Tokyo, while conservative media in Japan decried the fact that a Japanese vessel had abandoned a survey in its claimed waters due to pressure from China.[112] The *Shoyo* was again confronted in September 2010 280 kilometers (151 nautical miles) northwest of Okinawa by the *Haijian 51*, and in early 2012 Chinese vessels twice demanded that the JCG vessels *Takuyo* and *Shoyo* cease their survey activities in contested waters.[113] Curiously, the Chinese media reported that the Japanese vessels were "expelled" from Chinese waters.[114] Such activities by China are reminiscent of the efforts by the PLAN to intimidate the *Ramform Victory* during its survey of the median line in 2004–5.

The experiences of the *Shoyo* reveal the dangers of greater maritime activity by claimant states in disputed waters, particularly between military vessels. In early April 2010, a Chinese naval flotilla composed of two Kilo-class submarines and eight surface vessels conducted military drills southeast of Miyako Island and subsequently traveled past Okinawa into the Pacific Ocean. Japan dispatched two MSDF destroyers to shadow the flotilla, the largest to ever pass near Japan. On two occasions during the voyage, which lasted more than two weeks, Chinese helicopters approached to within 90 meters of the Japanese vessels.[115] Chinese sources maintained that the drills occurred on the high seas, while the Japanese media speculated that the drills were further evidence of China's ambitions to operate beyond the first island chain.[116] Tokyo recognized that the drills occurred on the high seas, but it complained to Beijing that the two approaches by helicopters were dangerous. PLAN vessels transited the same waters in March 2011 and were again accused of dangerous approaches with helicopters.[117] Chinese naval operations on the high seas and EEZ are accepted under both countries' interpretation of international law. However, the near collisions could spark a political crisis.[118] As with other elements of its maritime activity, these activities have become more frequent. Chinese military vessels passed through Japanese waters en route to the Pacific in June and November 2011 and in April, October, November, and December 2012.[119]

There is little doubt that Japan perceives these activities as a challenge to its reference point in its maritime environment and there are signs it is prepared to resist China in the East China Sea. When the *Shoyo* was confronted in September 2010, at the height of the crisis over the collision between the Chinese fishing boat and the JCG, the *Shoyo* stayed on station for a further two hours rather than abandon its work.[120] An MLIT official describes this as a demonstration of the consensus in the Japanese government that the *Shoyo* needed to demonstrate Tokyo's interpretation of what Japan is permitted to do in its claimed waters.[121] Subsequent surveys in early 2012 by the *Takuyo* and *Shoyo* also ignored Chinese warnings to cease their activities. That China's near-permanent presence in the territorial sea of the disputed islands has not yet yielded a more assertive response from Japan could be attributed to Japanese concerns about escalation of tensions with China. Japan will likely continue to strengthen its posture, while encouraging dialogue with China. The evidence presented in this book suggests that China will be receptive and seek to manage tensions, rather than escalate further, for fear of emboldening Japan.

The discussion above suggests that both claimants believe their jurisdictional claims are supported by the exercise of state practice. Although UNCLOS suggests that the exercise of coastal state jurisdiction cannot form the basis for a claim to maritime space, both claimants seem more convinced by Geoffrey Till's observation that "local navies have a basic national duty to exercise maritime sovereignty since it is a fundamental principle of international law that for sovereignty to be recognized, it needs to be exercised."[122] This sentiment is echoed by Meng Xiangqing of the National Defense University's Strategic Studies Institute: "In international law, there are two conventions regarding disputed sea areas; one is to see whether you have effective management there; and the second is that actual control is superior to historical proof. For example, we say that this sea area has historically been ours, but this alone is no use, it depends on whether we have actual control there. China's maritime monitoring must demonstrate its presence and express effective jurisdiction in the sea areas under its jurisdiction."[123]

This sentiment seems to confuse demonstration of unopposed administration of islands, through evidence of *effectivités*, with the exercise of coastal state jurisdiction over a claimed ocean space. The former supports a sovereignty claim; the latter cannot support a jurisdictional claim because claims to maritime space are based on possession of land, not the sea. Nevertheless, Chinese vessels have made a habit of setting a behavioral standard in East Asian waters that reflect Chinese claims. Likewise, Japan's threat to drill in 2005 was necessary to convey its entitlements to explore for resources in its EEZ; similarly, the change in the *Shoyo*'s behavior between May and September 2010 reflected a shift in Japanese understanding of the consequences of backing down. Viewed in this context, it is nearly impossible to separate, in a political sense, the material aspects of disputed space from the symbolic aspects. All aspects of disputed space have adopted a strategic quality due to the need to maintain maximum flexibility in the exercise of jurisdiction. Combined with the domestic barriers to cooperation that stem from the contested-symbolic aspects of disputed space, the chances of cooperation seem remote. Since the 2010 crisis, leaders in Beijing and Tokyo have been engaged in a process of trying to establish a status quo that supports their objectives in the East China Sea. The next section advances a possible trade-off that could establish a status quo that meets portions of both claimants' objectives for the East China Sea.

Ways Forward in the Sino-Japanese Maritime Relationship

At first glance, the recent phase of tensions in the East China Sea seems to belie the cooperative track record presented in this book. This record reveals that China and Japan are capable of managing tensions over the East China Sea but, of particular importance, not without a period of tension before commencing dispute management efforts. Escalation has been averted in the past, and cooperation characterized by a deeper degree of interaction in an issue area has been more successful at moderating underlying tensions. Gradual measures to build confidence and strategic trust seem to resonate with Chinese interlocutors.[124] Despite the tensions since September 2010, Sino-Japanese interactions on maritime issues, which are so important for lasting cooperation, remain robust despite occasional interruptions caused by crises.

For instance, despite recurrent tensions, bilateral talks toward the implementation of the 2008 agreement have endured. A series of high-level visits took place in May and June 2010 that seemed to galvanize momentum for renewed discussion of the implementation of the 2008 consensus on resource development.[125] Then–prime minister Hatoyama Yukio attended the Shanghai Expo, and Premier Wen Jiabao visited Japan for three days at the end of May. Director-general-level discussions were held on July 27 in Tokyo that focused on writing the treaty called for by the consensus. These were the first such meetings since the consensus was announced in June 2008, and they were greeted with a degree of skepticism by the Japanese.[126] Beijing canceled subsequent talks in response to the September 2010 collision near the Senkaku/Diaoyu Islands. Upon assuming the office of prime minister in August 2011, Noda Yoshihiko called for a resumption of the talks, and there was speculation that China would reciprocate, possibly under the auspices of the defunct bilateral consultations on the UN Convention on the Law of Sea.[127] East China Sea issues were discussed in an informal meeting between Sugiyama Shinsuke, director-general of MOFA's Asian and Oceanian Affairs Bureau, and Chinese vice foreign minister Zhang Zhijun in late January 2011.[128] Vice ministerial talks in late February 2011 built further momentum. When Kan and Wen met in Tokyo in May 2011, both expressed an interest in restarting resource exploitation talks and in creating a maritime communication mechanism. This was reiterated by foreign ministers Yang and Matsumoto in July 2011.[129]

As for the conduct of vessels at sea, the need for better communication between defense ministries was recognized in November 2009 in talks between defense ministers Liang Guanglie and Kitazawa Toshimi. The two pledged improved military transparency through a nine-point plan that includes port visits, annual security dialogues, a hotline, and planned joint search-and-rescue exercises.[130] Progress toward a maritime mechanism was renewed following the confrontations between Chinese and Japanese vessels in the spring of 2010. Hatoyama complained to Wen about the incidents at their meeting in May 2010, and the two agreed to accelerate talks on a maritime mechanism.[131] In August 2010 Beijing invited Tokyo to negotiate an agreement on "maritime measures" that would involve sharing frequencies, annual meetings, and the establishment of a hotline between branches of the two sides' militaries.[132] Chinese officials requested an informal chat between defense ministers Liang and Kitazawa during the ASEAN Defense Ministers' Meeting in Hanoi in October 2010, at which they reaffirmed this commitment, despite the ongoing crisis triggered by the collision near the Senkaku/Diaoyu Islands.[133] Director-general-level discussions were held between defense officials in late April 2013, despite the poor state of the relationship at this time. Future discussions on both the resources issue and the communications issue could take place under the auspices of the high-level dialogue on maritime issues set up by Noda and Wen in December 2011.[134]

It is notable that the nascent discussion on improving communication between naval forces was not a casualty of the diplomatic freeze that followed the 2010 Senkaku/Diaoyu crisis. The challenge, at least from the Japanese perspective, is that the Chinese seem unmoved by the clear need for some kind of crisis management mechanism. For instance, the Chinese Maritime Safety Administration conducted three search-and-rescue exercises with the JCG in 2004, 2010, and March 2011.[135] Although a useful confidence-building measure, the Chinese Maritime Safety Administration is not the primary source of tension with Japan, as are the CMS and FLEC. It is thus a shame that this agency was not included in the amalgamation of Chinese coast guard agencies in 2013. Further, a hotline between navies would not be useful in a confrontation between a CMS helicopter and an MSDF destroyer, as occurred in March 2011.[136] Fortunately, working-level discussions toward a maritime communications mechanism held in Beijing in June 2012 featured multiple agencies, including the CMS, FLEC, and JCG, as well as defense and foreign affairs officials. These meetings were wide ranging and discussed follow-on meetings, the specifics of a hotline, and the beginnings of an "unalerted" encounters agreement.[137] The "high-level consultations on maritime affairs" established by Noda and Wen met in Hangzhou in May 2012.[138] Discussions toward developing a maritime communication mechanism were one of the primary deliverables to come out of the first meeting between the defense chiefs in two years that took place on July 26, 2012, in Tokyo. These developments indicate that the Sino-Japanese capacity to engage in pragmatic efforts to mitigate tensions should not be underestimated. This is no better demonstrated than by the "secret" meetings that took place between vice foreign ministers Kawai Chikao and Zhang Zhijun at the height of the 2012 crisis over the Senkaku/Diaoyu Islands.[139]

This pattern of dispute management suggests that there is still considerable interest in Beijing and Tokyo in removing maritime issues as a source of discord. Resolution of the underlying sovereignty issue may be far-fetched, but there is reason to be optimistic that the two parties could be interested in trade-offs that satisfy some aspect of the territorial objectives outlined in figure 6.1. A promising way forward is a trade-off that addresses the two outstanding issues in the maritime relationship: resource exploitation and the conduct of vessels at sea. Linking these two aspects of disputed maritime jurisdiction in this way builds on the recognition in both China and Japan that the issues of resource development and interaction between state vessels at sea are connected. Such a trade-off is more feasible than the grand bargains that are often proposed for the wider China–Japan relationship. For instance, Reinhard Drifte has outlined a bargain in which Japan would compromise on its claims to the Senkaku/Diaoyu Islands in order to gain "access to a secure EEZ with maximum size."[140] Robert Dujarric has argued that Japan should settle its Takeshima and Northern Territories disputes with South Korea and Russia in exchange for the construction of an anti-China coalition.[141] However, both these proposals seem ambitious given the domestic consequences to compromise on sovereignty issues that is an inherent part of territorial disputes. Rather, trade-offs within the exercise of coastal state maritime jurisdiction are more feasible.

As illustrated above, China is constrained by the 2008 consensus, which cannot be implemented due to the contested-symbolic and strategic costs of resource exploitation in the JDZ. Continued development of fields not covered by the consensus, such as Tianwaitian, is greeted critically by Japan and comes at the cost to bilateral relations. Furthermore, the politicization of East China Sea resources has impeded their development; China has not yet dared exploit resources on the east side of the median line. Japan cannot access resources in the disputed area without Chinese acquiescence, and in any event it has little economic interest in the hydrocarbons in the area. Its resistance to Chinese drilling efforts is motivated by strategic concerns over the exercise of jurisdiction, not the production of resources. The case could be made therefore that Japan could agree to abrogate the June consensus—which neither party wants, but which favors Japan on paper—in exchange for an agreement on sharing jurisdiction in the contested area of the East China Sea. This would include a mechanism that fosters greater transparency between Chinese and Japanese state vessels operating in the East China Sea, including the notification of large naval deployments and the use of common frequencies when in proximity to the other. This agreement could contain within it an understanding that further expressions of jurisdictional competence by coast guard vessels do not prejudice either party's claims to the East China Sea, an arrangement not unlike that contained within the fisheries agreement. Each party would only apply its law to vessels flying its own flag. Indeed, this is in fact already taking place because neither party seems willing to take steps to escalate the dispute by enforcing its will on state vessels from the other country. Agreeing that these activities do not prejudice each party's claims removes the political tension from the relationship because it would remove the perceived legal requirement to demonstrate effective occupation of maritime space and sidestep the strategic barrier to cooperation. Properly explained to domestic audiences as an exercise of sovereignty, this tradeoff could sidestep the contested-symbolic element as well.

Under this arrangement, China would be free of the June 2008 consensus and be able to conduct drilling operations in prospective areas of the East China Sea with the understanding that such activities do not in fact strengthen China's claim to maritime space, given that jurisdiction is shared. This agreement in fact costs Japan very little. It does not lose access to offshore oil and gas resources, because these are of little economic value to it, but it gains the security associated with greater transparency between coast guard and military vessels. A critic might argue that this could result in a larger number of Chinese ships operating near Japan. However, there is little evidence that this would not occur anyway. As it stands, there is little Japan can do to police the number of Chinese ships near Japan; as one Japanese official put it, this cannot be helped and must be accepted.[142] Furthermore, greater East China Sea resource production by China serves the Japanese interest of keeping Chinese factories humming and keeping Japanese-owned manufacturing operating free of brownouts and power shortages. It would also have a depressing effect on regional prices of natural gas, of which Japan consumes a great deal, particularly due to the shutdown of its nuclear plants. This quid pro quo could improve the tone of Sino-Japanese interactions at sea. Given Japan's growing willingness to confront Chinese ships on the basis of the exercise of jurisdiction, Beijing may soon become aware that an incident at sea is a realistic possibility. Recall that more credible Japanese threats to exercise its jurisdiction have coerced cooperation from China in the past.

Such a quid pro quo requires domestic political leadership to overcome the contested-symbolic costs of compromise. Chinese leaders can frame the agreement as a gain of the resource rights to the East China Sea and cast new protocols regarding the interaction between ships at sea as the coming of age of the PLAN. It will be more difficult for Japanese politicians to sell such a deal domestically. With a free media, the notion of abandoning oil and gas rights will be hotly debated. However, such debates may also arrive at the conclusion that Japan has little to gain on the resources front and much to gain on the strategic front by creating safer navigation in its surrounding seas. Indeed, if framed as an exercise of Japanese sovereignty, such an agreement would undermine conservative anxiety about Japanese weakness vis-à-vis China.

This idea is not without shortcomings. First, it could be argued that an "incidents at sea"–type arrangement between China and Japan is not feasible. US–Chinese efforts to develop the Military Maritime Consultative Agreement as a truly transparent process have largely been unsuccessful. Many doubt China's willingness to enter into binding efforts to build transparency; it may be more interested in the symbolism. According to Japanese strategists, the Chinese see interactions on a "maritime mechanism" as part of a broader trust-building exercise between China and Japan, rather than as a method to improve communication channels between the two militaries.[143] This is also a complaint leveled by US naval officials at their Chinese counterparts. Furthermore, such an agreement might be too difficult for China to implement. It has five marine enforcement agencies that do the job of the JCG, which is an oft-cited barrier to greater transparency by Japanese officials.[144] It remains to be seen whether a unified Chinese coast guard is more coherent.[145] Finally, it could be argued that surrendering Japan's oil and gas rights to the East China Sea simply delays an inevitable conflict over other deep sea resources. However, each of these faults simply reinforces the need for an arrangement that strengthens the Sino-Japanese maritime relationship so that it can overcome future challenges.

Conclusion: Toward Maritime Order

The pattern of behavior revealed in this book is not consistent with that between two states seeking to amicably settle their differences and move toward a brighter future. There is a considerable amount of distrust between China and Japan that crosses economic, strategic, political, and cultural ties. Nevertheless, the two countries' demonstrated willingness to engage in brinkmanship, while avoiding escalation to war, implies that they are in fact capable of coexisting in the narrow confines of maritime East Asia. Perhaps the best way to view the China–Japan maritime relationship is as a process of building a maritime order. Beijing and Tokyo are engaging in an implicit negotiation over the formal and informal rules of conduct with regard to their contested maritime spaces.[146] In the period since the 2010 collision, the two sides have been trying to establish a status quo that reflects their preference for their maritime environment. The two have a track record of cooperation over the challenges that arise from their competing jurisdictional claims. These have been only moderately successful in some cases, yet have been able to prevent conflict.

If a trade-off such as that outlined above is out of the question, the outcome is likely the continuation of the complex pattern of interaction and signaling between China and Japan as to how far each can push the boundaries in their contested maritime space. Is an explicit agreement on the norms and rules of maritime behavior possible? Given the bevy of confrontations between Chinese and Japanese maritime assets, a formal understanding on acceptable behavior seems unlikely. However, informal agreements have mitigated the effects of some of the toughest issues in Sino-Japanese relations in the past. Indeed, one needs look no farther than Deng Xiaoping's modus vivendi on the Senkaku/Diaoyu Islands that underwrote the relative stability in the East China Sea until 2002. Beyond the maritime domain, the Yasukuni Shrine issue has been at peace since 2006 because Japanese leaders became aware that the issue was causing considerable damage to the advancement of the bilateral relationship. The consensus that sitting prime ministers should not visit Yasukuni is fragile, and if Japanese perceptions of China continue to deteriorate, it may yet again emerge as a salient issue in the bilateral relationship. Yet perhaps these informal agreements about agreed-on standards of behavior are the best that can be hoped for in a relationship plagued by unsettled historical issues, shifting power dynamics, and perceptions of competition. Interactions on dispute management resumed less than two months after the 2012 nationalization of the Senkaku/Diaoyu Islands.

Shared jurisdiction, perhaps as part of a broader maritime order, is a peaceful way forward for the Sino-Japanese maritime relationship. The sovereignty of the Senkaku/Diaoyu Islands and the delimitation of the East China Sea will likely remain disputed because neither will be depoliticized. Japanese leaders have little incentive to pursue delimitation because they are aware that China's claim to an extended continental shelf, and Chinese sovereignty over the Senkaku/Diaoyu Islands, would limit Japan's EEZ claim in the East China Sea.[147] Third-party arbitration is therefore as unlikely as unilateral renunciation or bilateral negotiations on delimitation. But a functioning maritime order could establish a status quo that satisfies the bulk of each party's territorial objectives, thereby averting future crises.

Notes

1. Sasakawa, "Why Is an Ocean Policy Think Tank Required Now?"; Kisugi and Nakahara, "To Everyone Involved with the Ocean from the Newsletter Editorial Committee."

2. For a more complete history of Marine Day, see "Marine Day and the Basic Ocean Law." See also "Japan Celebrates its Oceans," *The Economist*, July 19, 2010.

3. "Gov't Panel Eyes Unification of Marine Policies," *Yomiuri Shimbun*, December 6, 2006; "Basic Sea Law Set to Unify Ocean Policies," *Yomiuri Shimbun*, July 21, 2007.

4. "Diet Passes Bills to Protect Japan EEZ," *Asahi Shimbun*, April 21, 2007; author interview "Q."

5. "Basic Law of the Sea," *Japan Times*, May 29, 2007. This was corroborated by a bureaucrat seconded to the Ocean Policy Headquarters in 2011.

6. In particular, MLIT officials are seen to be hawkish on China, while MOFA officials are not. Author interview "Q."

7. Government of Japan, *Law on the Exclusive Economic Zone and the Continental Shelf* (Law No. 74 of 1996), article 3(1).

8. "Japan to Establish Law Aimed at Cracking Down on Suspicious Ships," Kyodo News, February 26, 2008; Okuwaki, "Basic Act on Ocean Policy and Japan's Agenda for Legislative Improvement," 181–83; "Coast Guard Enhancements OK'd," Kyodo News, February 29, 2012.

9. Hughes, *Japan's Security Agenda*, 171; Samuels, "'New Fighting Power!,'" 110.

10. See the collected opinions given by Hue and Suzuki, "Japan to Revise Mining Law, Seeking $3.6 Trillion in Undersea Resources."

11. "Japan Plans to Tighten Controls on Mineral Resources with Law Change," Associated Press, March 10, 2011.

12. "Bill Eyed to Ban EEZ Exploration," Kyodo News, October 28, 2010.

13. Government of Japan, *Basic Plan on Ocean Policy*, 30.

14. Quoted in "'50 Mine Law Update Eyed to Tap Seabed," *Japan Times*, March 9, 2011.

15. Author interview "Y," July 27, 2011, Tokyo.

16. Author interview "V."

17. Conversations with Japanese officials, Tokyo, June and July 2011.

18. Author interview "Q."

19. Drifte, "Politics of the East China Sea Gas Dispute," 15.

20. Author interviews "Q" and "S"; Sakamoto, "Japan–China Dispute over Maritime Boundary Delimitation," 103.

21. Author interview "T," July 4, 2011, Tokyo. This is supported by an informal poll the author conducted before delivering remarks on this subject at Temple University Japan, in Tokyo on July 19, 2011.

22. Author interview "Z."

23. Author interview "T." See also MOFA, "Japan–China Foreign Ministers' Meeting (Summary)."

24. JDA, "National Defense Program Guidelines for FY 2005–2009," 8–9; Samuels, *Securing Japan*, 168–69.

25. JDA, *Defense of Japan 2004,* 118; JDA, *Defense of Japan,* 67.

26. Yoshihara and Holmes, "Japanese Maritime Thought," 38; Fouse, "Japan's FY 2005 National Defense Program Outline," 3.

27. MOD, *Summary of National Defense Program Guidelines, FY 2011.*

28. "With Eye on China, Defense Ministry to Bolster Southern Flank," *Nihon Keizai Shimbun,* October 9, 2007; "Info Gathering Boost Eyed for East China Sea," *Yomiuri Shimbun,* October 24, 2006.

29. Doi, "Japan to Keep Closer Watch Over Its Skies." This is a sensitive issue in Japan because Japanese forces were apparently unaware of a Ming-class submarine transiting the Osumi Strait in 2003 and had to be alerted by US forces. "Protecting Japan, Part III: China Winning Undersea War," *Yomiuri Shimbun,* June 9, 2004.

30. MOD, *Defense of Japan 2010,* 152; "Government Plans to Cut GSDF Quota to 154,000 Members," Kyodo News, December 13, 2010; Fackler, "With Its Eye on China, Japan Builds Up Military"; Katsumata and Yoshimura, "Upgrade of Brigade Targets China Threat."

31. "Beefed Up Okinawa Border Eyed," Kyodo News, July 20, 2010.

32. This argument does not necessarily support the argument that Japan is pursuing a more "normal" security policy. The shifts noted above are limited to China when considered in the context of overall Japanese security policy. See Oros, *Normalizing Japan.*

33. Mochizuki, "Japan's Shifting Strategy toward the Rise of China," 754.

34. Katsumata, "Defense Bills Waste of Time until Constitution Debated."

35. Woolley, *Japan's Navy*; Sakuja, "Japanese Maritime Self-Defense Force," 807–19; Pekkanen and Kraus, "Japan's "Coalition of the Willing,'"" 429–44.

36. MOD, *Defense of Japan 2010,* 62.

37. Ibid.; "China: Ships Near Disputed Islands Were on Patrol," Associated Press, December 9, 2008.

38. "Surveying? Encroaching Chinese Ships Circled Uotsuri Island One and a Half Times, Probably Entered from Coast Guard Blind Spot," *Sankei Shimbun,* December 22, 2008.

39. Bush, *Perils of Proximity,* 73–75.

40. Ibid., 74.

41. "China Boats Enter Water off Senkakus," *Yomiuri Shimbun,* August 25, 2011.

42. Toshiyuki, "Can JGSDF Operate as Marine?"

43. Author interview "C."

44. Author interview "G."

45. The United States has long been ambivalent about the role of the Senkaku/Diaoyu Islands and the East China Sea dispute in the United States–Japan alliance. Recall the confusion following Walter Mondale's comments in 1996 that the United States' stance on the disputed islands was similar to its security guarantee to Taiwan (strategic ambiguity). The State Department did not comment on the issue, but Assistant Secretary of Defense Kurt Campbell stated unequivocally that the alliance did cover the islands while on a visit to Japan. See Dumbaugh et al., *China's Maritime Territorial Claims,* 24–28.

46. "Japan Condemns China's Copter's Approach to MSDF Destroyer," Kyodo News, March 29, 2011.

47. Kumagai, "Japan Looks to Offshore Methane Hydrates to Cut Reliance on Energy Imports."

48. "New Maritime Laws Well Overdue," *Yomiuri Shimbun*, April 21, 2007.

49. "PGS to Sell Seismic Ship to Japan Government," Reuters, March 26, 2007.

50. "Abe Pauses on Senkakus Postings," Kyodo News, December 23, 2012.

51. See "US Fudges Senkaku Security Pact Status," Kyodo News, August 17, 2010.

52. Christensen, "Advantages of an Assertive China," 59.

53. Wu, "China in 2010," 29; Economy and Segal, "G2 Mirage," 14–23; Brown and Hsing, *Trying to Read the New "Assertive" China Right*; Swaine, "Perceptions of an Assertive China." For a critical assessment, see Johnston, "How New and Assertive Is China's New Assertiveness?" 7–48.

54. Shambaugh, "China Engages Asia," 64–99; Kurlantzick, *Charm Offensive.*

55. See Hughes, "Reclassifying Chinese Nationalism," 601–20.

56. Tiberghien, "Diaoyu Crisis of 2010," 70–78.

57. Guo, "China Protests over Sea Collision."

58. Fu, "Be Vigilant against the Danger of Neo-Militarism in Japan."

59. Reilly, *Strong Society, Smart State*; Stockmann, "Who Believes Propaganda?" 269–89.

60. Hughes, "Japan in the Politics of Chinese Leadership Legitimacy," 245–66; Reilly, "China's Online Nationalism toward Japan," 45–72.

61. Author interview "O." See also Kawasaki, "Widening Anti-Japan Protests Centered in Inland Areas"; and Saeki, "China Readies for Diplomatic Warfare."

62. On new actors in the making of Chinese foreign policy, see Jakobson and Knox, *New Foreign Policy Actors in China.*

63. See Cheung, "Influence of the Gun," 61–90; and Swaine, "Chinese Decision Making regarding Taiwan," 289–336.

64. Author interview "U," Tokyo, July 4, 2011.

65. Pomfret, "Dispute with Japan Highlights China's Foreign-Policy Power Struggle."

66. Li, "Evolution of China's Naval Strategy and Capabilities," 144–69.

67. State Council of the People's Republic of China, *China's National Defense in 2006.*

68. Zhang, "China Adjusts Its Maritime Power Strategy at the Right Moment."

69. Chen, "Effectively Cope with the New Rivalry for Sea Power in the Peripheral Areas"; Xiao, "Claimant Countries Concerned in the Nansha Dispute Seeking to Capture Sea Areas by Force Triggers Arms Race."

70. "Imperative for China to Break Out of the 'First Island Chain,'" *Wen Wei Po*, June 20, 2011.

71. "CPC Central Committee's Proposal on Formulating the 12th Five-Year Program on National Economic and Social Development," Xinhua News, October 30, 2010.

72. "China: Measures Aim to Bolster Control of Maritime Interests," *OSC Analysis*, May 31, 2007.

73. Yang, "China's New Maritime Interests."

74. State Oceanic Administration, *China National Offshore Development Report 2011.*

75. Hille, "Hu Calls for China to Be 'Maritime Power'."

76. Chia and Ma, "'Defense Presence' Should Be Built Up to Protect Maritime Rights."

77. Goldstein, "Chinese Coast Guard Development," 6.

78. Masuda et al., *NIDS China Security Report 2012.*

79. ICG, "Stirring up the South China Sea (I)."

80. Ma, "China Marine Surveillance Maneuvers Multi-Pronged Approaches Protecting Its Maritime Rights; Yang, "China's New Maritime Interests," 2.

81. Jin and Ma, "Stronger Fleet for Fishery Administration."

82. "Summary: JFJB Reporter Boards China Marine Surveillance Ship to Chunxiao Field," *Jiefangjun Bao,* May 25, 2011.

83. Manicom, "Beyond Boundary Disputes," 46–53.

84. Thayer, "China's New Wave of Aggressive Assertiveness in the South China Sea"; Schofield and Storey, *South China Sea Dispute.*

85. Author interview "R"; Author interview "W," July 13, 2011, Tokyo.

86. Author interview "S."

87. Author interview "U."

88. Gao, "Note on the 2008 Cooperation Consensus between China and Japan," 296.

89. "Japan Watching If China Breached Deal in Disputed Gas Field," *Petroleum World,* December 9, 2009.

90. "Japan Threatens China with Measures If Gas Recovery Accord Violated," ITAR-TASS, January 17, 2010; "Okada Warns China on Gas Drilling Pact," Kyodo News, January 18, 2010.

91. "China Has Sovereignty over Disputed Gas Field, Yang Tells Okada," Associated Press, January 18, 2010.

92. "Edano Slams Reported China Drilling in Gas Field," Kyodo News, March 8, 2011; Yamaguchi, "Japan Protests to China over Undersea Gas Drilling."

93. This terminology is important in the Chinese language. *Hézuò kāifā* (cooperative development) implies one party participating in the project of another, while *Gòngtóng fāzhǎn* (joint development) implies that sovereignty is shared between the two parties. "China Emphasizes Sovereignty over Chunxiao Oil and Gas Field, Opposes the Saying of Joint Development," *Zhongguo Xinwen She,* January 19, 2010.

94. Author interview "N," Tokyo, June 17, 2011.

95. Author interview "S."

96. Ibid.

97. Minemura, "China to Establish Permanent Senkaku Patrols"; Feng, "Major General Jin Yinan: Diaoyu Islands Sovereignty Patrols to Normalize"; "China to Boost Surveillance Flights over Disputed East China Sea Areas," Kyodo News, January 27, 2012.

98. MOD, *Defense of Japan 2012,* 58–59.

99. Author's total based on calculations from Kyodo News Service.

100. "China Boats Enter Water off Senkakus," *Yomiuri Shimbun,* August 25, 2011.

101. "China Set to Increase Patrols over Disputed Senkaku Islands," Kyodo News, March 20, 2012; "PRC FM Spokesman: Activities of Patrol Boats Located Near Islands 'Lawful,'" Xinhua News, March 16 2012.

102. "Chinese Boats Enter Waters off Senkakus / Gov't Protests Intrusion to Beijing Envoy," *Yomiuri Shimbun*, July 12, 2012.

103. This has been the Chinese characterization of these activities since the first time Chinese vessels entered the territorial sea in December 2008. See MFA, "Foreign Ministry Spokesman Liu Jianchao's Remarks on Chinese Marine Surveillance Ships Entering the Waters near the Diaoyu Islands."

104. Hille and Nakamoto, "China Raises Stakes over Disputed Islands"; "China Has Seized Diaoyu Momentum," *Global Times*, October 31. 2012; "Chinese Intruders Tell Coast Guard to Get Out," Kyodo News, October 31, 2012.

105. "China to Boost Surveillance Flights over Disputed East China Sea Areas," Kyodo News, January 27, 2012.

106. "China Raises Dispute over Senkakus into Airspace Above," *Asahi Shimbun*, December 14, 2012. See also "Navy Fleet Returns from West Pacific Training," Xinhua News, December 11, 2012; and Yang, "PLA Warships in Drill near Diaoyu Waters."

107. Chinese MFA, "Foreign Ministry Spokesperson Hong Lei's Regular Press Conference on October 31, 2012."

108. "Diaoyu Islands Enters a New Stage," *Global Times*, December 14, 2012.

109. "JCG Stretched Thin over Senkakus," *Yomiuri Shimbun*, October 4, 2012; "Coast Guard Worried about Prolonged Senkaku Row," NHK, October 29, 2012.

110. "Japan to Establish 'Senkaku Unit' to Deal with China's Provocations in the Sea," *Sankei Shimbun*, December 24, 2012; "Chinese Ships Seen in Disputed Waters for First Time since LDP's Win," Agence France-Presse, December 21, 2012,

111. Goldstein, *Five Dragons Stirring Up the Sea*, 19.

112. "Unless the Prime Minister Protests over the Chinese Survey Vessel, It Will Create Problems for the Future," *Sankei Shimbun*, May 11, 2010.

113. "Chinese Vessel Asks Survey Ship to Stop," Kyodo News, September 12, 2010; "Chinese Ship Asks Japan Ship to Stop Surveys Amid Tense Row, Agence France-Press, September 11, 2010; "China Again Seeks Halt of Japan's Marine Research off Okinawa," Kyodo News, February 29, 2012.

114. "China Expels Japanese Survey Boats," Xinhua News, February 22, 2012.

115. "Chinese Navy Helicopter Circles MSDF Ship Again," *Mainichi Shimbun*, April 22, 2010.

116. See, respectively, Luo, "Regular Training on the High Seas Organized by the Chinese Navy Poses No Threat to Other Countries"; and "Japan Says Chinese Submarines, Ships Seen Near Okinawa."

117. Watanabe, "Four Chinese Warships Pass through Waters off Okinawa"; Dickie and Hille, "Japan Protests over China Military Incident."

118. The fact that these drills often occur within the EEZ of Okinotorishima is seen by some as evidence of China's rejection of Japan's claim that this rock is entitled to an EEZ. See Yoshikawa, "Okinotorishima: Just the Tip of the Iceberg," 2; and Hiramatsu, "Aim of the Chinese Submarine in Waters near Japan."

119. "Japan to Monitor Chinese Navy Vessels Near Okinawa," Kyodo News, June 10 2011; "China Warships Pass," Kyodo News, November 24 2011; Cole, "Chinese Navy Vessels Spotted Close to Japanese Coast"; Ng, "Chinese Warships Cross Waters Near Japan's Okinawa Islands"; Minemura, "China Taunts Japan with 'Aircraft Carrier' Exercise."

120. "Chinese Ship Asks Japan Ships to Stop Surveys amid Tense Row," Agence France-Presse, September 11, 2010.

121. Author interview "X," July 27, 2011, Tokyo.

122. Till, "The Navies of the Asia-Pacific in a Revolutionary Age," 36. Till does not distinguish between the limited sovereignty states exercise over the territorial sea and jurisdiction over the EEZ. For an analysis of this issue, see Kim, *Maritime Delimitation and Interim Arrangements*, 72–74.

123. Quoted by Huang, "Rough Waves in China's Territorial Seas."

124. Author interviews "I" and "N."

125. Sakai, "First Negotiations Held for Gas Field Deliberations but No Clear Outlook for Final Decision."

126. Przystup, "Japan–China Relations: Troubled Waters," 8.

127. "China Urges Reviving Sea Boundary Talks," Kyodo News, November 29, 2011.

128. Ma, "Meeting Signals Improved Ties"; "Japan, China officials Discuss North Korea, East China Sea Gas Project," *Mainichi Shimbun*, January 31, 2011.

129. "Matsumoto, Yang Address Sea Spats," Kyodo News, July 5, 2011.

130. "'Full Text' of PRC-Japan Joint Press Communiqué on Liang Guanglie-Kitazawa Talks," Xinhua Domestic Service, November 27, 2009; "China, Japan Plan First Joint Military Exercise," Reuters, November 27, 2009. This section draws on data published by James Przystup, John Bradford, and James Manicom, "Japan–China Maritime Confidence-Building and Communications Mechanisms."

131. Kurashige and Minemura, "Japan, China to Finally Enter Gas Field Talks."

132. "Beijing Proposes Maritime Measures," Kyodo News, August 15, 2010. There is some dispute as to whether the hotline would be between political or military leaders.

133. "Japan, China Defense Chiefs Agree on Liaison Mechanism to Avoid Conflicts," Kyodo News, October 12, 2010.

134. "Noda, Wen Unite on Keeping Koreas Stable," Kyodo News, December 26, 2011.

135. Shen and Chen, "Chinese 'Haixun 21' Carries Out Preparations for Going to Japan for Rescue Efforts."

136. "China Denies Helicopter Flying Too Close to Japanese Destroyer," Xinhua News, March 31, 2011.

137. "Hotline with China Eyed to Avoid Clashes at Isles," Kyodo News, July 28, 2012; "China's Brooding Dragons Complicate Standoffs at Sea," *Sentaku*, translated by *Japan Times*, June 12, 2012.

138. Zhang, "Beijing, Tokyo Agree to Hold Second Rounds of Maritime Consultations Later This Year."

139. "Diplomats Met Secretly in Shanghai," Kyodo News, October 25, 2012, Westlake, "Secret Meetings Held in Shanghai between China, Japan Officials";

"Chinese Foreign Ministry Official Visits Japan to Negotiate Diaoyu Island Dispute," *Zhongguo Xinwen She,* October 11, 2012.

140. Drifte, "Future of the Japanese–Chinese Relationship," 72.

141. Dujarric, "Japan's Territorial Claims Are Detrimental to Its National Interests"; Dujarric, "Enhancing Japan's Position in the Senkaku Dispute."

142. Author interview "U." This sanguine view was echoed by a member of a Japanese think tank; author interview "W."

143. Iida et al., *NIDS China Security Report,* 35–36.

144. Author interview "K," June 12, 2011, Tokyo.

145. "Dragons Unite," *The Economist,* March 16, 2013.

146. For a discussion of the term "order," see Alagappa, "Study of International Order," 33–69.

147. Author interview "S."

Conclusion

Building Maritime Order in the East China Sea

DESPITE PERIODS of severe tension, the evidence presented in this book suggests that China and Japan are quite capable of managing the tensions that arise from their contested sovereignty and jurisdiction in the East China Sea. Beijing and Tokyo have repeatedly articulated some kind of consensus on a point of difference and, however briefly, have adjusted their behavior in accord with the actual or anticipated preferences of the other party. As illustrated by the MVM, in each instance this point of consensus has addressed only one dimension of disputed space and has left the others unresolved. This reluctance to pursue deeper, binding cooperation can be explained by the different functions that each dimension of disputed space performs for state leaders. As the dispute has progressed, different aspects of disputed maritime space have become more important to the leaders of both countries. Nevertheless, grounds for optimism remain because the two sides engage in a familiar pattern of guarded crisis behavior followed by cooperative interactions on issues of discord.

The sources of Sino-Japanese tensions over maritime space lie in the two parties' shifting interpretations of their preferred status quo in the East China Sea, their reference point. This status was typically challenged by virtue of China's emergence as a maritime power. Tacit cooperation over the disputed Senkaku/Diaoyu Islands—in the form of Deng Xiaoping's 1978 modus vivendi and the post-1996 agreement not to be provoked by nationalist groups—collapsed as both parties perceived efforts by the other to alter this understanding. By contrast, challenges to the reference point galvanized cooperative action over the jurisdictional aspects of the East China Sea dispute. In 1995–96, China's emergence as a fisheries power threatened the future of the Japanese offshore fisheries industry and exposed the challenges associated with the delimitation of the East China

Sea. In the years 1999–2000, China's marine survey and military training activities heralded the beginning of a more active Chinese presence in the seas near Japan. Finally, between 2003 and 2008, China's efforts to develop natural gas resources at the Chunxiao gas field raised concerns in Japan about "resources theft" and accentuated the urgency of the exercise of jurisdiction in contested maritime space.

In the latter three cases, Japan pursued a cooperative strategy once the Chinese challenge created a set of circumstances that altered Japan's interpretation of its reference point for a given jurisdictional issue in the East China Sea. In the case of fisheries and marine surveys, Japanese policy was determined by existing path dependencies until acted upon by actors outside the central policymaking apparatus. In the case of resources development, Tokyo's reaction was driven from the center as a consequence of the centralization of Japan's China policy under Prime Minister Koizumi and a growing awareness of the challenge that China presented in the waters around Japan. Following each Japanese "awakening," Tokyo attempted to convince Beijing to alter its behavior in a fashion amenable to Japanese interests, which Beijing reciprocated. Cooperation, it seems, follows crisis.

Cooperation in the East China Sea Dispute

The cooperative track record between China and Japan in the East China Sea belies the expectation that the two countries are teetering on the brink of war over their disputed maritime space. Rather, there are grounds for optimism, despite the deterioration of the maritime relationship since September 2010, even as Japan loosens the restrictions on the exercise of its maritime jurisdiction.

Island Sovereignty

Cooperation over the Senkaku/Diaoyu Islands was achieved by establishing an informal set of circumstances under which China and Japan could pursue their wider diplomatic prerogatives. Due to the contested-symbolic sensitivity of this issue, cooperation could only ever be tacit. Deng's modus vivendi, articulated in 1978, underwrote stability for two and a half decades. Chinese and Japanese elites frequently reminded each other of the validity of Deng's modus vivendi during times of crisis over the disputed islands. Cooperation endured because Japanese leaders, such as Prime Minister

Miyazawa, framed their crisis management efforts in a way that recognized their interest in the status quo. However, in a change that was indicative of the fragile nature of tacit cooperation, the consensus began to erode in 2002 amid a deteriorating bilateral relationship in which China perceived Japan to be altering the basis of the agreement by consolidating its hold over the islands. China has subsequently increased its presence near the islands, and it has established a near-permanent presence in the islands' territorial sea in an effort to undermine Japan's claim. That these vessels are agents of the state rather than secondary political actors, like nationalist groups, indicates that Beijing seeks to take the policy initiative away from nationalist groups and exercise its sovereign prerogative to defend "maritime rights and interests." This in turn acts as a legitimizing tool for the CCP.

In the wake of the 1996 crisis, officials also agreed not to be provoked by nationalist groups. This tacit cooperation also relied on signaling—as Prime Minister Koizumi did by releasing detained Chinese nationalists in 2004—that each party interpreted the consensus to be binding. However, like its predecessor, this agreement collapsed as crises triggered by the broader maritime relationship undermined each party's perception that the other was committed to cooperation. This case is indicative of the difficulty of cooperating over the contested-symbolic dimensions of maritime space. Prime Minister Noda's decision to nationalize the islands in 2012, rather than allow them to be purchased by Ishihara, further illustrates the end of this trend. Chinese leaders dismissed the efforts of the nationalist politician Nishimura Shingo to land on the islands in 1997, but they chose not to ignore the provocation from a Japanese nationalist in September 2012. The experience of cooperation over the islands seems to support hypothesis H2 (see chapter 1), that cooperation over contested-symbolic issues will be reciprocal, but informal and fragile.

Fisheries

China's emergence as a fisheries power challenged Japan's reference point as the dominant fisheries state in East Asia. Fishing by an increasingly capable, and unregulated, Chinese industry threatened Japan's offshore fisheries industry, which had become more vital to Japan following the decline of its distant water counterpart. The Japanese fisheries lobby convinced Tokyo to ratify UNCLOS and declare an EEZ, which was necessary to extend Japanese authority over its offshore areas. From the Chinese standpoint, although it stood to lose from the application of fishery regulations to Japanese coastal waters, its primary aim was the delimitation of the maritime boundary with Japan. When this proved impossible, Chinese policymakers proceeded because establishing jurisdiction supported efforts to gain some recognition of China's enormous maritime claims and enshrine some sense of the favorable fisheries status quo. Shared interests over an economic issue, fisheries resources, proved sufficient for reaching an agreement. Policymakers were able to sidestep the strategic aspect of the disputed Senkaku/Diaoyu Islands because of the precedent set by previous fisheries agreements. Bargaining efforts were supported by the forty-two-year relationship between the two sides on fisheries issues. This case seems to support hypothesis H1, that cooperation over economic issues will be reciprocal, formal, and enduring.

Marine Surveys

In February 2001, China and Japan agreed to notify one another when conducting marine research in "waters of concern" to the other. In practice the agreement was designed to address more frequent Chinese activity in Japan's waters, in the form of both marine research activities and naval activities. Similar to the case of the fisheries agreement, domestic political pressure—from the defense sector, the media, and public opinion—played an important role in alerting policymakers to the shifting status quo in the East China Sea. However, whereas Japan sought new international legal tools to address fisheries issues—by ratifying UNCLOS—its options vis-à-vis Chinese vessels were limited by domestic constraints. Combined with the nature of China's maritime claim and the type of activities in which its vessels were engaged, shortcomings in Japanese law made a more assertive stance impossible. Japanese leaders thus used ODA pressure, a coercive approach, to encourage their Chinese counterparts to address the survey issue. That this resulted in little real cooperation supports hypothesis H3, that cooperation over strategic issues will be coercive, informal, and short-lived. In the words of the MVM, strategic issues, such as the costs of conceding jurisdiction, and concerns over military freedom of operation prevented cooperation over China's activities.

Resource Development

No other aspect of the maritime relationship reinforced the perception in Japan that its maritime environment had undergone a dramatic shift as much as the Chunxiao gas field issue. Like previous cases, there existed a climate within Japan that called for action on the issue of Chinese resource development in the East China Sea. The central government was quick to involve itself, and policy was directed from the Prime Minister's Office and METI. Following Chinese intransigence through 2004, as in the case of marine research, Japanese leaders attempted to coerce a change in Chinese behavior by conducting surveys and by threatening to drill in the disputed area. Beijing reciprocated Japan's overtures when it calculated that doing so would allow it to enshrine some aspect of the status quo in the East China Sea and improve relations with Japan. A favorable status quo was one that allowed China to exploit resources on its side of the median line, and prevented unilateral resource development by Japan. Following Koizumi's ultimatum and Japan's efforts to remove the institutional and legal limits on EEZ drilling in 2007, Beijing broke the two-year deadlock in negotiations by offering to be flexible on the median line. However, the implementation of the 2008 consensus has been impeded by the contested-symbolic and strategic dimensions of the disputed space. The contested-symbolic dimension—evidenced by the anticipated audience costs incurred through compromise with an "other"—has delayed implementation of the agreement. Furthermore, both sides are concerned about the strategic implications of the consensus for their maritime claims.

The very existence of a cooperative track record speaks to Beijing's and Tokyo's capacity to manage their differences. However, all agreements have only addressed the acute issues involved and have left the underlying sovereignty and delimitation issues unresolved. All three were driven by a desire somewhere within the Japanese state for action on a perceived challenge from China; China's reciprocity was a function of whether it perceived a favorable postcooperation status quo.

Empirical Patterns

The case studies reveal four empirical patterns that shed light on the future of cooperation in the East China Sea. First, Japan's response to China's maritime challenges has become progressively more centralized, as Japan has become a more "maritime-oriented" state. Early reactions typically originated outside the central policymaking apparatus, either on the part of bureaucracy or in response to public opinion and media pressure. Concomitantly, Japanese leaders have become progressively less "reactive" when faced with Chinese challenges to their reference point.[1]

Tokyo's resistance to the EEZ regime shifted following pressure from the fisheries lobby. Japan's use of coercive diplomacy to convince China to negotiate on the marine survey issue reflected a shift in Japanese bureaucratic attitudes toward China. By contrast, Tokyo's reaction to the discovery of the drilling platform at Chunxiao in 2004 was led from the center from the beginning, particularly by Nakagawa and Koizumi, and was supported by the media and popular opinion. Resisting China in the East China Sea is now a widely held foreign policy preference that was illustrated by the near-national consensus on this issue in Japan's lower house election in 2012.[2] Candidates disagreed on appropriate strategies for resisting China, not on the issue of whether resisting China is a sound policy choice. This belies expectations that Japan will continue or has ever been compliant vis-à-vis China in the East China Sea dispute.[3]

Second, once driven to act, Japan typically adopted a coercive posture vis-à-vis China if reciprocity was not immediately forthcoming. Coercive cooperation represents the limits of Japan's ability to directly influence Chinese behavior because Japanese constitutional limitations undermine the credibility of threats to use force. However, as illustrated in chapter 6, these have loosened in recent years. Chapter 5 argues that these shifts increased the credibility of Japan's threats to China, which coerced Chinese cooperation. Nevertheless, structural barriers to Japanese coercion remain. No institutional reform can change the fact that the most economical way for a Japanese company to access the East China Sea's gas is to buy it from China. Early signs from the Abe government are that Japan is considering a number of ways to assert itself, up to and including constitutional revision.[4]

Third, China's acceptance of Japan's terms was a product of its efforts to defend its own reference point. Cooperation over the Senkaku/Diaoyu Islands supported China's efforts to keep the issues sidelined to focus on other priorities. As it became a more active maritime power, China's adherence to Deng's modus vivendi ended when it perceived Japanese efforts to consolidate its hold over the disputed islands. By agreeing to renegotiate the fisheries order to reflect the new EEZ regime, Beijing ensured that UNCLOS, which provided the basis for China's extensive maritime claims, became the building block of the regional maritime order. In particular this order included its preferred method of claiming maritime space: natural prolongation. Using UNCLOS's language, as well as that contained within its own reservations upon ratification, China has claimed jurisdiction in waters as far as the Okinawa Trough, has challenged American interpretations of freedom of navigation, and has denied Japanese claims that selected rock formations in the Pacific Ocean are entitled to the full complement of maritime zones.[5] By articulating its understanding of the Law of the Sea, Beijing can claim the moral high ground while barely adjusting the behavior criticized by Japan. By incorporating the median line into the 2008 JDZ, Beijing has effectively shelved the basis for Japanese criticism of its resource exploitation activities. Furthermore, it has been able to continue its maritime expansion in other ways.

Fourth, cooperation was more successful when negotiations were lengthy and covered multiple levels of government. A greater frequency and depth of interactions were consistent with more robust cooperative agreements. All cooperative outcomes were the product of differing degrees of interaction. The deepest and most long standing was the fisheries dispute. Interaction had occurred over a fifty-year period, and had often occurred independently of government. Consequently, it is hardly surprising that the fisheries agreement has been the most successful of the three.[6] By comparison, the notification agreement was concluded following two rounds of talks, and has been a spectacular failure. The fisheries agreement is a formal treaty, whereas the notification agreement is a *note verbale.* By this logic there are grounds for optimism about the 2008 consensus on resource development; it was preceded by concerted efforts by bureaucratic-level actors to pursue a cooperative solution to the Chunxiao issue, independent of the official freeze on bilateral contact. Chinese and Japanese director-general-level negotiators met eleven times, and lower-level bureaucrats had working group meetings on legal issues, resource development and greater transparency between civilian maritime agencies. Once a breakthrough was achieved, senior-level interactions became more frequent and more positive, beginning with ministerial meetings in Beijing in early December 2007. Senior cabinet and executive meetings on the issue occurred six times subsequently en route to the announcement of the declaration in June 2008. Chinese and Japanese leaders remained rhetorically committed to implementing the agreement until the deterioration of the maritime relationship in September 2010, which has been driven by prominence of the "relational" features of contested space, sidelined this agreement.

The pattern of behavior supports the observation that crisis breeds cooperation. There are grounds for optimism that policymakers in both countries recognize the value of cooperation. As outlined in chapter 6, Japanese and Chinese leaders have repeatedly pursued high-level dialogue on outstanding maritime issues, including resource development and establishing a maritime communication mechanism, despite a deteriorating bilateral relationship. Even in the wake of the 2012 crisis, Japanese and Chinese officials held working-level discussions in Shanghai and Beijing in an effort to find clarity and maintain an open channel of communication.[7] The case for cautious optimism rests therefore on the pattern of cooperation that has defined past interaction at sea. Although cooperation has been only moderately successful at mitigating tensions that stem from unsettled boundary delimitation, it has successfully defused crises and averted escalation. Chapter 6 outlined a potential trade-off, whereby both China and Japan could be satisfied with the status quo in the East China Sea.

The Value of Space and the Durability of Cooperation

The salience of maritime space offers insights into the limits on cooperation. In three of the four cases, cooperation was severely limited by the relational aspects of the disputed maritime space. Although it lasted for more than two decades, cooperation on the Senkaku/Diaoyu Islands was weak due to the purely contested-symbolic nature of the issue. All remaining agreements contained at least some tangible quality—fisheries, marine surveys, and hydrocarbons—which can be shared, at least in theory. Neither instance of tacit cooperation vis-à-vis sovereignty over the Senkaku/Diaoyu Islands survived a serious test. Although Beijing did not explicitly articulate a strategy to create a new status quo until after the 2012 crisis over the islands, Beijing perceived subtle shifts by Japan beginning in 2002 as just such an effort. Chinese sources celebrate the fact that although China did not trigger the 2012 crisis, it was able to exploit that opportunity to increase its physical presence near the Senkaku/Diaoyu Islands.[8] This occurred despite the fact that Japan's efforts to consolidate its hold over the islands since 2002 could reasonably be explained as an effort to keep Japanese nationalists off the islands and reduce tensions. This was strikingly revealed during the 2012 crisis, when it appeared that Chinese officials either could not comprehend or did not care that Japan's nationalization was an effort to keep the islands out of the hands of Japan's most controversial nationalist figure. In light of the prominence of political symbolism in Sino-Jananese relations, that there was any cooperation over the islands at all is a testament to the collective will of Chinese and Japanese leaders to manage their differences.

Strategic issues have witnessed the weakest degree of cooperation. The notification agreement failed to modify Chinese behavior for more than six months because China determined that to have abided by the agreement would have sacrificed its longer-term objectives in the strategically vital waters around Japan. Despite a more formal cooperative arrangement, efforts to negotiate the treaty to implement the 2008 consensus have failed due to concerns in China that the agreement undermines its claims to the wider East China Sea because the JDZ straddles the median line, a contested-symbolic and strategic concern. The latter indicates the conflation of tangible and intangible aspects of disputed space. Chinese leaders agreed to the JDZ and stressed that it did not undermine their jurisdictional claims. Yet it was the intangible challenge presented by domestic criticism and potential audience costs from compromise with Japan over an issue of national sovereignty that prevented treaty negotiations. In contrast, the fisheries issue and the islands issue were free of strategic concerns and witnessed the longest periods of cooperation. This supports the logic of cooperation illustrated by the spectrum of cooperation outlined in chapter 1. Cooperation is most difficult over strategic issues.

Conclusion

The prospects for sharing the contested jurisdiction in the East China Sea are poor if they become tainted by relational concerns, particularly strategic issues. The findings suggest that the strategic implications of maritime space present the most significant barrier to cooperation. One pathway toward circumventing this problem is to engage in trade-offs between issue areas. As proposed by chapter 6, Japan's interest in East China Sea resources is less about the resource wealth itself and more about the Beijing's recognition of the legitimacy of Japan's entitlement to exercise jurisdiction in its EEZ. Japanese leaders became willing to exploit the East China Sea's resources not because of a change in Japan's energy needs but because they feared a Chinese fait accompli in the disputed space. Beijing and Tokyo are not prepared to settle the resources issue at the expense of their wider claims to the East China Sea. In this context it may be possible for Japan to exchange an aspect of maritime space that is unpopular in China and useless to Japan for greater transparency and better conduct at sea from Chinese vessels. Properly implemented, this could alleviate a major threat to regional security, improve regional energy security, and improve Sino-Japanese maritime relations. Although concerns of Chinese cheating will abound, Japan's progress toward a more assertive posture may be enough to again coerce Chinese compliance with an agreement that satisfies Beijing's reference point in the East China Sea.

Japan should abrogate the 2008 consensus in exchange for improved transparency at sea with Chinese vessels as a first step toward building the recognition that jurisdiction can be shared in contested maritime areas. On the basis of the deepening degree of working-level discussions, it seems that Beijing and Tokyo are aware of this as well. In any event, barring a coherent effort by both parties to address their contested-symbolic attachment to the disputed islands or to ameliorate their deteriorating security relationship, lasting cooperation in the East China Sea will remain elusive. Nevertheless, the track record explored herein suggests that China and Japan are able to manage escalatory pressures through established practices that remove or sidestep issues that are a source of tension.

Notes

1. Manicom, "Japan's Ocean Policy," 307–26. For the original formulation, see Calder, "Japanese Foreign Economic Policy Formation," 519.
2. Ozawa, "Nationalism Rears Head Ahead of Poll"; Nakamoto, "Abe Talks Tough on China before Election"; Cai, "Japanese Candidates Debate China Policy."
3. Dreyer, """Sino-Japanese Territorial and Maritime Disputes," 93.
4. Yoshida, "Senkaku Intrusions Seen as Testing Abe."
5. Manicom, "China's Claims to an Extended Continental Shelf in the East China Sea," 9–11.
6. This agreement was successful compared with other agreements between China and Japan in the East China Sea. This is not an attempt to compare the agreement with other fisheries agreements in Northeast Asia or to weigh its success at achieving a sustainable fisheries industry.
7. "Diplomats Met Secretly in Shanghai," Kyodo News, October 25, 2012.
8. "Diaoyu Islands Enters a New Stage," *Global Times*, December 14, 2012.

Bibliography

Primary Sources

During two field trips in 2008 and 2011, totaling three and a half months, semi-structured interviews were conducted on a not-for-attribution basis with officials and scholars in China and Japan. To ensure candid views, anonymity was promised.

"A," author interview, January 29, 2008, Tokyo.
"B," author interview, February 1, 2008, Tokyo.
"C," author interview, February 4, 2008, Yokohama.
"D," author interview, January 14, 2008, Beijing.
"E," author interview, January 18, 2008, Beijing.
"F," author interview, January 25, 2008, Beijing.
"G," author interview, January 29, 2008, Tokyo.
"H," author interview, January 30, 2008, Tokyo.
"I," author interview, January 15, 2008, Beijing.
"J," author interview, January 24, 2008, Beijing.
"K," author interview, June 13, 2011, Tokyo.
"L," author interview, June 15, 2011, Tokyo.
"M," author interview, June 16, 2011, Tokyo.
"N," author interview, June 17, 2011, Tokyo.
"O," author interview, June 20, 2011, Tokyo.
"P," author interview, June 20, 2011, Tokyo.
"Q," author interview, June 28, 2011, Tokyo.
"R," author interview, June 29, 2011, Tokyo.
"S," author interview, June 30, 2011, Tokyo.
"T," author interview, July 4, 2011, Tokyo.
"U," author interview, July 4, 2011, Tokyo.
"V," author interview, July 8, 2011, Tokyo.
"W," author interview, July 13, 2011, Tokyo.
"X," author interview, July 27, 2011, Tokyo.
"Y," author interview, July 27, 2011, Tokyo.
"Z," author interview, July 28, 2011, Tokyo.

Secondary Sources

"Abe Pauses on Senkakus Postings." Kyodo News, December 23, 2012.

Acharya, Amitav. *Constructing a Security Community in Southeast Asia: ASEAN and the Problem of Regional Order.* London: Routledge, 2001.

Adler, Emanuel, and Michael Barnett. *Security Communities.* Cambridge: Cambridge University Press, 1998.

AFP-Jiji. "Rightwingers Land on Senkakus, Hoist Flags." *Japan Times,* August 20, 2012.

Alagappa, Muthiah. "The Study of International Order: An Analytical Framework." In *Asian Security Order: Instrumental and Normative Features,* edited by Muthiah Alagappa. Stanford, CA: Stanford University Press, 2003.

Akaha, Tsuneo. "A Cybernetic Analysis of Japan's Fishery Policy Process." In *Japan and the New Ocean Regime,* edited by Robert L. Friedheim. Boulder, CO: Westview Press, 1984.

———. "Fishery Relations in Northeast Asia." In *UN Convention on the Law of the Sea and East Asia,* edited by Dalchoong Kim, Choon-ho Park, Seo-Hang Lee, and Jin-Hyun Paik. Seoul: Institute of East and West Studies at Yonsei University, 1996.

———. *Japan in Global Ocean Politics.* Honolulu: University of Hawaii Press and Law of the Sea Institute at University of Hawaii, 1985.

———. "Muddling through Successfully: Japan's Post-War Ocean Policy and Future Prospects." *Marine Policy* 19, no. 3 (1995): 171–83.

Akao, Nobutoshi. "Resources and Japan's Security." In *Japan's Economic Security,* edited by Nobutoshi Akao. New York: St. Martin's Press, 1983.

Akiyama, Masahiro. "Use of Seas and Management of Ocean Space: Analysis of the Policy Making Process for Creating the Basic Ocean Law." *Ocean Policy Studies* no. 5 (2007): 1–28.

Albin, Cecilia. *Justice and Fairness in International Negotiation.* Cambridge: Cambridge University Press, 2001.

Allee, Todd L., and Paul K. Huth. "When Are Governments Able to Reach Negotiated Settlement Agreements? An Analysis of Dispute Resolution in Territorial Disputes, 1919–1985." In *Approaches, Levels and Methods of Analysis in International Politics: Crossing Boundaries,* edited by Harvey Starr. New York: Palgrave Macmillan, 2006.

"Ambassador to China Slams Ishihara's Senkakus Plan." *Japan Times,* June 8, 2012.

Anderson, Benedict. *Imagined Communities: Reflections on the Origin and Spread of Nationalism,* 2nd ed. London: Verso, 1991.

Andrews-Speed, Philip. *Energy Policy and Regulation in the People's Republic of China.* The Hague: Kluwer Law International, 2004.

"Anger Builds over EEZ Violations." *Japan Times,* July 22, 2004.

Anonymous. "China Expects Offshore Production to Buttress Overall Output Target." *Oil & Gas Journal* 99, no. 51 (2001): 58–65.

Anonymous. "China's Upstream Programs Advance Onshore and Offshore." *Oil & Gas Journal* 93, no. 39 (1995): 29–34.

Anonymous. "The East China Sea: The Role of International Law in the Settlement of Disputes." *Duke Law Journal* 1973, no. 4 (1973): 823–65.

Anonymous. "Japanese Energy Policy Focuses on Supply Security." *Oil & Gas Journal* 103, no. 8 (2005): 32–35.

ANRE (Agency for Natural Resources and Energy). *Fiscal 2005 Annual Energy Report (Outline)*. Tokyo: METI, 2006.

———. *New National Energy Strategy (Digest)*. Tokyo: METI, 2006.

Aoki, Naoki. "China Accuses Japan of 'Provocation' Ahead of Machimura Visit." Kyodo News, April 14, 2005.

———. "Japan, China Remain Apart on Gas but Proposal Tabled." Kyodo News, May 31, 2005.

Arase, David. "Japan, the Active State? Security Policy after 9/11." *Asian Survey* 47, no. 4 (2007): 560–83.

———."Japanese ODA Policy toward China: The New Agenda." In *Japan's Relations with China: Facing a Rising Power*, edited by Peng Er Lam. London: Routledge, 2006.

"ASDF Scrambles Up 60% in '05; Chinese Intrusions Jump 8-Fold." *Yomiuri Shimbun*, April 22, 2006.

"Asia and Australasia." *Petroleum Economist*, February 7, 2013.

"Asian Development Bank Approves Loan to Develop Ping Hu Oil/Gasfield in East China Sea." *Petroleum Economist*, February 28, 1996.

Au, Kung-wing. "The East China Sea Issue: Japan-China Talks for Oil and Gas." *East Asia* 25 (2008): 223–41.

Austin, Greg. *China's Ocean Frontier: International Law, Military Force and National Development*. St. Leonards, Australia: Allen & Unwin, 1998.

Austin, Greg, and Stuart Harris. *Japan and Greater China: Political Economy and Military Power in the Asian Century*. London: Hurst & Co., 2001.

Axelrod, Robert. *The Evolution of Cooperation*. New York: Basic Books, 1984.

Axelrod, Robert, and Robert O. Keohane. "Achieving Cooperation under Anarchy: Strategies and Institutions." In *Cooperation under Anarchy*, edited by Kenneth A. Oye. Princeton, NJ: Princeton University Press, 1986.

Bailey, Jennifer L. "States, Stocks and Sovereignty: High Seas Fishing and the Expansion of State Sovereignty." In *Conflict and the Environment*, edited by Nils Petter Gleditsch. Dordrecht: Kluwer Academic Publishers, 1997.

Ball, Desmond. "Arms and Affluence: Military Acquisitions in the Asia-Pacific Region." *International Security* 18, no. 3 (1993–94): 78–112.

"Barring of Diaoyu Offenders 'Unreasonable.'" *China Daily*, October 18, 2006.

"Basic Law of the Sea." *Japan Times*, May 29, 2007.

"Basic Sea Law Set to Unify Ocean Policies." *Yomiuri Shimbun,* July 21, 2007.

Bateman, Sam. "Hydrographic Surveying in the EEZ: Differences and Overlaps with Marine Scientific Research." *Marine Policy* 29, no. 2 (2005): 163–74.

———. "UNCLOS and Its Limitations as the Foundation for a Regional Maritime Security Regime." *Korean Journal of Defense Analysis* 19, no. 3 (2007): 27–56.

"Beefed-Up Okinawa Border Eyed." Kyodo News, July 20, 2010.

Beer, William T., and Tsuneo Watanabe. "Mori Continues to React, Not Lead after Election." *Japan Watch,* September 20, 2000.

Beier, J. Marshall. "Bear Facts and Dragon Boats: Rethinking the Modernization of Chinese Naval Power." *Contemporary Security Policy* 26, no. 2 (2005): 287–316.

"Beijing Proposes Maritime Measures." Kyodo News, August 15, 2010.

"Beijing, Tokyo Scrapping over Territorial Sea Rights." *Mainichi Daily News,* June 10, 1999.

Berejekian, Jeffrey. "The Gains Debate: Framing State Choice." *The American Political Science Review* 91, no. 4, (1997): 789–805.

Berger, Thomas. "Set for Stability? Prospects for Conflict and Cooperation in East Asia." *Review of International Studies* 26, no. 3 (2000): 405–28.

"Bill Eyed to Ban EEZ Exploration." Kyodo News, October 28 2010.

Bin, Shan. "Japan Steps Up Military Expansion at Sea." *Jiefangjun Bao,* February 4, 2002. World News Connection CPP-2002-02-04-000044.

Bitzinger, Richard. "A New Arms Race? The Political Economy of Maritime Military Modernization in the Asia-Pacific." *Economics of Peace and Security Journal* 4, no. 2 (2009): 32–37.

Blanchard, Jean-Marc F. "China's Peaceful Rise and Sino-Japanese Territorial and Maritime Tensions." In *China's "Peaceful Rise" in the 21st Century: Domestic and International Conditions,* edited by Sujian Guo. Aldershot, UK: Ashgate, 2006.

———. "An Island of Friction in a Sea of Problems: China and the Diaoyu (Senkaku) Islands and East China Sea Disputes." Paper presented at Annual Meeting of Association of Chinese Political Studies, San Francisco, July 30–31, 2005.

———. "Linking Border Disputes and War: An Institutionalist-Statist Theory." *Geopolitics* 10, no. 4 (2005): 688–711.

Bong, Youngshik. "Flashpoints at Sea? Legitimization Strategy and East Asian Island Disputes." PhD thesis, University of Pennsylvania, 2002.

BP. *BP Statistical Review of World Energy 2008.* Houston: BP, 2008.

———. *BP Statistical Review of World Energy 2012.* Houston: BP, 2012.

Brooke, James. "For Japan and China, Strains from a Line in the Sea." *New York Times,* April 14, 2005.

Brown, David. *Contemporary Nationalism: Civic, Ethnocultural and Multicultural Politics.* London: Routledge, 2000.

Brown, Kerry, and Loh Su Hsing. *Trying to Read the New "Assertive" China Right.* Chatham House Asia Programme Paper 02. London: Chatham House, 2011.

Bush, Richard C. *Perils of Proximity: China-Japan Security Relations.* Washington, DC: Brookings Institution Press, 2010.

Bussert, James C. "Oil May Be Focal Point of Sino-Japanese Dispute." *Signal* 61, no. 3 (2006): 33–36.

Buszynski, Leszek. *Asia Pacific Security—Values and Identity.* London: Routledge-Curzon, 2003.

Buzan, Barry. *A Sea of Troubles? Sources of Dispute in the New Ocean Regime.* Adelphi Paper 143. London: Oxford University Press for International Institute for Strategic Studies, 1978.

Cai, Hong. "Japanese Candidates Debate China Policy." *China Daily*, November 29, 2012.

Calabrese, John. "In the Shadow of Uncertainty: Japan's Energy Security and Foreign Policy." *Pacific and Asian Journal of Energy* 12, no. 1 (2002): 81–101.

Calder, Kent E. *Asia's Deadly Triangle: How Arms, Energy and Growth Threaten to Destabilize Asia Pacific.* London: Nicholas Brealey, 1996.

———. "China and Japan's Simmering Rivalry." *Foreign Affairs* 85, no. 2 (2006): 129–39.

———. "Coping with Energy Insecurity: China's Response in a Global Perspective." *East Asia*, 23, no. 3 (2006): 49–66.

———. "The Institutions of Japanese Foreign Policy." In *The Process of Japanese Foreign Policy: Focus on Asia*, edited by Robert L. Grant. London: Royal Institute of International Affairs, 1997.

———. "Japanese Foreign Economic Policy Formation: Explaining the Reactive State." *World Politics* 40, no. 4 (1988): 517–41.

"Cancellation of Japan Loan Would Hurt Ties, Says China Paper." Kyodo News, August 28, 2000.

Carlson, Allen. *Unifying China, Integrating with the World: Securing Chinese Sovereignty in the Reform Era.* Stanford, CA: Stanford University Press, 2005.

Chang, Maria Hsia, and Xiaoyu Chen. "The Nationalist Ideology of the Chinese Military." *Journal of Strategic Studies* 21, no. 1 (1998): 44–64.

Chapman, J. W. M. "Energy and Food Security." In *Japan's Quest for Comprehensive Security: Defence, Diplomacy, Dependence*, edited by J. W. M. Chapman, R. Drifte, and I. T. M. Gow. New York: St. Martin's Press, 1982.

Chen, Chunmei, "Use of Oceans Faces Legal Restrictions." *China Daily*, June 26, 1996.

Chen, Stephen. "Anti-Japanese Protesters Assail Beijing's Gas Pact." *South China Morning Post*, June 19, 2008.

Chen, Xiangyang, "Effectively Cope with the New Rivalry for Sea Power in the Peripheral Areas." *Liaowang*, July 24, 2010. World News Connection 201007241477.1_d77302f2191d0d0f.

———. "Judging the New Game of the Diaoyu Islands." *Liaowang*, October 25, 2012. World News Connection 201210251477.1_1d7500e22ed29f1f.

Cheng, Joseph Y. S. "Normalization of Sino-Japanese Relations: China's Bargaining Position regarding the Taiwan Question." *Asia Quarterly*, no. 4 (1980): 245–72.

Cheng, Tao. "The Sino-Japanese Dispute over the Tiao-Yu-Tai (Senkaku) Islands and the Law of Acquisition." *Virginia Journal of International Law* 14, no. 2 (1974): 221–66.

Cheong, Ching. "China–Japan Deal on East China Sea: Tokyo Seen as Having the Upper Hand." *Straits Times*, June 21, 2008.

Cheung, Tai Ming. "The Influence of the Gun: China's Central Military Commission and Its Relationship with the Military, Party and State Decision-Making Systems." In *The Making of Chinese Foreign and Security Policy in the Era of Reform*, edited by David M. Lampton. Stanford, CA: Stanford University Press, 2001.

Cheung, Tai Ming, and Charles Smith. "Rocks of Contention." *Far Eastern Economic Review*, November 1, 1990.

Chia, Lei, and Ma Hao-liang. "'Defense Presence' Should Be Built Up to Protect Maritime Rights." *Ta Kung Pao*, March 8, 2011. World News Connection 201103081477.1_b06605693edee079.

"China Again Seeks Halt of Japan's Marine Research off Okinawa." Kyodo News, February 29, 2012.

"China Allows Rowdy Anti-Japanese Protests." Associated Press, October 18, 2010.

"China Boats Enter Water off Senkakus." *Yomiuri Shimbun*, August 25, 2011.

"China to Boost Surveillance Flights over Disputed East China Sea Areas." Kyodo News, January 27, 2012.

"China Breaks Accord, Conducts Drilling in the 'Kashi' Gas Field in the East China Sea." *Sankei Shimbun*, January 4, 2009. World News Connection 200901041477.1_fd1201d3fa889d32.

"China Bringing Okinawa 'within Range': What Underlies Oilfield Development in the East China Sea." *Sentaku*, January 2006. FBIS JPP-2006-01-13-016001.

China Defence Today. "851 (Dongdiao 232) Electronic Intelligence Ship." www.sinodefence.com/navy/research_survey/851.asp.

———. "Research & Survey Vessels." www.sinodefence.com/navy/research_survey/default.asp.

———. "Type 625c Oceanographic Survey Ship." www.sinodefence.com/navy/research_survey/type625c.asp.

"China Denies Helicopter Flying Too Close to Japanese Destroyer." Xinhua News, March 31, 2011. World News Connection 201103311477.1_14a70035bc2a6283.

"China Does Not Recognize Exclusive Economic Zone Unilaterally Announced by Japan." *Zhongguo Xinwen She*, September 14, 2000. World News Connection FBIS-CHI-2000-0914.

"China Emphasizes Sovereignty over Chunxiao Oil and Gas Field, Opposes the Saying of Joint Development." *Zhongguo Xinwen She*, January 19, 2010. World News Connection 201001191477.1_aec90045b448fe30.

"China Expels Japanese Survey Boats." Xinhua News, February 22, 2012.

"China Has Seized Diaoyu Momentum." *Global Times*, October 31, 2012.

"China Has Sovereignty over Disputed Gas Field, Yang Tells Okada." Associated Press, January 18, 2010.

"China Interferes with Survey of Natural Resource in East China Sea; Transmits Sound Waves and Makes Abnormal Approach." *Sankei Shimbun*, March 28, 2005. World News Connection 2005-03-28-1477.1_031b0076ac301f2d.

"China, Japan Plan First Joint Military Exercise." Reuters, November 27, 2009.

"China, Japan Reach Principled Consensus on East China Sea Issue." Xinhua News, June 18, 2008.

"China: Measures Aim to Bolster Control of Maritime Interests." *OSC Analysis*, May 31, 2007. World News Connection 200705311477.1_46b002e82b57d797.

"China Naval Visits in E. China Sea Cause for Concern: Sankei." Kyodo News, April 18, 2000.

"China: 'Peaceful Rise in Light and Shadow.'" In *East Asian Strategic Review 2005*. Tokyo: National Institute for Defense Studies, 2005.

"China Prepares for Implementation of Sino-Japan Fishing Pact." Japan Economic Newswire, March 23, 2000.

"China Pressed for Skipper's Release." Kyodo News, November 27, 2011.

"China Raises Dispute over Senkakus into Airspace Above." *Asahi Shimbun*, December 14, 2012.

"China Says Warship Operations Irrelevant to Loans from Japan." Kyodo News, August 25, 2000.

"China's Brooding Dragons Complicate Standoffs at Sea." *Sentaku*, translated by *Japan Times*, June 12, 2012.

"China Set to Increase Patrols over Disputed Senkaku Islands." Kyodo News, March 20, 2012.

"China: Ships Near Disputed Islands Were on Patrol." Associated Press, December 9, 2008.

"China Should Give Notice of Maritime Research: Kono." *Japan Times*, September 9, 2000.

"China Slams Blocking of Activists." *Japan Times*, October 31, 2007.

"China: Towards a Less Cooperative, More Assertive Posture." In *East Asian Strategic Review 2011*. Tokyo: National Institute for Defense Studies, 2011.

"China Urges Reviving Sea Boundary Talks." Kyodo News, November 29, 2011.

"China Warships Pass." Kyodo News, November 24, 2011.

"Chinese Boats Enter Waters Off Senkakus / Gov't Protests Intrusion to Beijing Envoy." *Yomiuri Shimbun*, July 12, 2012.

"Chinese Foreign Ministry Official Visits Japan to Negotiate Diaoyu Island Dispute." *Zhongguo Xinwen She*, October 11, 2012. World News Connection 201210111477.1_941d00111885331a.

"Chinese Intruders Tell Coast Guard to Get Out." Kyodo News, October 31, 2012.

Chinese Ministry of Foreign Affairs. "China's Maritime Demarcation and Bilateral Fishery Affairs." 2001. www.fmprc.gov.cn/eng/wjb/zzjg/tyfls/tyfl/2626/2628/t15476.htm.

———. "Foreign Ministry Spokesman Liu Jianchao's Remarks on Chinese Marine Surveillance Ships Entering the Waters near the Diaoyu Islands." December 9, 2008. www.fmprc.gov.cn/eng/xwfw/s2510/2535/t525428.shtml.

———. "Foreign Ministry Spokesperson Hong Lei's Regular Press Conference on October 31, 2012." 2012. www.fmprc.gov.cn/eng/xwfw/s2510/t984549.htm.

———. "Foreign Ministry Spokesperson Jiang Yu's Regular Press Conference on June 17, 2008." 2008. www.fmprc.gov.cn/ce/cemy/eng/fyrth/t448663.htm.

"Chinese Naval Ships on Rise Near Japan." *Japan Times*, March 22, 2000.

"Chinese Navy Helicopter Circles MSDF Ship Again." *Mainichi Shimbun*, April 22, 2010.

"Chinese Official Raps Japan's 'Provocative' Action over Gas Dispute." Kyodo News, June 7, 2006.

"Chinese Research Ship Sighted near Senkaku Isles." *Yomiuri Shimbun*, February 5, 2007.

"Chinese Ship Asks Japan Ship to Stop Surveys amid Tense Row." Agence France-Press, September 11 2010.

"Chinese Ship Leaves Japan's Economic Waters off Kyushu." Kyodo News, August 29, 2000.

"Chinese Ships Seen in Disputed Waters for First Time since LDP's Win." Agence France-Presse, December 21 2012,

"Chinese Skipper Nabbed off Nagasaki after Chase." *Japan Times*, November 8, 2011.

"Chinese Spy Boat in Pacific off Tokyo Last Month: Paper." Japan Economic Newswire, June 10, 2000.

"Chinese Vessel Asks Survey Ship to Stop." Kyodo News, September 12, 2010.

"Chinese Vessel Leaves Okinawa Waters after Warnings." Agence France-Presse, May 2, 1997. World News Connection FBIS-EAS-97–122.

"Chinese Warship Pointed Gun at Japanese Patrol Plane in Sept." Kyodo News, October 2, 2005.

Chino, Keiko. "Yonaguni Island in Crisis parts 1, 2&3." *Sankei Shimbun*, October 16–18, 2009. World News Connection 200910181477.1_247c05538757c432.

Chiozza, Giacomo, and Ajin Choi. "Guess Who Did What: Political Leaders and the Management of Territorial Disputes, 1950–1990." *Journal of Conflict Resolution* 47, no. 3 (2003): 251–78.

Chisholm, Anthony H., and Rodney Tyers. "Food Security: An Introduction and Overview." In *Food Security: Theory, Policy and Perspectives from Asia and the Pacific Rim*, edited by Anthony H. Chisholm and Rodney Tyers. Lexington, MA: Lexington Books, 1982.

Chiu, Hungdah. "An Analysis of the Sino-Japanese Dispute over the T'iaotutai Islets (Senkaku Gunto)." *Chinese Yearbook of International Law and Affairs* 15 (1998): 9–31.

Christensen, Thomas J. "The Advantages of an Assertive China: Responding to Beijing's Abrasive Diplomacy." *Foreign Affairs,* 90, no. 2 (2011): 54–67.

Chung, Chien-peng. "The Diaoyu/Tiaoyutai/Senkaku Islands Dispute: Domestic Politics and the Limits of Diplomacy." *American Asian Review* 16, no. 3 (1998): 135–64.

———. *Domestic Politics, International Bargaining and China's Territorial Disputes.* London: RoutledgeCurzon, 2004.

———. "Resolving China's Island Disputes: A Two-Level Game Analysis." *Journal of Chinese Political Science* 12, no. 1 (2007): 49–70.

Churchill, R. R., and A. V. Lowe. *The Law of the Sea,* 3rd ed. Manchester: Manchester University Press, 1999.

Cliff, Roger, Mark Burles, Michael S. Chase, Derek Eaton, and Kevin L. Pollpeter. *Entering the Dragon's Lair: Chinese Antiaccess Strategies and Their Implications for the United States.* Santa Monica, CA: RAND Corporation, 2007.

"Coast Guard Enhancements OK'd." Kyodo News, February 29, 2012.

"Coast Guard Worried about Prolonged Senkaku Row." NHK, October 29, 2012.

Colaresi, Michael, Karen Rasler, and William R. Thompson. *Strategic Rivalries in World Politics.* Cambridge: Cambridge University Press, 2008.

Cole, Bernard D. "Beijing's Strategy of Sea Denial." *China Brief* 6, no. 23 (2006): 2–4.

———. "Chinese Naval Modernization and Energy Security." Paper presented at 2006 Pacific Symposium, Washington, June 20, 2006.

———. *The Great Wall at Sea: China's Navy Enters the 21st Century.* Annapolis, MD: Naval Institute Press, 2001.

———. Oil for the Lamps of China: Beijing's 21st-Century Search for Energy. McNair Paper 67. Washington, DC: National Defense University Press, 2003.

———. "Right-Sizing the Navy: How Much Naval Force Will Beijing Deploy?" In *Right Sizing the People's Liberation Army Navy: Exploring the Contours of China's Military,* edited by Roy Kamphausen and Andrew Scobell. Carlisle, PA: Strategic Studies Institute, US Army War College, 2007.

Cole, J. Michael. "China and Japan Turn the Screw over Island Dispute." *China Brief* 12, no. 18 (September 2012): 2–5.

———. "Chinese Navy Vessels Spotted Close to Japanese Coast." *Jane's Defense and Security Report,* May 3, 2012.

Collins, Gabriel B., Andrew S. Erickson, Lyle Goldstein, and William Murray, eds. *China's Energy Strategy: The Impact on Beijing's Maritime Policies.* Annapolis, MD: Naval Institute Press, 2008.

"Commentary Accuses Japan of Historical 'Cover-Ups'." Xinhua News, July 24, 1996. FBIS-CHI-96–143.

"Conflict at Sea with Chinese Vessel." *Joongang Daily*, March 5, 2011.

Corcoran, Tom, and Tomoko Hosoe. "Japan Gov't to Assume More Aggressive Energy Role." Reuters, August 6, 2006.

"CPC Central Committee's Proposal on Formulating the 12th Five-Year Program on National Economic and Social Development." Xinhua News, October 30, 2010. World News Connection 201010301477.1_0a16fe24c4569374.

Curtin, J. Sean. "New Sino-Japanese Strain over Disputed Islands." *Asia Times Online*, March 30, 2004. www.atimes.com/atimes/Japan/FC27Dh01.html. Accessed March 15 2006.

———. "Sea of Confrontation: Japan-China Territorial and Gas Dispute Intensifies." *Asia Times*, October 19, 2005. www.nautilus.org/aesnet/2005/OCT2605/JF_ChinaSea.pdf.

"DA Pressured Not to Announce PRC Ships Activity near Japan due to 'Delicate' Ties." *Sankei Shimbun*, July 14, 2001. World News Connection JPP-2001-07-15-000024.

Daiki, Shibuichi. "The Yasukuni Shrine Dispute and the Politics of Identity in Japan." *Asian Survey* 45, no. 2 (2005): 197–215.

Deans, Phil. "Contending Nationalisms in the Diaoyutai/Senkaku Dispute." *Security Dialogue* 31, no. 1 (2000): 119–31.

———. "The Diaoyutai/Senkaku Dispute: The Unwanted Controversy," *Kent Papers in Politics and International Relations* 6 (1996). www.kent.ac.uk.politics/research/kentpapers/deans.html.

"Diaoyu Islands Enters a New Stage." *Global Times*, December 14, 2012.

Dickie, Mure, and Kathrin Hille. "Japan Protests over China Military Incident." *Financial Times*, March 8, 2011.

Dickson, Bruce J. "Dilemmas of Party Adaptation: The CCP's Strategies for Survival." In *State and Society in 21st Century China: Crisis, Contention and Legitimation*, edited by Peter Hays Gries and Stanley Rosen. London: RoutledgeCurzon, 2004.

Diehl, Paul F. "What Are They Fighting For? The Importance of Issues in International Conflict Research." *Journal of Peace Research* 29, no. 3 (1992): 333–44.

"Diet Passes Bills to Protect Japan EEZ." *Asahi Shimbun*, April 21, 2007.

"Diet to See Video of Senkaku Run-in." *Japan Times*, October 28, 2010.

DiFilippo, Anthony. "How Tokyo's Security Policies Discount Public Opinion: Toward an Alternative Security Agenda." *Pacifica Review: Peace, Security and Global Change* 14, no. 1 (2002): 23–48.

Ding, Arthur S. "China's Energy Security Demands and the East China Sea: A Growing Likelihood of Conflict in East Asia?" *China and Eurasia Forum Quarterly* 3, no. 3 (2005): 35–38.

"Diplomats Met Secretly in Shanghai." Kyodo News, October 25, 2012.

Division for Ocean Affairs and the Law of the Sea. "Law of the Sea Information Circular No. 28." Office of Legal Affairs, United Nations, New York, October 2008.

———. "Submission by the People's Republic of China concerning the Outer Limits of the Continental Shelf beyond 200 Nautical Miles in Part of the East China Sea." December 14 2012. www.un.org/depts/los/clcs_new/submissions_files/submission_ chn_63_20 12.htm.

Doi, Takateru. "Japan to Keep Closer Watch over Its Skies." *Asahi Shimbun*, October 8, 2010.

Donaldson, John W., and Martin Pratt. "International Boundary Developments: Boundary and Territorial Trends in 2004." *Geopolitics* 10, no. 2 (2005): 398–427.

Downs, Erica S. "China." In *The Brookings Foreign Policy Studies Energy Security Series*. Washington, DC: Brookings Institution, 2006. www.brookings.edu/reports/2006/12china.aspx.

Downs, Erica S., and Phillip C. Saunders. "Legitimacy and the Limits of Nationalism: China and the Diaoyu Islands." *International Security* 23, no. 3 (1998–99): 114–46.

"Dragons Unite." *The Economist*, March 16, 2013.

Dreyer, June Teufel. "China's Military Strategy regarding Japan." In *China's Military Faces the Future*, edited by James R. Lilley and David Shambaugh. Armonk, NY: M. E. Sharpe, 1999.

———. "Sino-Japanese Territorial and Maritime Disputes." In *Beijing's Power and China's Neighbors: Twenty Neighbors in Asia*, edited by Bruce A. Elleman, Stephen Kotkin, and Clive Schofield. Armonk, NY: M. E. Sharpe, 2013.

Drifte, Reinhard. "The Ending of Japan's ODA Loan Programme to China: All's Well That Ends Well?" *Asia-Pacific Review* 13, no. 1 (2006): 94–117.

———. "From 'Sea of Confrontation' to 'Sea of Peace, Cooperation and Friendship'? Japan Facing China in the East China Sea." *Japan Aktuell*, no. 3 (2008): 27–51.

———. "The Future of the Japanese-Chinese Relationship: The Case for a Grand Political Bargain." *Asia-Pacific Review* 16, no. 2 (2009): 55–74.

———. *Japanese-Chinese Territorial Disputes in the East China Sea: Between Military Confrontation and Economic Cooperation*. Working Paper 24. London: Asia Research Centre at London School of Economics and Political Science, 2008.

———. *Japan's Security Relations with China since 1989*. London: RoutledgeCurzon, 2003.

———. "The Politics of the East China Sea Gas Dispute: Ongoing Discussion between China and Japan." In *Peace in Northeast Asia: Resolving Japan's Territorial and Maritime Disputes with China, Korea and the Russian Federation*, edited by Thomas J. Schoenbaum. Cheltenham, UK: Edward Elgar, 2008.

"Drillship Enters Senkaku Area." *Petroleum Economist*, March 1, 1996.

Duan, Tingzhi. "Review of Japanese Government's Granting of Test Exploitation Authorization from the Angle of International Law." *Beijing Liaowang*, August 3, 2005. World News Connection 2005-08-03-1477.1_e59b0210ffcadaec.

Dujarric, Robert. "Enhancing Japan's Position in the Senkaku Dispute." *PacNet*, no. 50, October 15, 2010.

———. "Japan's Territorial Claims Are Detrimental to Its National Interests." *Asahi Shimbun*, January 13, 2011.

Dumbaugh, Kerry, David Ackerman, Richard Cronin, Shirley A. Kan, and Larry A. Niksch. *China's Maritime Territorial Claims: Implications for U.S. Interests.* CRS Report for Congress RL31183. Washington, DC: Congressional Research Service, 2001.

Dupont, Alan. *East Asia Imperiled: Transnational Challenges to Security.* Cambridge: Cambridge University Press, 2001.

Dutton, Peter A. "Carving up the East China Sea." *Naval War College Review* 60, no. 2 (2007): 49–72.

———. "International Law and the November 2004 'Han Incident.'" *Asian Security* 2, no. 2 (2006): 87–101.

Dzurek, Daniel J. "Effect of the Diaoyu/Senkaku Islands on Maritime Delimitation." In *Borderlands under Stress*, edited by Martin Pratt and Janet Allison Brown. London: Kluwer Law International, 2000.

East Asian Strategic Review 2000. Tokyo: National Institute for Defense Studies, 2000.

East Asian Strategic Review 2001. Tokyo: National Institute for Defense Studies, 2001.

East Asian Strategic Review 2002. Tokyo: National Institute for Defense Studies, 2002.

Eckstein, Harry. "Case Study and Theory in Political Science." In *Strategies of Inquiry: Handbook of Political Science Vol. 7*, edited by Fred I. Greenstein and Nelson W. Polsby. Reading, Ma: Addison-Wesley, 1975.

Economy, Elizabeth, and Adam Segal. "The G2 Mirage: Why the US and China Are Not Ready to Upgrade Ties." *Foreign Affairs* 88, no. 3 (May–June 2009): 14–23.

"Edano Slams Reported China Drilling in Gas Field." Kyodo News, March 8, 2011.

"Editorial: A Defensive Report." *Mainichi Daily News*, August 4, 2000.

"Editorial: Japan, China Should Negotiate Gas Development Deal." *Nihon Keizai Shimbun*, October 22, 2004.

"Editorial: Joint Project with China." *Japan Times*, January 29, 2009.

"Editorial: Urges Tokyo to Limit PRC Vessel Access to Economic Zone." *Sankei Shimbun* July 21, 2001. World News Connection JPP-2001-07-22-000025.

EIA (Energy Information Administration). "East China Sea." US Department of Energy, updated September 25, 2012. www.eia.doe.gov/emeu/cabs/East_China_Sea/Background.html.

———. "East China Sea: Country Analysis Brief." US Department of Energy, 2008. www.eia.doe.gov/emeu/cabs/East_China_Sea/Background.html.

———. "Privatization and the Globalization of Energy Markets." US Department of Energy, 1996. www.eia.doe.gov/emeu/pgem/contents.html.

Emery, K. O., Yoshikazu Hayashi, Thomas W. C. Hilde, Kazuo Kobayashi, Ja Hak Koo, C. Y. Meng, Hiroshi Niino, J. H. Osterhagen, L. M. Reynolds, John W. Wageman, C. S. Wang, and Sung Jin Yang. "Geological Structure and Some

Water Characteristics of the East China Sea and the Yellow Sea." *Technical Bulletin* 2 (1969): 3–41.

Emmers, Ralf. *Geopolitics and Maritime Territorial Disputes in East Asia.* London: Routledge, 2010.

"Energy White Paper States for First Time Gas Fields Issue 'Important.'" *Sankei Shimbun,* May 19, 2005. World News Connection 2005-05-19-1477.1_00ac00162a638c16.

ESSG (Energy Security Study Group). "Interim Report." Agency for Natural Resources and Energy (Japan). 2007. www.enecho.meti.go.jp/english/archives_2006.htm.

Esteban, Mario. "The Management of Nationalism during the Jiang Era (1994–2002) and Its Implications on Government and Regime Legitimacy." *European Journal of East Asian Studies* 5, no. 2 (2006): 181–214.

Fackler, Martin. "Japan Isle in Sea of Contention Weights Fist versus Open Hand." *New York Times,* February 10, 2011.

———. "With Its Eye on China, Japan Builds Up Military." *New York Times,* February 28, 2011.

Faiola, Anthony. "Japan–China Oil Dispute Escalates." *Washington Post,* October 22, 2005.

Fan, Yongming. "Searching for Common Interests between China and Japan: A Chinese View." *Journal of Contemporary China* 17, no. 55 (2008): 375–82.

FAO (Food and Agriculture Organization of the United Nations). "Fisheries and Aquaculture Information and Statistics Service." www.fao.org/figis/servlet/TabSelector.

———. "Fishery and Aquaculture Country Profile: China." www.fao.org/fishery/countrysector/FI-CP_CN/en.

Fearon, James D. "Bargaining, Enforcement and International Cooperation." *International Organization* 52, no. 2 (1998): 269–305.

———. "Domestic Political Audiences and the Escalation of International Disputes," *American Political Science Review* 88, no. 3 (1994): 577–92.

Feng, Yao. "Major General Jin Yinan: Diaoyu Islands Sovereignty Patrols to Normalize." *Wen Wei Po,* March 15, 2011. World News Connection 201103151477.1_2d8502db362691c9.

Feng, Zhaokui. "Factors Shaping Sino-Japanese Relations." *Contemporary International Relations,* 2001.

"Fewer Japanese Feel Friendly toward China." *Yomiuri Shimbun,* December 25, 2005.

"'50 Mine Law Update Eyed to Tap Seabed." *Japan Times,* March 9, 2011.

Finnemore, Martha. *National Interests in International Society.* Ithaca, NY: Cornell University Press, 1996.

Fisheries Agency. *FY 2005 Trend in Fisheries.* Ministry for Forestry, Fisheries, and Agriculture, 2006.

"Fishermen Seek Early Establishment of Exclusive Zone." Japan Economic Newswire, February 28, 1996.

"Fishery Leader Urges Talks to Be Completed within 1 Year." Japan Economic Newswire, February 20, 1996.

"Fishing Industry Unions to Vote for 200-Mile Zone." Japan Economic Newswire, November 21, 1995.

"Foreign Ministry Spokesperson Discusses Diaoyutai Issue." *People's Daily*, July 25, 1996, FBIS-CHI-96–144.

"Foreign Ministry Spokesperson Jiang Yu's Remarks." Embassy of the People's Republic of China in the Republic of Ghana. http://gh.china-embassy.org/eng/fyrth/t777814.htm.

Forster, Hector. "Japan Seeks Oil Security in Iraq, Indonesia after Iran Setback." Bloomberg News, October 27, 2006.

Fouse, David. "Japan's FY 2005 National Defense Program Outline: New Concepts, Old Compromises." *Asia-Pacific Security Studies* 4, no. 3 (2005).

Fravel, M. Taylor. "China's Search for Military Power." *Washington Quarterly* 31, no. 3 (2008): 125–41.

———. "Explaining Stability in the Senkaku (Diaoyu) Islands Dispute." In *Getting the Triangle Straight: Managing China-Japan-US Relations*, edited by Gerald Curtis, Ryosei Kokubun, and Wang Jisi. Washington, DC: Brookings Institution Press, 2010.

———. "Regime Insecurity and International Cooperation: Explaining China's Compromises in Territorial Disputes." *International Security* 30, no. 2 (2005): 46–83.

———. *Strong Borders, Secure Nation: Cooperation and Conflict in China's Territorial Disputes.* Princeton, NJ: Princeton University Press, 2008.

French, Howard W. "A Sense of Community Elusive for East Asia." *International Herald Tribune*, June 19, 2008.

Fridley, David. "Natural Gas in China." In *Natural Gas in Asia: The Challenges of Growth in China, India, Japan and Korea*, edited by Ian Wybrew-Bond and Jonathan Stern. Oxford: Oxford University Press, 2002.

Fu, Zhiwei. "Be Vigilant against the Danger of Neo-Militarism in Japan." *Jiefangjun Bao*, October 28, 2012. World News Connection 201210281477.1_5ed300fd3b97f443.

"Fukuda, Hu Agree to Boost Ties / Joint Statement Future-Oriented; Gas Issue 'Close to Resolution.'" *Yomiuri Shimbun*, May 8, 2008.

Fukui, Haruhiro. "How Japan Handled UNCLOS Issues: Does Japan Have an Ocean Policy?" In *Japan and the New Ocean Regime*, edited by Robert L. Friedheim. Boulder CO: Westview Press, 1984.

"'Full Text' of PRC-Japan Joint Press Communiqué on Liang Guanglie-Kitazawa Talks." Xinhua Domestic Service, November 27, 2009. World News Connection 200911271477.1_267000ad7bb56580.

Gao, Jianjun. "A Note on the 2008 Cooperation Consensus between China and Japan in the East China Sea." *Ocean Development and International Law* 40, no. 3 (2009): 291–303.

Gao, Zhiguo, and Jilu Wu. "Key Issues in the East China Sea: A Status Report and Recommended Approaches." Paper presented at Conference on Seabed Petroleum in the East China Sea: Geological Prospects, Jurisdictional Conflicts and Paths to Cooperation, Beijing, April 12–13, 2005.

"Gas Field Agreement Helps Japan–China Ties." *Yomiuri Shimbun*, June 19, 2008.

George, Alexander L., and Andrew Bennett. *Case Studies and Theory Development in the Social Sciences*. Cambridge, MA: MIT Press, 2005.

Glaser, Charles L. "Realists as Optimists: Cooperation as Self-Help." *Security Studies* 5, no. 3 (1996): 122–63.

Glaubitz, Joachim. "Anti-Hegemony Formulas in Chinese Foreign Policy," *Asian Survey* 16, no. 3 (1976): 205–15.

Glosny, Michael A. "Strangulation from the Sea? A PRC Submarine Blockade of Taiwan." *International Security* 28, no. 4 (2004): 125–60.

Goddard, Stacie. "Uncommon Ground: Indivisible Territory and the Politics of Legitimacy." *International Organization* 60, no. 1 (2006): 35–68.

Goertz, Gary, and Paul F. Diehl. *Territorial Changes and International Conflict*. London: Routledge, 1992.

Goldstein, Avery. "China in 1996: Achievement, Assertiveness, Anxiety." *Asian Survey* 37, no. 1 (1997): 29–42.

Goldstein, Lyle J. "Chinese Coast Guard Development: Challenge and Opportunity." *China Brief* 9, no. 23 (2009): 5–8.

———. *Five Dragons Stirring Up the Sea*. China Maritime Study 5. Newport, RI: US Naval War College, 2010.

Goldstein, Lyle, and Vitaly Kozyrev. "China, Japan and the Scramble for Siberia." *Survival* 48, no. 1 (2006): 163–78.

Goldstein, Lyle, and William Murray. "Undersea Dragons: China's Maturing Submarine Force." *International Security* 28, no. 4 (2004): 161–96.

Gorham, Michael. "Japan's Policy of Food Security: An Alternative Strategy." *Federal Reserve Bank of San Francisco Economic Review* (1979): 31–45.

Gourevitch, Peter Alexis. "Squaring the Circle: The Domestic Sources of International Cooperation." *International Organization* 50, no. 2 (1996): 349–73.

"Government Aims at Fresh Start in Negotiations on Gas Field Development, Fears China Creating Fait Accompli." *Sankei Shimbun*, November 10, 2004. World News Connection JPP-2004-11-16-000043.

Government of Japan. *Basic Plan on Ocean Policy*. Tokyo: Government of Japan, 2008.

———. *Law on the Exclusive Economic Zone and the Continental Shelf*. Law No. 74 of 1996. Tokyo: Government of Japan, 1996.

"Government Plans to Cut GSDF Quota to 154,000 Members." Kyodo News, December 13, 2010.

"Gov't Foot-Dragging on China Gas Rig Blamed on Ministry Sectionalism." *Yomiuri Shimbun*, June 20, 2004.

"Gov't-Funded Pipeline for China." *Yomiuri Shimbun*, February 25, 2005.

"Gov't Hastens to Identify Mystery Sub / Presumed Chinese Vessel May Be Linked to Gas Field Development." *Yomiuri Shimbun*, November 11, 2004.

"Gov't Offers Beijing New Gas Deal." *Yomiuri Shimbun*, February 6, 2008.

"Gov't Panel Eyes Unification of Marine Policies." *Yomiuri Shimbun*, December 6, 2006.

"Gov't Starts Survey of EEZ Riches." *Yomiuri Shimbun*, July 8, 2004.

"Gov't Welcomes Japan–China Agreement on Fisheries Pact." Kyodo News, March 6, 2000.

Graham, Euan. *Japan's Sea Lane Security 1940–2004: A Matter of Life and Death?* London: Routledge, 2006.

Green, Michael J. *Japan's Reluctant Realism: Foreign Policy Challenges in an Era of Uncertain Power.* New York: Palgrave, 2001.

Green, Michael J., and Benjamin L. Self. "Japan's Changing China Policy: From Commercial Liberalism to Reluctant Realism." *Survival* 38, no. 2 (1996): 35–58.

Greenfield, Jeanette. *China's Practice in the Law of the Sea.* Oxford: Clarendon Press, 1992.

Grieco, Joseph M. "Anarchy and the Limits of Cooperation: A Realist Critique of the Newest Liberal Institutionalism." In *Controversies in International Relations Theory: Realism and the Neoliberal Challenge*, edited by Charles W. Kegley Jr. Belmont, CA: Wadsworth/Thomson, 1995.

———. *Cooperation among Nations: Europe, America and Non-Tariff Barriers to Trade.* Ithaca, NY: Cornell University Press, 1990.

———. "Realist Theory and the Problem of International Cooperation: Analysis with an Amended Prisoner's Dilemma Model." *Journal of Politics* 50, no. 3 (1988): 600–624.

Gries, Peter Hays. *China's New Nationalism: Pride, Politics and Diplomacy.* Berkeley: University of California Press, 2004.

———. "China's 'New Thinking' on Japan." *China Quarterly*, no. 184 (2005): 831–50.

Guo, Qiang. "China Protests over Sea Collision." *Global Times*, September 8, 2010.

Guo, Rongxing. "Territorial Disputes and Seabed Petroleum Exploitation: Some Options for the East China Sea." CNAPS Visiting Fellow Working Paper. Washington, DC: Brookings Institution, 2010.

Gupta, Sourabh. "An 'Early Summer': Sino-Japanese Cooperation in the East China Sea." *Nautilus Policy Forum Online*, vol. 08–10A (2008). www.nautilus.org/fora/security/08010Gupta.html.

Haas, Ernst B. "Nationalism: An Instrumental Social Construction." *Millennium: Journal of International Studies* 22, no. 3 (1993): 505–45.

Hagstrom, Linus. *Japan's China Policy: A Relational Power Analysis.* London: Routledge, 2005.

———. "'Power Shift' in East Asia? A Critical Reappraisal of Narratives on the Diaoyu/Senkaku Islands Incident in 2010." *Chinese Journal of International Politics* 5 (2012): 267–97.

———. "Quiet Power: Japan's China Policy in Regard to the Pinnacle Islands." *Pacific Review* 18, no. 2 (2005): 159–88.

Hall, Kenji. "The Japan–China Oil Slick." *Business Week,* November 11, 2005.

Harrison, Selig S. *China, Oil, and Asia: Conflict Ahead?* New York: Columbia University Press, 1977.

———. "Quiet Struggle in the East China Sea." *Current History* 101, no. 656 (2002): 271–77.

———. "Seabed Petroleum in Northeast Asia: Conflict or Cooperation?" Paper presented at Conference on Seabed Petroleum in the East China Sea: Geological Prospects, Jurisdictional Conflicts and Paths to Cooperation, Beijing, April 12–13, 2005.

Hassner, Ron E. "The Path to Intractability: Time and the Entrenchment of Territorial Disputes." *International Security* 31, no. 3 (2006/07): 107–38.

———. *War on Sacred Grounds.* Ithaca, NY: Cornell University Press, 2009.

Haward, Marcus, and Anthony Bergin. "The Political Economy of Japanese Distant Water Tuna Fisheries." *Marine Policy* 25, no. 2 (2001): 91–101.

Hayashi, Moritaka. "Japan: New Law of the Sea Legislation." *International Journal of Marine and Coastal Law* 12, no. 4 (1997): 570–80.

———. "Military and Intelligence-Gathering Activities in the EEZ: Definition of Key Terms." *Marine Policy* 29, no. 1 (2005): 123–37.

———. "Regional Fisheries Management in the East China Sea." In *Recent Developments in the Law of the Sea and China,* edited by Myron H. Nordquist, John Norton Moore, and Kuen-chen Fu. Leiden: Martinus Nijhoff, 2006.

Hayashi, Yuichi. *Japan Fishery Products Annual Report.* Washington, DC: USDA Foreign Agricultural Service, 2007.

He, Yinan. "History, Chinese Nationalism and the Emerging Sino-Japanese Conflict." *Journal of Contemporary China* 16, no. 50 (2007): 1–24.

———. "Ripe for Cooperation or Rivalry? Commerce, Realpolitik, and War Memory in Contemporary Sino-Japanese Relations." *Asian Security* 4, no. 2 (2008): 162–97.

———. *The Search for Reconciliation: Sino-Japanese and German-Polish Relations since World War II.* Cambridge: Cambridge University Press, 2009.

Hellman, Gunther, and Benjamin Herborth. "Fishing in the Mild West: Democratic Peace and Militarised Inter-State Disputes in the Transatlantic Community." *Review of International Studies* 34, no. 3 (2008): 481–506.

Hensel, Paul R. "Contentious Issues and World Politics: The Management of Territorial Claims in the Americas, 1816–1992." *International Studies Quarterly* 45, no. 1 (2001): 81–109.

Hensel, Paul R., Sara McLaughlin Mitchell, Thomas E. Sowers II, and Clayton L. Thyne. "Bones of Contention: Comparing Territorial, Maritime, and River Issues." *Journal of Conflict Resolution* 52, no. 1 (2008): 117–43.

Herberg, Mikkal. "Asia's Energy Insecurity: Cooperation or Conflict?" In *Strategic Asia 2004–05: Confronting Terrorism in the Pursuit of Power*, edited by Ashley J. Tellis and Michael Wills. Seattle: National Bureau of Asian Research, 2004.

Herrmann, Wilfried A. "Chinese Military Strategy and Its Maritime Aspects." *Naval Forces* 20, no. 2 (1999): 14–17.

Hille, Kathrin. "Hu Calls for China to Be 'Maritime Power.'" *Financial Times*, November 8, 2012.

Hille, Kathrin, and Michiyo Nakamoto. "China Raises Stakes over Disputed Islands." *Financial Times*, October 30, 2012.

Hiramatsu, Shigeo. "The Aim of the Chinese Submarine in Waters near Japan: With Taiwan in Mind, Preparing to Block US Aircraft Carriers." *Seiron*, November 17, 2004. World News Connection JPP-2004–1117–000009.

———. "China Aims to Advance into the Pacific Ocean; I Would Like to Pay Attention to Its Active Marine Survey Activities." *Seiron*, July 21, 2003. World News Connection JPP-2003–07–23–000069.

———. "China's Naval Advance: Objectives and Capabilities." *Japan Review of International Affairs* 8, no. 2 (1994): 118–32.

Hiwatari, Nobuhiro. "Japan in 2005." *Asian Survey* 46, no. 1 (2006): 22–36.

Hobsbawn, E. J. *Nations and Nationalism since 1870: Programme, Myth, Reality*. Cambridge: Cambridge University Press, 1990.

Holmes, James R., and Toshi Yoshihara. *Chinese Naval Strategy in the 21st Century: The Turn to Mahan*. London: Routledge, 2008.

"Hotline with China Eyed to Avoid Clashes at Isles." Kyodo News, July 28, 2012.

Howarth, Peter. *China's Rising Sea Power: The PLA Navy's Submarine Challenge*. London: Frank Cass, 2006.

Hsiung, James C. "Sea Power, Law of the Sea, and a Sino-Japanese East China Sea 'Resource War.'" In *China and Japan at Odds: Deciphering the Perpetual Conflict*, edited by James C. Hsiung. New York: Palgrave Macmillan, 2007.

Huang, Alexander Chieh-cheng, "The Chinese Navy's Offshore Active Defense Strategy: Conceptualization and Implications." *Naval War College Review* 47, no. 3 (1994): 7–32.

Huang, Haixia, "Rough Waves in China's Territorial Sea." *Liaowang*, May 7, 2009. World News Connection 200905071477.1_b8cd0521654d35d9.

Hudson, Valerie M. *Foreign Policy Analysis: Classic and Contemporary Theory*. Lanham, MD: Rowan & Littlefield, 2007.

Hue, Jae, and Ichiro Suzuki. "Japan to Revise Mining Law, Seeking $3.6 Trillion in Undersea Resources." Bloomberg News, March 8, 2011.

Hughes, Christopher R. "Japan in the Politics of Chinese Leadership Legitimacy: Recent Developments in Historical Perspective." *Japan Forum* 20, no. 2 (2008): 245–66.

———. "Reclassifying Chinese Nationalism: The Geopolitik Turn." *Journal of Contemporary China* 20, no. 71 (2011): 601–20.

Hughes, Christopher W. "Japanese Military Modernization: In Search of a 'Normal' Security Role." In *Strategic Asia 2005–06: Military Modernization in an Era of Uncertainty*, edited by Ashley J. Tellis and Michael Wills. Seattle: National Bureau of Asian Research, 2005.

———. *Japan's Security Agenda: Military, Economic and Environmental Dimensions.* Boulder, CO: Lynne Rienner, 2004.

Hughes, Christopher W., and Ellis S. Krauss. "Japan's New Security Agenda." *Survival* 49, no. 2 (2007): 157–76.

Huth, Paul K. *Standing Your Ground: Territorial Disputes and International Conflict.* Ann Arbor: University of Michigan Press, 1996.

Huth, Paul K., and Todd L. Allee. *The Democratic Peace and Territorial Conflict in the Twentieth Century.* Cambridge: Cambridge University Press, 2002.

———. "Domestic Political Accountability and the Escalation and Settlement of International Disputes." *Journal of Conflict Resolution* 46, no. 6 (2002): 775–90.

Iida, Masafumi, Makoto Saito, Yasuyuki Sugiura, and Masayuki Masuda. *NIDS China Security Report.* Tokyo: National Institute for Defense Studies, 2011.

Iitake, Koichi. "Lawmakers Set Sights on Visit to Senkaku Islands." *Asahi Shimbun*, August 4, 1999.

"Impact on China-Japan Ties." *Zhongguo Tongxun She*, September 22, 2004. World News Connection CPP-2004-09-22-000217.

"Imperative for China to Break out of the 'First Island Chain.'" *Wen Wei Po*, June 20, 2011. World News Connection 201106201477.1_0574080a8a6f85ef.

"Info Gathering Boost Eyed for East China Sea." *Yomiuri Shimbun*, October 24, 2006.

Inoguchi, Takashi. "National Identity and Adapting to Integration: Nationalism and Globalization in Japan." In *Nationalism and Globalization: East and West*, edited by Leo Suryadinata. Singapore: Institute of Southeast Asian Studies, 2000.

International Crisis Group (ICG). "Northeast Asia's Undercurrents of Conflict." *Asia Policy Report*, no. 108 (2005).

———. "Stirring Up the South China Sea (I)." *Asia Policy Report*, no. 223 (2012).

International Energy Agency. *World Energy Outlook 2012.* Paris: Organization for Economic Cooperation and Development and International Energy Agency, 2012.

———. *Global Offshore Oil Prospects to 2000.* Paris: International Energy Agency, 1996.

"Interview with New Cabinet Members: Defense Agency Director General Kazuo Torashima." *Sankei Shimbun,* July 17, 2000. World News Connection FBIS-EAS-2000–0717.

"Island Row Might Hamper Ratification of Sea Convention." Japan Economic Newswire, December 16, 1995.

Jakobson, Linda, and Dean Knox. *New Foreign Policy Actors in China.* SIPRI Policy Paper 10. Stockholm: Stockholm International Peace Research Institute, 2010.

"Japan Arrests China Boat Captain for Illegal Fishing." Reuters, December 20, 2011.

"Japan Asks China to Investigate East China Sea Incident." Kyodo News, December 16, 1991.

"Japan Bans Political Group from Sailing for Disputed Islands." Kyodo News, March 27, 2004.

"Japan Celebrates Its Oceans." *The Economist,* July 19, 2010.

"Japan, China Agree on 2-Month Maritime Notice System." Kyodo News, February 19, 2001.

"Japan, China to Continue Informal Fishery Talks Wednesday." Kyodo News, April 9, 1996.

"Japan, China Defense Chiefs Agree on Liaison Mechanism to Avoid Conflicts." Kyodo News, October 12, 2010.

"Japan–China Gas Deal Leaves Key Issues Unresolved." *Nihon Keizai Shimbun,* June 19, 2008.

"Japan–China Gas Field Talks Upgraded to Minister Level." *Yomiuri Shimbun,* November 13, 2007.

"Japan, China Hope to Resolve Fishing Dispute Next Week." Kyodo News, November 4, 1999.

"Japan, China to Ink New Fisheries Pact Soon." Japan Economic Newswire, September 3, 1997.

"Japan, China Make Progress toward New Fishery Accord." Kyodo News, April 22, 1997.

"Japan, China Officials Discuss North Korea, East China Sea Gas Project." *Mainichi Shimbun,* January 31, 2011.

"Japan, China Strike Deal on Gas Project Areas in Disputed E. China Sea." Kyodo News, June 16, 2008.

"Japan Condemns China's Copter's Approach to MSDF Destroyer." Kyodo News, March 29, 2011.

"Japan Confirms China Pumps Gas or Oil in E. China Sea." Kyodo News, September 20, 2005.

"Japan DA Chief on PRC Navy Ships in Japanese Waters." *Sankei Shimbun,* July 15, 2000. World News Connection FBIS-EAS-2000–0715.

"Japan Deported Chinese Protestors under Political Pressure." Kyodo News, April 2, 2004.

"Japan to Establish Law Aimed at Cracking Down on Suspicious Ships." Kyodo News, February 26, 2008.

"Japanese Article Says Tokyo Broke 'Secret' Islets Pact with China." Agence-France Presse, October 18, 2010.

"Japanese Consortium Wins Blocks 41/17 and 42/03 in East China Sea." *Petroleum Economist*, January 19, 1994.

"Japanese Daily Notes Kono's Visit to PRC Helped Promote Bilateral Relations." *Sankei Shimbun*, September 2, 2000. World News Connection JPP-2000–09–02–000036.

"Japanese Editorial Excerpts." Kyodo News, August 27, 2000.

"Japanese Editorial Excerpts." Kyodo News, August 28, 2000.

"Japanese Editorial Excerpts." Kyodo News, October 27, 2004.

"Japanese Editorial Excerpts." Kyodo News, April 15, 2005.

"Japanese Fishermen Assail Agreements with Korea, China." *Wall Street Journal*, April 3, 1997.

"Japan to Establish 'Senkaku Unit' to Deal with China's Provocations in the Sea." *Sankei Shimbun*, December 24, 2012.

"Japan Eyes More Protest over China's Pipeline to Disputed Gas Fields." Kyodo News, August 27, 2004.

"Japan Foreign Minister Defends PRC Marine Survey in EEZ." *Sankei Shimbun*, June 21, 2001. World News Connection FBIS-EAS-2001–0621.

"Japan to Go on Exploring Gas Resources in E. China Sea." Kyodo News, September 30, 2004.

"Japan to Monitor Chinese Navy Vessels near Okinawa." Kyodo News, June 10, 2011.

"Japan Moves to Drill in the East China Sea." *Japan Times*, January 17, 2005.

"Japan Plans to Tighten Controls on Mineral Resources with Law Change." Associated Press, March 10, 2011.

"Japan Protests China Gas Field Moves." *Asahi Shimbun*, January 6, 2009.

"Japan Protests China's Imminent Production at Chunxiao Field." Kyodo News, August 10, 2005.

"Japan Regrets China Move to Produce Gas in E. China Sea." Kyodo News, August 31, 2005.

"Japan Regrets Timing of Chinese Claim on Islands." Kyodo News, March 2, 1992.

"Japan Says Chinese Submarines, Ships Seen Near Okinawa." *Taipei Times*, April 14, 2010.

"Japan Should Build Lighthouse, Heliport in Senkakus—Minister." Kyodo News, April 3, 2004.

"Japan Should Tackle China Sea Gas Project Carefully." *Nihon Keizai Shimbun*, April 15, 2005.

"Japan's Move in the East China Sea Makes Conflict 'Inevitable': Report." *People's Daily*, July 16, 2005.

"Japan's Provocation in East China Sea Very Dangerous." *Renmin Ribao*, July 21, 2005. World News Connection 2005–07–21–1477.1_9ccc0365f08ed963.

"Japan Threatens China with Measures If Gas Recovery Accord Violated." ITAR-TASS, January 17, 2010.

"Japan Vice Defense Minister: DA to Monitor PRC Vessel Near Sea of Japan." *Sankei Shimbun*, July 18, 2000. World News Connection FBIS-EAS-2000–0718.

"Japan Voices Concern about Chinese Naval Activities around Japan." Japan Economic Newswire, June 20, 2000.

"Japan Watching If China Breached Deal in Disputed Gas Field." *Petroleum World*, December 9, 2009.

"JCG Stretched Thin over Senkakus." *Yomiuri Shimbun*, October 4, 2012.

JDA (Japanese Defense Agency). *Defense of Japan*. Tokyo: Japanese Defense Agency, 1977.

———. *Defense of Japan 1998*. Tokyo: Japan Times Ltd., 1998.

———. *Defense of Japan 1999*. Tokyo: Urban Connections, 1999.

———. *Defense of Japan 2000*. Tokyo: Urban Connections, 2000.

———. *Defense of Japan 2001*. Tokyo: Urban Connections, 2001.

———. *Defense of Japan 2002*. Tokyo: Urban Connections, 2002.

———. *Defense of Japan 2004*. Tokyo: Inter Group Corp., 2004.

———. *Defense of Japan 2005*. Tokyo: Japanese Defense Agency, 2005.

———. *Defense of Japan 2006*. Tokyo: Japanese Defense Agency, 2006.

———. "National Defense Program Guidelines for FY 2005–2010." www.kantei.go.jp/foreign/policy/2004/1210taikou_e.html.

Jennings, Ralph. "China Protests Japan's Decision to Drill E. China Sea Gas." Kyodo News, July 15, 2005.

———. "China Wants to Continue Gas Exploration Dispute with Japan." Kyodo News, October 26, 2004.

———. "Sea Area Disputed by China, Japan May Offer Little Oil or Gas." Kyodo News, March 25, 2005.

Jervis, Robert. "Realism, Neoliberalism, and Cooperation: Understanding the Debate." In *Progress in International Relations Theory: Appraising the Field*, edited by Colin Elman and Miriam Fendius Elman. Cambridge, MA: MIT Press, 2003.

Ji, You. *The Armed Forces of China*. St. Leonards, NSW: Allen & Unwin, 1999.

Ji, You, and You Xu. "In Search of Blue Water Power: The PLA Navy's Maritime Strategy in the 1990s." *Pacific Review* 4, no. 2 (1991): 137–49.

Jiang, Wenran. "East Asia's Troubled Waters, Part I." 2006. http://yaleglobal.yale.edu/display.article?id=7302.

———. "New Dynamics of Sino-Japanese Relations." *Asian Perspective* 31, no. 1 (2007): 15–41.

Jimbo, Ken. *Japan's Security Strategy toward China: Integration, Balancing and Deterrence in the Era of Power Shift*. Tokyo: Tokyo Foundation, 2011.

Jin, Zhu, and Ma Liyao. "Stronger Fleet for Fishery Administration." *China Daily*, November 17, 2010.

Johnston, Alistair Iain. "How New and Assertive Is China's New Assertiveness?" *International Security* 37, no. 4 (2013): 7–48.

Johnston, Douglas M. *The Theory and History of Ocean Boundary-Making*. Montreal: McGill–Queens University Press, 1988.

Johnston, Douglas M., and Mark J. Valencia. *Pacific Ocean Boundary Problems: Status and Solutions*. Dordrecht: Martinus Nijhoff Publishers, 1991.

Kacowicz, Arie M. "The Problem of Peaceful Territorial Change." *International Studies Quarterly* 38, no. 2 (1994): 219–54.

"Kan Administration Criticized over Spat with China." *Asahi Shimbun*, September 28, 2010.

Kanehara, Nobukatsu, and Yutaka Arima. "Japan's New Agreement on Fisheries with the Republic of Korea and with the People's Republic of China." *Japanese Annual of International Law* 42 (1999): 1–31.

Kang, Joon-Suk. "The United Nations Convention on the Law of the Sea and Fishery Relations between Korea, Japan and China." *Marine Policy* 27, no. 2 (2003): 111–24.

Katada, Saori N. "Why Did Japan Suspend Foreign Aid to China? Japan's Foreign Aid Decision-Making and Sources of Aid Sanction." *Social Science Japan Journal* 4, no. 1 (2001): 39–58.

Katsumata, Hidemichi. "Defense Bills Waste of Time until Constitution Debated." *Yomiuri Shimbun*, April 23, 2004.

Katsumata, Hidemichi, and Ryuhei Yoshimura. "Upgrade of Brigade Targets China Threat." *Yomiuri Shimbun*, April 8, 2010.

Katzenstein, Peter J., and Nobuo Okawara. "Japan and Asia-Pacific Security." In *Rethinking Security in East Asia: Identity, Power and Efficiency*, edited by J. J. Suh, Peter J. Katzenstein, and Allen R. Carlson. Stanford, CA: Stanford University Press, 2004.

Kawakami, Osamu. "Mutual Gas Benefit Stressed / East China Sea Exploration Pact Highlights Japan-China Ties." *Yomiuri Shimbun*, June 20, 2008.

Kawasaki, Hideki, and Junya Hashimoto. "Maritime Law a Start to Securing Interests." *Yomiuri Shimbun*, April 22, 2007.

Kawasaki, Masumi. "Widening Anti-Japan Protests Centered in Inland Areas; Demonstrations Also Fuelled by Citizen Discontent over Economic Gaps, Authorities' Control Ineffective." *Sankei Shimbun*, October 25, 2010.

Keohane, Robert O. *After Hegemony: Cooperation and Discord in the World Political Economy*. Princeton, NJ: Princeton University Press, 1984.

Kim, Duk-Ki. *Naval Strategy in Northeast Asia: Geostrategic Goals, Policies and Prospects*. London: Frank Cass, 2000.

Kim, Sun Pyo. *Maritime Delimitation and Interim Arrangements in North East Asia*. The Hague: Martinus Nijhoff, 2004.

———. "The UN Convention of the Law of the Sea and New Fisheries Agreements in Northeast Asia." *Marine Policy* 27, no. 2 (2003): 97–109.

Kim, Young C. "Japanese Policy towards China: Politics of the Imperial Visit to China in 1992." *Pacific Affairs* 74, no. 2 (2001): 225–42.

Kimura, Masato, and David Welch. "Specifying 'Interests': Japan's Claim to the Northern Territories and Its Implications for International Relations Theory." *International Studies Quarterly* 42, no. 2 (1998): 213–44.

Kisugi, Shin, and Hiroyuki Nakahara. "To Everyone Involved with the Ocean from the Newsletter Editorial Committee." *OPRF Newsletter*, July 20, 2000.

Kitamura, Jun. "The US Military's Perception of Japan and National Strategies That Japan Should Have: Proposal for the Future of the Japan–US Alliance." *Seiron*, January 22, 2006, World News Connection 2006-01-22-1477.1_07111ce7ee56cf73.

Klare, Michael T. *Resource Wars*. New York: Henry Holt & Co., 2002.

Koike, Masanari, Gento Moji, and Waleed H. Albedaiwi. "Overseas Oil-Development Policy of Resource-Poor Countries: A Case Study from Japan." *Energy Policy* 36, no. 5 (2008): 1764–75.

Koji, Murata. "Domestic Sources of Japanese Policy towards China." In *Japan's Relations with China: Facing a Rising Power*, edited by Peng Er Lam. London: Routledge, 2006.

Kojima, Tomoyuki. "Japan's China Policy." In *Japan and China: Rivalry or Cooperation in East Asia?* edited by Peter Drysdale and Dong Dong Zhang. Canberra: Australia–Japan Research Centre, 2000.

———. "To Make China a Responsible Major Power: Japan's ODA Programs for China as Diplomatic Strategy." *Gaiko Forum*, January 2001, 38–45. World News Connection FBIS-CHI-2001-0110.

Komori, Yoshihisa. "Latest Intrusion of PRC Vessels in Japanese EEZ to Have Serious Impact." *Sankei Shimbun*, September 8, 2000. World News Connection FBIS-EAS-2000-0908.

Koo, Min Gyo. "Scramble for the Rocks: The Dokto/Takeshima, Senkaku/Diaoyu, and Paracel and Spratly Islands Disputes." PhD thesis, University of California, 2005.

———. "The Senkaku/Diaoyu Dispute and Sino-Japanese Political-Economic Relations: Cold Politics and Hot Economics?" *Pacific Review* 22, no. 2 (2009): 205–32.

"Korea Alarmed by China–Japan Deal on East China Sea." *Korea Herald*, June 23, 2008.

Kotler, Mindy L. Naotaka Sugawara, and Tetsuya Yamada. "Chinese and Japanese Public Opinion: Searching for Moral Security." *Asian Perspective* 31, no. 1 (2007): 93–125.

Kumagai Takeo. "Japan, China to Start East China Sea Talks; Information to Be Exchanged on Shirakaba Field." *Platt's Oilgram*, March 30, 2007.

———. "Japan Looks to Offshore Methane Hydrates to Cut Reliance on Energy Imports." *Platt's*, November 22, 2010.

Kupchan, Charles. *How Enemies Become Friends: The Sources of Stable Peace*. Princeton, NJ: Princeton University Press, 2010.

Kurashige, Nanae, and Kenji Minemura. "Japan, China to Finally Enter Gas Field Talks," *Asahi Shimbun*, June 1, 2010

Kuriyama, Takakazu. "Both Sides Need to Make Efforts to Maintain Status Quo." *Asahi Shimbun*, December 26, 2012.

Kurlantzick, Joshua. *Charm Offensive: How China's Soft Power Is Transforming the World*. New Haven, CT: Yale University Press, 2007.

Kwon, Park Hee. *The Law of the Sea and Northeast Asia: A Challenge for Cooperation*. The Hague: Kluwer Law International, 2000.

Lai, Hongyi Harry. "China's Oil Diplomacy: Is It a Global Security Threat?" *Third World Quarterly* 28, no. 3 (2007): 519–37.

Lam, Peng Er. "Mediating Geopolitics, Markets and Regionalism: Domestic Politics in Japan's Post-Cold War Relations with China." In *Regional Cooperation and Its Enemies in Northeast Asia: The Impact of Domestic Forces*, edited by Edward Freidman and Sung Chull Kim. London: Routledge, 2006.

Lanteigne, Marc. "China's Maritime Security and the 'Malacca Dilemma.'" *Asian Security* 4, no. 2 (2008): 143–61.

"Lawmakers Inspect China's Gas Projects in the E. China Sea." Kyodo News, April 10, 2005.

"Lawmakers View Disputed Senkaku Islands." Kyodo News, June 11, 2012.

"LDP Delays China Loans over Encroaching Ships." Kyodo News, August 24, 2000.

Lee, Chae-Jin. *Japan Faces China: Political and Economic Relations in the Postwar Era*. Baltimore: Johns Hopkins University Press, 1976.

Lee, Wei-chin. "Trouble under the Water: Sino-Japanese Conflict of Sovereignty on the Continental Shelf in the East China Sea." *Ocean Development and International Law* 18, no. 5 (1987): 585–611.

Lehman, Jean-Pierre. "Japanese Attitudes towards Foreign Policy." In *The Process of Japanese Foreign Policy: Focus on Asia*, edited by Robert L. Grant. London: Royal Institute of International Affairs, 1997.

Levy, Jack S. "Prospect Theory and the Cognitive-Rational Debate." In *Decision-Making on War and Peace: The Cognitive-Rational Debate*, edited by Nehemia Geva and Alex Mintz. Boulder, CO: Lynne Rienner, 1997.

———. "Prospect Theory and International Relations: Theoretical Applications and Analytical Problems." *Political Psychology* 13, no. 2 (1992): 283–310.

Lewis, John Wilson, and Xue Litai. *China's Strategic Seapower: The Politics of Force Modernization in the Nuclear Age*. Stanford, CA: Stanford University Press, 1994.

Li, Nan. "The Evolution of China's Naval Strategy and Capabilities: From 'Near Coast' to 'Near Sea' to 'Far Sea.'" *Asian Security* 5, no. 2 (2009): 144–69.

———. "The PLA's Evolving Warfighting Doctrine, Strategy and Tactics, 1985–95: A Chinese Perspective." *China Quarterly,* no. 146 (1996): 443–63.

Li, Victor H. "China and Offshore Oil: The Tiao-Yu Tai Dispute." In *China's Changing Role in the World Economy,* edited by Bryant G. Garth. New York: Praeger, 1975.

Liao, Yameng. "China Refuses to Accept the Idea of 'Middle Line' but Proposes 'Common Development' as a Solution to the Recent Row between China and Japan over the Gas Field on the East China Sea." *Wen Wei Po,* July 11, 2004. World News Connection CPP-2004-07-12-000048.

Lind, Jennifer. *Sorry States: Apologies in International Politics.* Ithaca, NY: Cornell University Press, 2008.

Lindkvist, Knut Bjorn, Torbjorn Trondsen, and Jinghua Xie. "Restructuring the Chinese Seafood Industry, Global Challenges and Policy Implications." *Marine Policy* 32, no. 3 (2008): 432–41.

Linge, G. J. R. "The Kuriles: The Geo-Political Spanner in the Geo-Economic Works." *Australian Geographical Studies* 33, no. 1 (1995): 116–32.

Liu, Huadi. "Japan's Sinister Designs in Illegally Leasing Diaoyu Dao." *Jiefangjun Bao,* January 20, 2002. World News Connection CPP-2003-01-20-000029.

Liu, Jiangping, and Feng Xianhui. "Going Global: Dialogue Spanning 600 Years." *Liaowang,* September 8, 2005. World News Connection 2005-09-08-1477.1_89870599299e4719.

Liu, Ning-che. "Masses in Four Mainland Cities Stage Protests Defending the Diaoyu Islands." *Wen Wei Po,* February 17, 2005. World News Connection 200502171477.1_c67f00c61bf30e85.

Liu, Rongzi. "Exploitation and Management of the Fishery Resources and Regional Cooperation in the Yellow Sea and the East China Sea." In *Ocean Affairs in Northeast Asia and Prospects for Korea-China Maritime Cooperation,* edited by Dalchoong Kim, Jiao Yongke, Jin-Hyun Paik, and Chen Degong. Seoul: Institute of East and West Studies at Yonsei University, 1994.

Liu, Yi-chien. "China's 21st-Century Navy Prospects." *Ta Kung Pao,* September 1, 1999. World News Connection FBIS-CHI-1999-1011.

Lo, Chi-Kin. *China's Policy towards Territorial Disputes: The Case of the South China Sea Islands.* London: Routledge, 1989.

Lu, Baosheng, and Guo Hongjun. "Okinawa: 'Hub' of the Pacific." *Jiefangjun Bao,* June 22, 2003. World News Connection CPP-2003-06-23-000084.

Ludwig, Noel A., and Mark J. Valencia. "Building North-East Asian Maritime Regimes: Will Japan Take the Lead?" *Marine Policy* 19, no. 2 (1995): 83–96.

Luo, Zheng. "Regular Training on the High Seas Organized by the Chinese Navy Poses No Threat to Other Countries." *Jiefangjun Bao,* April 26, 2010. World News Connection 201004261477.1_a02400fd6137870a.

Ma, Haoliang, "China Marine Surveillance Maneuvers Multi-Pronged Approaches Protecting Its Maritime Rights." *Ta Kung Pao,* May 12, 2011. World News Connection 201105121477.1_77f5034cabb4c67a.

Ma, Liyan. "Meeting Signals Improved Ties." *China Daily*, February 1, 2011.

Ma, Ying-jeou. *Legal Problems of Seabed Boundary Delimitation in the East China Sea*, vol. 62. Baltimore: Occasional Papers/Reprints Series in Contemporary Asian Studies, 1984.

Mack, Andrew. *Island Disputes in Northeast Asia*. Working Paper 1997/2. Canberra: Department of International Relations, Australian National University, 1997.

Mallory, Tabitha Grace. "China's Distant Water Fishing Industry: Evolving Policies and Implications." *Marine Policy* 38 (March 2013): 99–108.

Manicom, James. "Beyond Boundary Disputes: Understanding the Nature of China's Challenge to Maritime East Asia." *Harvard Asia Quarterly* 12, nos. 3–4 (2010): 46–53.

———. "China's Claims to an Extended Continental Shelf in the East China Sea: Meaning and Implications." *China Brief* 9, no. 14 (2009): 9–11.

———. "China's Strategy in the East China Sea: Contested Jurisdiction and National Reunification." In *China's Near Seas Strategy*, China Maritime Study 12. Newport, RI: US Naval War College, 2014.

———. "Growing Nationalism and Maritime Jurisdiction in the East China Sea." *China Brief* 10, no. 21 (2010): 9–11.

———. "The Interaction of Material and Ideational Factors in the East China Sea Dispute: Impact on Future Dispute Management." *Global Change, Peace and Security* 20, no. 3 (2008): 375–91.

———. "Japan's Ocean Policy: Still the Reactive State?" *Pacific Affairs* 83, no. 2 (2010): 307–26.

———. "Sino-Japanese Cooperation in the East China Sea: Limitations and Prospects." *Contemporary Southeast Asia* 30, no. 3 (2008): 455–78.

———. "Strategic Policy, Economic Opportunities and Cooperation in the East China Sea Dispute." *Economics and Politics of Security Journal* 4, no. 4 (July 2009): 38–44.

Manicom, James, and Andrew O'Neil. "Sino-Japanese Strategic Relations: Will Rivalry Lead to Confrontation?" *Australian Journal of International Affairs* 63, no. 2 (2009): 213–32.

"Marine Day and the Basic Ocean Law." August 8, 2007. www.nippon-foundation.or.jp/eng/current/20070808MarineDay.html.

"Maritime Row Unlikely to Be Resolved before Zhu's Visit." Kyodo News, October 7, 2000.

MARPAC (Maritime Forces Pacific, Royal Canadian Navy). "In Focus: Strategic Isles of the East China Sea." February 2011.

Marquand, Robert. "Japan–China Tensions Rise over Tiny Islands." *Christian Science Monitor*, February 11, 2005.

Martin, Lisa L. *Coercive Cooperation: Explaining Multilateral Economic Sanctions*. Princeton, NJ: Princeton University Press, 1992.

Masuda, Masayuki. "Japan's Changing ODA Policy towards China." *China Perspectives*, no. 47 (2003). http://chinaperspectives.revues.org/document358.html.

Masuda, Masayuki, Masafumi Iida, Yasuyuki Sugiura, and Shinji Yamaguchi. *NIDS China Security Report 2012*. Tokyo: National Institute for Defense Studies, 2012.

Matsui, Yoshiro. "International Law of Territorial Acquisition and the Dispute over the Senkaku (Diaoyu) Islands." *Japanese Annual of International Law* 40 (1997): 3–31.

"Matsumoto, Yang Address Sea Spats." Kyodo News, July 5, 2011.

McDevitt, Michael. "The Strategic and Operational Context Driving PLA Navy Building." In *Right Sizing the People's Liberation Army: Exploring the Contours of China's Military*, edited by Roy Kamphausen and Andrew Scobell. Carlisle, PA: Strategic Studies Institute, US Army War College, 2007.

McVadon, Eric A. "China's Maturing Navy." *Naval War College Review* 59, no. 2 (2006): 90–107.

Mendl, Wolf. *Japan's Asia Policy: Regional Security and Global Interests*. London: Routledge, 1995.

Midford, Paul. *Rethinking Japanese Public Opinion and Security: From Pacifism to Realism?* Stanford, CA: Stanford University Press, 2011.

Midlarsky, Manus I. "Identity and International Conflict." In *Handbook of War Studies II*, edited by Manus I. Midlarsky. Ann Arbor: University of Michigan Press, 2000.

Milner, Helen. "International Theories of Cooperation among Nations: Strengths and Weaknesses." *World Politics* 44, no. 3 (1992): 466–96.

Minemura, Kenji. "China to Establish Permanent Senkaku Patrols." *Asahi Shimbun*, December 20, 2010.

———. "China Taunts Japan with 'Aircraft Carrier' Exercise." *Asahi Shimbun*, November 29, 2012.

Minister's Secretariat Statistics Department, MAFF (Ministry of Agriculture, Forestry, and Fisheries). "Fishery Production." www.maff.go.jp/toukei/abstract/1_9/44a.htm.

Mintz, Alex, and Karl DeRouen Jr. *Understanding Foreign Policy Decision Making*. Cambridge: Cambridge University Press, 2010.

Mitchell, Sara McLaughlin, and Brandon C. Prins. "Beyond Territorial Contiguity: Issues at Stake in Militarized Interstate Disputes." *International Studies Quarterly* 43, no. 1 (1999): 169–83.

Mitzen, Jennifer. "Ontological Security in World Politics: State Identity and the Security Dilemma." *European Journal of International Relations* 12, no. 3 (2006): 341–70.

Miyamoto, Akira. "Natural Gas in Japan." In *Natural Gas in Asia: The Challenges of Growth in China, India, Japan and Korea*, edited by Ian Wybrew-Bond and Jonathan Stern. Oxford: Oxford University Press, 2002.

Miyashita, Akitoshi. "Where Do Norms Come From? Foundations of Japan's Postwar Pacifism." *International Relations of the Asia-Pacific* 7, no. 1 (2007): 99–120.

"Miyazawa Opposes China's Territorial Claim." *Jiji Press English News Service*, February 27, 1992.

Miyoshi, Masahiro. "New Japan–China Fishery Agreement: An Evaluation from the Point of View of Dispute Management." *Japanese Annual of International Law* 41 (1998): 30–43.

Mochizuki, Mike M. "Japan's Long Transition: The Politics of Recalibrating Grand Strategy." In *Domestic Political Change and Grand Strategy*, edited by Ashley J. Tellis and Michael Wills. Seattle: National Bureau of Asian Research, 2007.

———. "Japan's Shifting Strategy toward the Rise of China." *Journal of Strategic Studies* 30, nos. 4–5 (2007): 739–76.

MOD (Japanese Ministry of Defense). *Defense of Japan 2007.* Tokyo: Japan Ministry of Defense, 2007.

———. *Defense of Japan 2010.* Tokyo: Japanese Ministry of Defense, 2010.

———. *Defense of Japan 2012.* Tokyo: Japanese Ministry of Defense, 2012.

———. *Summary of National Defense Program Guidelines, FY 2011.* Tokyo: Japanese Ministry of Defense, 2010.

MOFA (Japanese Ministry of Foreign Affairs). *Diplomatic Blue Book 2005.* www.mofa.go.jp/policy/other/bluebook/2005/index.html.

———. *Diplomatic Blue Book 2006.* www.mofa.go.jp/policy/other/bluebook/2006/index.html.

———. "Japan–China Cooperation in the East China Sea." June 18, 2008. www.mofa.go.jp/mofaj/area/china/higashi_shina/press.html.

———. "Japan–China Foreign Ministers' Meeting (Summary)." July 24, 2001. www.mofa.go.jp/region/asia-paci/china/meet0107.html.

———. "日中外相会談 (概要) [Japan–China Foreign Minister's Meeting (Summary)]." July 4, 2011. www.mofa.go.jp/mofaj/kaidan/g matsumoto/china1107/jc_gk1107.

———. "Japan–China Foreign Minister's Meeting." August 28, 2000. www.mofa.go.jp/region/asia-paci/china/fmv0008/meet_4.html.

———. "Meeting between the Japan Coast Guard and the State Oceanic Administration of China." July 20, 2007. www.mofa.go.jp/announce/announce/2007/7/1174543_830.html.

———. "Press Conference 18 June 2004." www.mofa.go.jp/announce/press/2004/6/0618.html. Accessed May 5 2008.

———. "Press Conference 22 June 2004." www.mofa.go.jp/announce/press/2004/6/0622.html.

———. "Press Conference 19 September 2000." www.mofa.go.jp/announce/press/2000/9/919.html.

———. "Press Conference 3 October 2000." www.mofa.go.jp/announce/press/2000/10/1003.html.

———. "Q&A on the Senkaku Islands." www.mofa.go.jp/region/asia-paci/senkaku/qa_1010.html.

———. "Strategy and Approaches of Japan's Energy Diplomacy." www.mofa.go.jp/policy/energy/diplomacy.html.

Moon, Gwang-lip. "Chinese Sailors Admit Ramming Coast Guard Ship." *Joongang Daily*, December 24, 2010.

"More Japanese View China Unfavorably." *Yomiuri Shimbun*, December 19, 2004.

MSA (Japanese Maritime Safety Agency). "Annual Report on Maritime Safety 1998." www.kaiho.mlit.go.jp/e/tosho/apoms1.pdf.

Murayama, Masaya, and Toshu Noguchi. "Japan–China Boundary Issue: Resources an Additional Factor Aggravating Dispute; China Aims at Making EEZ Fait Accompli." *Sankei Shimbun*, June 8, 2004. World News Connection JPP-2004–06–08–000053.

"Mysterious Ships Run for North Korean Waters." *Mainichi Daily News*, March 25, 1999.

"Nakagawa Reveals 4 Gas Fields Eyed for Joint Efforts." *Yomiuri Shimbun*, October 4, 2005.

Nakamoto, Michiyo. "Abe Talks Tough on China before Election." *Financial Times*, November 30, 2012.

Nakamoto, Michiyo, and Mure Dickie. "Japan and China near Gas Fields Accord." *Financial Times*, June 16, 2008.

Nakazawa, Kensuke. "Gov't Slow to Wake up to Potential of EEZ." *Yomiuri Shimbun*, August 27, 2004.

Nash, John. "The Bargaining Problem." *Econometrica* 18 (1950): 155–62.

"Navy Fleet Returns from West Pacific Training." Xinhua News, December 11, 2012.

Negishi, Mayumi. "Japan Proposes Joint Use of Deposits in East China Sea Fields." *Japan Times*, October 2, 2005.

———. "Japan Ready to Drill in Disputed Waters." *Japan Times*, April 2, 2005.

Nemeth, Stephen C., Sara McLaughlin Mitchell, Elizabeth A. Nyman, and Paul R. Hensel. "Ruling the Sea: Institutionalization and Privatization of the Global Ocean Commons." Paper presented at International Studies Association 49th Annual Convention, San Francisco, 2007.

"New Aid to China: The Incoherent Japanese Diplomacy without Strategies." *Sankei Shimbun*, August 18, 2000. World News Connection FBIS-CHI-2000–0818.

"New Maritime Laws Well Overdue." *Yomiuri Shimbun*, April 21, 2007.

"Newly Assertive China Wanted the Senkaku Stunt to Succeed." *Asahi Shimbun*, August 16, 2012.

Newman, David. "Real Spaces, Symbolic Spaces: Interrelated Notions of Territory in the Arab-Israeli Conflict." In *A Roadmap to War: Territorial Dimensions of International Conflict*, edited by Paul F. Diehl. Nashville: Vanderbilt University Press, 1999.

"News Briefs International: China." *Platt's Oilgram*, April 20, 2006.

Ng, Teddy. "Chinese Warships Cross Waters near Japan's Okinawa Islands." *South China Morning Post*, October 17, 2012.

"Nihon Senkaku Mitsuhyaku atta" [Japan Had a Secret Agreement over the Senkaku Islands]. *Aera, Asahi Shimbun Weekly*, October 25, 2010.

Niimi, Reiko. "The Problem of Food Security." In *Japan's Economic Security*, edited by Nobutoshi Akao. New York: St. Martin's Press, 1983.

Nishiyama, Kiriko. "Japanese Destroyer Tracks 'Suspected' Chinese Spy Ship Passing through Tsugaru-Kaikyo Strait." Agence France-Presse, May 25, 2000. World News Connection FBIS-EAS-2000–0525.

"Noda Team Moves Swiftly to Curtail Senkaku Controversy." *Asahi Shimbun*, August 17, 2012.

"Noda, Wen Unite on Keeping Koreas Stable." Kyodo News, December 26, 2011.

"Nonaka Asks China to Address Maritime Intrusions." Kyodo News, June 12, 2000.

"Number of Illegal Ships More Than Doubles." Kyodo News, September 20, 1999.

"ODA to China: Bold Review Based on Guidelines Necessary." *Sankei Shimbun*, May 12, 2000. World News Connection FBIS-EAS-2000–05–13.

Odgaard, Liselotte. "Perception, Pragmatism, and Political Will: Maritime Disputes and Balances of Power in the Asia-Pacific." *Asian Perspective* 26, no. 4 (2002): 113–43.

Office of International Policy Planning Division, Ministry of Forestry, Fisheries, and Agriculture. "Abstract of Statistics on Agriculture, Forestry and Fisheries in Japan." www.maff.go.jp/toukei/abstract/index.htm.

"Oil and Gas in Troubled Waters; Japan and China." *The Economist*, October 8, 2005.

"Oil Rivals See Value of Cooperation." *Nihon Keizai Shimbun*, July 5, 2004.

"Okada Warns China on Gas Drilling Pact." Kyodo News, January 18, 2010.

Okubo, Yoshio. "Political Pulse: Time Gov't Stood up to China over EEZ Oil, Gas Reserves." *Yomiuri Shimbun*, July 10, 2004.

Okuwaki, Naoya. "The Basic Act on Ocean Policy and Japan's Agenda for Legislative Improvement." *Japan Yearbook of International Law* 51 (2008): 164–216.

O'Neal, John R., and Bruce Russet. "The Classical Liberals Were Right: Democracy, Interdependence, and Conflict, 1950–1985." *International Studies Quarterly* 41, no. 2 (1997): 267–94.

Ong, David, and B. A. Hamzah. "Disputed Maritime Boundaries and Claims to Offshore Territories in the Asia Pacific Region." In *Calming the Waters: Initiatives for Asia Pacific Maritime Cooperation*, edited by Sam Bateman and Stephen Bates. Canberra: Strategic and Defence Studies Centre at Australian National University, 1996.

Oros, Andrew. *Normalizing Japan: Politics, Identity and the Evolution of Security Practice.* Stanford, CA: Stanford University Press, 2009.

O'Rourke, Ronald. *China Naval Modernization: Implications for US Navy Capabilities: Background and Issues for Congress.* CRS Report for Congress RL33153. Washington, DC: Congressional Research Service, 2007.

Ota, Fumio. "How Should Japan Respond to Chinese Maritime Expansion?" *Japanese Dynamism no. 26.* Tokyo: Tokyo Foundation, 2005.

Ozawa, Harumi. "Nationalism Rears Head Ahead of Poll." *Japan Times,* December 8, 2012.

Paik, Jin-Hyun. "Exclusive Economic Zones and Maritime Boundary Delimitations in Northeast Asia." In *The Seas Unite: Maritime Cooperation in the Asia Pacific Region,* edited by Sam Bateman and Stephen Bates. Canberra Paper on Strategy and Defence 118. Canberra: Strategic and Defence Studies Centre at Australian National University, 1996.

———. "Exploitation of Natural Resources: Potential for Conflict in Northeast Asia." In *Calming the Waters: Initiatives for Asia-Pacific Maritime Cooperation,* edited by Sam Bateman and Stephen Bates. Canberra Paper on Strategy and Defence 114. Canberra: Strategic and Defence Studies Centre at Australian National University, 1996.

———. "Fisheries Regime in Northeast Asia: Current Situation and Prospects." In *Ocean Affairs in Northeast Asia and Prospects for Korea-China Maritime Cooperation,* edited by Dalchoong Kim, Jiao Yongke, Jin-Hyun Paik, and Chen Degong. Seoul: Institute of East and West Studies at Yonsei University, 1994.

Pak, Chi Young. "Resettlement of the Fisheries Order in Northeast Asia Resulting from the New Fisheries Agreements among Korea, Japan, and China." *Korea Observer* 30, no. 4 (1999): 587–622.

Park, Choon-ho Park. *East Asia and the Law of the Sea.* Seoul: Seoul National University Press, 1985.

Pekkanen, Robert, and Ellis S. Kraus. "Japan's 'Coalition of the Willing' on Security Policies." *Orbis* 49, no. 3 (2005): 429–44.

Penn, Michael. "The Battle of Azadegan: Japan, Oil and Independence." *Japan Focus,* 2005. www.japanfocus.org/_Michael_Penn-The_Battle_of_Azadegan__Japan e_Oil_and_Independence_/.

Peterson, Alexander M. "Sino-Japanese Cooperation in the East China Sea: A Lasting Arrangement?" *Cornell Journal of International Law* 42 (2010): 441–74.

Petzet, Alan. "Exploration, Production Futures Bright for East China Sea." *Oil & Gas Journal* 97, no. 32 (1999): 80–82.

"PGS to Sell Seismic Ship to Japan Government." Reuters, March 26, 2007.

Pilling, David. "Japan Strikes Easier Tone on Gas Disputes." *Financial Times,* November 5, 2005.

"Planning National Strategies-Resources and Energy / China Warnings Went Unheeded." *Yomiuri Shimbun,* April 28, 2005.

"Planning National Strategies-Resources and Energy / More Open China a Threat to Japan." *Yomiuri Shimbun,* April 13, 2005.

Pomfret, John. "Dispute with Japan Highlights China's Foreign-policy Power Struggle." *Washington Post,* September 24, 2010.

———. "The Risk of War in the Far East." *Washington Post,* February 8, 2013.

Potter, David, and Sudo Sueo. "Japanese Foreign Policy: No Longer Reactive?" *Political Studies Review* 1, no. 3 (2003): 317–32.

"PRC Declaration on Sea Baselines for Paracel Islands." *People's Daily,* May 16, 1996. FBIS-CHI-96-096.

"PRC FM Spokesman: Activities of Patrol Boats Located near Islands 'Lawful.'" Xinhua News, March 16, 2012. World News Connection 201203161477.1_1d4300248b160a24.

"PRC FM Spokesperson Warns Japan of 'Consequences' over Drilling Rights Decision." Agence France-Presse, April 14, 2005.

"PRC Naval Vessels Activities in East China Sea 'Drop Sharply' in 2006." *Sankei Shimbun,* November 4, 2006.

"PRC UNCLOS Ratification Statement." www.un.org/Depts/los/convention_agreements/convention_declara tions.htm.

Primeline Petroleum Corporation. "Lishui 36–1 (Vicky) Discovery." www.primelineenergy.com/s/Lishui36–1.asp.

"Protecting Japan, Part III: China Winning Undersea War." *Yomiuri Shimbun,* June 9, 2004.

Prizel, Ilya. *National Identity and Foreign Policy: Nationalism and Leadership in Poland, Russia, and Ukraine.* Cambridge: Cambridge University Press, 1998.

Przystup, James J. "Japan–China Relations: Looking beyond Koizumi." *Comparative Connections* 8, no. 1 (2006): 109–21.

———. "Japan–China Relations: Not the Best of Times." *Comparative Connections* 6, no. 3 (2004): 117–27.

———. "Japan–China Relations: Progress in Building a Strategic Relationship." *Comparative Connections* 10, no. 2 (2008): 119–32.

———. "Japan–China Relations: Spring Thaw." *Comparative Connections* 8, no. 2 (2006): 117–26.

———. "Japan–China Relations: Summer Calm." *Comparative Connections* 7, no. 3 (2005): 117–28.

———. "Japan–China Relations: Troubled Waters." *Comparative Connections* 12, no. 3 (October 2010): 101–14.

———. "Japan–China Relations: Troubled Waters II." *Comparative Connections* 12, no. 4 (January 2011): 117–30.

———. "Japan–China Relations: Trying to Get beyond Yasukuni." *Comparative Connections* 7, no. 1 (2005): 109–21.

———. "Japan–China Relations: Yasukuni Stops Everything." *Comparative Connections* 7, no. 4 (2006): 109–21.

Przystup, James J., John Bradford, and James Manicom. "Japan–China Maritime Confidence-Building and Communications Mechanisms." PacNet, no. 67. August 20, 2013.

Putnam, Robert D. "Diplomacy and Domestic Politics: The Logic of Two-Level Games." *International Organization* 42, no. 3 (1988): 427–60.

Qin, Amy, and Edward Wong. "Smashed Skull Serves as Grim Symbol of Seething Patriotism." *New York Times*, October 10, 2012.

"A Question of Meaning: China's State Visit to Japan Leaves Relations Strained." *The Economist*, December 5, 1998.

Rachman, Gideon. "The Shadow of 1914 Falls over the Pacific." *Financial Times*, February 4, 2013.

Ragland, Thomas R. "A Harbinger: The Senkaku Islands." *San Diego Law Review* 10, no. 3 (1973): 664–91.

Rasler, Karen, and William R. Thompson. "Contested Territory, Strategic Rivalries, and Conflict Escalation." *International Studies Quarterly* 50, no. 1 (2006): 145–68.

———. "Explaining Rivalry Escalation to War: Space, Position, and Contiguity in the Major Power Subsystem." *International Studies Quarterly* 44, no. 3 (2000): 503–30.

Reilly, James. "China's Online Nationalism toward Japan." In *Online Chinese Nationalism and China's Bilateral Relations*, edited by Simon Shen and Shaun Breslin. Lanham, MD: Lexington Books 2010.

———. *Strong Society, Smart State: The Rise of Public Opinion in China's Japan Policy*. New York: Columbia University Press, 2011.

Risse-Kappen, Thomas. "Public Opinion, Domestic Structure and Foreign Policy in Liberal Democracies." *World Politics* 43, no. 4 (1991): 479–512.

"Rivals Race Petrochina to Shanghai." *Petroleum Intelligence Weekly*, August 27, 2003.

Roach, J. Ashley. "China's Straight Baseline Claim: Senkaku (Diaoyu) Islands." *ASIL Insights* 17, no. 7 (February 13, 2013).

Ross, Robert S. "Geography of the Peace: East Asia in the Twenty-First Century." *International Security* 23, no. 4 (1999): 81–118.

Rousseau, David L. *Identifying Threats and Threatening Identities: The Social Construction of Realism and Liberalism*. Stanford, CA: Stanford University Press, 2006.

Roy, Denny. *China's Foreign Relations*. Lanham, MA: Rowman & Littlefield, 1998.

———. "Stirring Samurai, Disapproving Dragon: Japan's Growing Security Activity and Sino-Japan Security Relations." *Asian Affairs, an American Review* 31, no. 2 (2004): 86–101.

Rudd, Kevin. "East Asia . . . A Maritime Balkans of the 21st Century?" *Foreign Policy*, January 31, 2013. www.foreignpolicy.com/articles/2013/01/30/a_maritime_balkans...of_the_ 21st_century_east_asia.

Saeki, Satoshi. "China Readies for Diplomatic Warfare." *Yomiuri Shimbun*, September 24, 2010.

Sakai, Mitsuru. "First Negotiations Held for Gas Field Deliberations but No Clear Outlook for Final Decision, Negotiations Proceeding at Pace of China, Japan Being Pushed Around." *Sankei Shimbun*, August 9, 2010. World News Connection 201008091477.1_bf8703522c0ee301.

Sakamoto, Shigeki. "Japan-China Dispute over Maritime Boundary Delimitation: From a Japanese Perspective." *Japan Yearbook of International Law* 51 (2008): 98–118.

Sakuja, Vijay. "Japanese Maritime Self-Defense Force: *Kata* and *Katana*." *Strategic Analysis* 24, no. 4 (2000): 807–19.

Salameh, Mamdouh. "China, Oil and the Risk of Regional Conflict." *Survival* 37, no. 4 (1995–96): 133–46.

Samuels, Richard J. "'New Fighting Power!' Japan's Growing Maritime Capabilities and East Asian Security." *International Security* 32, no. 3 (2007–8): 84–112.

———. *Securing Japan: Tokyo's Grand Strategy and the Future of East Asia.* Ithaca, NY: Cornell University Press, 2007.

Sasajima, Masahiko. "Japan's Domestic Politics and China Policymaking." In *An Alliance for Engagement: Building Cooperation in Security Relations with China,* edited by Benjamin Self and Jeffrey W. Thompson. Washington, DC: Henry L. Stimson Center, 2002.

Sasakawa, Yohei. "Why Is an Ocean Policy Think Tank Required Now?" *OPRF Newsletter,* July 20, 2000.

Saseda, Hironori. "Youth and Nationalism in Japan." *SAIS Review* 26, no. 2 (2006): 109–22.

Saunders, Stephen, ed. *Jane's Fighting Ships 2008–2009.* Cambridge: Jane's Information Group, 2008.

Schelling, Thomas C. *The Strategy of Conflict.* Cambridge, MA: Harvard University Press, 1960.

Schofield, Clive, and Ian Storey. *The South China Sea Dispute: Increasing Stakes and Rising Tensions.* Washington, DC: Jamestown Foundation, 2009.

"Senkaku Visit Riles Japan, China." *Asahi Shimbun,* May 6, 1997.

Shambaugh, David. "China Engages Asia: Reshaping the Regional Order." *International Security* 29, no. 3 (2004–5): 64–99.

———. *Modernizing China's Military: Progress, Problems, and Prospects.* Stanford, CA: Stanford University Press, 2002.

Shaoul, Raquel. "An Evaluation of Japan's Current Energy Policy in the Context of the Azadegan Oil Field Agreement Signed in 2004." *Japanese Journal of Political Science* 6, no. 3 (2005): 411–37.

Shaw, Han-yi. *The Diaoyutai/Senkaku Islands Dispute: Its History and an Analysis of the Ownership Claims of the PRC, ROC and Japan.* Occasional Papers/Reprints Series in Contemporary Asian Studies, vol. 152. Baltimore: School of Law, University of Maryland at Baltimore, 1999.

"Shell, Unocal Exit East China Sea Project; CNOOC Says It Still Intends to Start Output in Mid-2005." *Platt's Oilgram,* September 30, 2004.

Shen, Wenmin, and Chen Hongguo. "Chinese 'Haixun 21' Carries Out Preparations for Going to Japan for Rescue Efforts." *Renmin Wang,* March 17, 2011. World News Connection 201103171477.1_f8a7011bb0f7492d.

Shi, Jiangtao. "Hu Warns Japan over Planned Purchase of Diaoyu Islands." *South China Morning Post*, September 10, 2012.

Shih, Chih-Yu. "Defining Japan: The Nationalist Assumption in China's Foreign Policy." *International Journal* 50, no. 1 (1995): 539–63.

Shih, Chun-yu. "Casting Doubts on Japan's Sinking of Suspicious Ship." *Ta Kung Pao*, December 26, 2001. World News Connection CPP-2001-12-26-000020.

Shin Joho Center. "USIA #2000-I20012: Foreign Companies/Relations with US/ Military Issues." May 18–22, 2000.

———. "USIA Poll # 2000-I20045: Economic Conditions/International Relations/ Military Issues/North Korea/Security." Roper Center, September 27–October 1, 2000.

Shinoda, Tomohito. "Becoming More Realistic in Post–Cold War: Japan's Changing Media and Public Opinion on National Security." *Japanese Journal of Political Science* 8, no. 2 (2007): 171–90.

———. *Koizumi Diplomacy: Japan's Kantei Approach to Foreign and Defense Affairs.* Seattle: University of Washington Press, 2007.

Shirk, Susan L. *China: Fragile Superpower.* Oxford: Oxford University Press, 2007.

Simmons, Beth A. "Capacity, Commitment, and Compliance: International Institutions and Territorial Disputes." *Journal of Conflict Resolution* 46, no. 6 (2002): 829–56.

———. "Rules over Real Estate: Trade, Territorial Conflict and International Borders as Institution." *Journal of Conflict Resolution* 49, no. 6 (2005): 823–48.

Smil, Vaclav. *Energy at the Crossroads: Global Perspectives and Uncertainties.* Cambridge, MA: MIT Press, 2003.

Smith, Roger. "Japan's High Seas Fisheries in the North Pacific Ocean: Food Security and Foreign Policy." In *Japan at the Millennium: Joining Past and Future*, edited by David W. Edgington. Vancouver: University of British Columbia Press, 2003.

Soeya, Yoshihide. "Japan: Normative Constraints versus Structural Imperatives." In *Asian Security Practice: Material and Ideational Influences*, edited by Muthiah Alagappa. Stanford, CA: Stanford University Press, 1998.

Solis, Mireya. "How Japan's Economic Class Views China and the Future of Asian Regionalism." *JIIA Policy Report*, 2006.

Song, Yann-huei Billy. "China's Ocean Policy: EEZ and Marine Fisheries." *Asian Survey* 29, no. 10 (1989): 983–98.

"South Korean Coastguard Killed by Chinese Fisherman." Reuters, December 12, 2011.

"Spokesperson: Vessel Leaves Disputed Area near Diaoyutai Islands." Agence France-Presse, February 15, 1996.

"Spokesperson Warns Japan over Lighthouse on Disputed Islands." *People's Daily*, July 18, 1996. FBIS-CHI-96-139.

Starr, Harvey. "International Borders: What They Are, What They Mean, and Why We Should Care." *SAIS Review* 26, no. 1 (2006): 3–10.

———. "Territory, Proximity, and Spatiality: The Geography of International Conflict." *International Studies Review* 7, no. 3 (2005): 387–406.

Starr, Harvey, and Benjamin A. Most. "The Substance and Study of Borders in International Relations Research." *International Studies Quarterly* 20, no. 4 (1976): 581–620.

State Council of the People's Republic of China. *China's National Defense in 2000.* Beijing: Information Office of the State Council of the People's Republic of China, 2000.

———. *China's National Defense in 2002.* Beijing: Information Office of the State Council of the People's Republic of China, 2002.

———. *China's National Defense in 2004.* Beijing: Information Office of the State Council of the People's Republic of China, 2004.

———. *China's National Defense in 2006.* Beijing: Information Office of the State Council of the People's Republic of China, 2006.

———. "Law on the Territorial Sea and the Contiguous Zone." February 25, 1992.

———. "Regulations of the People's Republic of China concerning the Exploitation of Offshore Petroleum Resources in Cooperation with Foreign Enterprises." 2001. www.asianlii.org/cn/legis/cen/laws/rotproccteoopricwfe1391.

State Oceanic Administration. *China National Offshore Development Report 2011.* April 29, 2011. www.f-paper.com/?i201553-%22China-National-Offshore-Development-Report-(2011)%22-starts-in-Beijing#.

"Status of the Convention and Its Implementing Agreements." www.un.org/Dept/los/legislationandtreaties/asia/htm.

Steinberg, Philip E. *The Social Construction of the Ocean.* Oxford: Oxford University Press 2001.

Stockmann, Daniela. "Who Believes Propaganda? Media Effects during the Anti-Japanese Protests in Beijing." *China Quarterly* 202 (June 2010): 269–89.

Stokke, Olav Schram. "Transnational Fishing: Japan's Changing Strategy." *Marine Policy* 15, no. 4 (1991): 231–343.

Su, Steven Wei. "The Territorial Dispute over the Tiaoyu/Senkaku Islands: An Update." *Ocean Development and International Law* 36, no. 1 (2005): 45–61.

Suettinger, Robert L. "The Rise and Descent of 'Peaceful Rise.'" *China Leadership Monitor* 12 (2004).

Suganuma, Unryu. *Sovereign Rights and Territorial Space in Sino-Japanese Relations: Irredentism and the Diaoyu/Senkaku Islands.* Honolulu: Association for Asian Studies and University of Hawaii Press, 2000.

Suh, J. J. "War-Like History or Diplomatic History? Contentions over the Past and Regional Orders in Northeast Asia." *Australian Journal of International Affairs* 61, no. 3 (2007): 382–402.

"Summary: JFJB Reporter Boards China Marine Surveillance Ship to Chunxiao Field." *Jiefangjun Bao,* May 25, 2011. World News Connection 201105251477.1_1ff0040102ff1faa.

"Surveying? Encroaching Chinese Ships Circled Uotsuri Island One and a Half Times, Probably Entered from Coast Guard Blind Spot." *Sankei Shimbun*, December 22, 2008. World News Connection 200812221477.1_fd270094 b1e18a37.

Suryanarayana, P. S. "Japan Raises Stake in East China Sea, Grants Rights for Drilling." *The Hindu*, April 14, 2005.

Sutter, Robert G. "China and Japan: Trouble Ahead?" *Washington Quarterly* 25, no. 4 (2002): 37–49.

———. "The PLA, Japan's Defense Posture, and the Outlook for China-Japan Relations." In *Shaping China's Security Environment: The Role of the People's Liberation Army*, edited by Andrew Scobell and Larry M. Wortzel. Carlisle, PA: Strategic Studies Institute, US Army War College, 2006.

Suzuki, Shogo. "Japan and China's Masochists." *The Diplomat*, November 11, 2010.

Swaine, Michael D. "Chinese Decision Making Regarding Taiwan, 1979–2000." In *The Making of Chinese Foreign and Security Policy in the Era of Reform*, edited by David M. Lampton. Stanford, CA: Stanford University Press, 2001.

———. "Perceptions of an Assertive China." *China Leadership Monitor*, no. 32 (2010).

Swartz, Wilfram Ken. "Global Maps of the Growth of Japanese Marine Fisheries and Fish Consumption." MS thesis, University of British Columbia, 2004.

"Taiwan Threatens to Board Chinese Ship." *Daily Collection of Maritime Press Clippings*, no. 133 (2005).

Takada, Akira. "Marine Scientific Research in the Exclusive Economic Zone and Japan-China Agreement for Prior Notification (1995–2001)." *Japanese Annual of International Law* 44 (2001): 134–50.

Takahara, Akio. "A Japanese Perspective on China's Rise and the East Asian Order." In *China's Ascent: Power, Security, and the Future of International Politics*, edited by Robert S. Ross and Zhu Feng. Ithaca, NY: Cornell University Press, 2008.

Takamine, Tsukasa. "Domestic Determinants of Japan's China Aid Policy: The Changing Balance of Foreign Policymaking Power." *Japanese Studies* 22, no. 2 (2002): 191–206.

———. *Japan's Development Aid to China: The Long-Running Foreign Policy of Engagement*. London: Routledge, 2006.

———. "A New Dynamism in Sino-Japanese Security Relations: Japan's Strategic Use of Foreign Aid." *Pacific Review* 18, no. 4 (2005): 439–62.

Tanaka, Takayuki. "Planning National Strategies: Marine Interests at Stake / Gas Field Policy Needs Clarity." *Yomiuri Shimbun*, June 1, 2006.

"Tang Jiaxuan, Kono Discuss Ties, Zhu's Visit, East China Sea Dispute." Xinhua Domestic Service, August 28, 2000. World News Connection FBIS-EAS-2000–1013.

Taniguchi, Tomohiko. "A Cold Peace: The Changing Security Equation in Northeast Asia." *Orbis* 49, no. 3 (2005): 445–57.

Tanner, J. J., and W. E. Kennett. "Petroleum Developments in Far East in 1971." *AAPG Bulletin* 56, no. 9 (1972): 1823–45.

"Teikoku to Drill despite Risk of China Action." *Japan Times*, August 27, 2005.

"Teikoku Oil Starts Gas-Drilling Preparations in the E. China Sea." *Nihon Keizai Shimbun*, September 6, 2005.

"10 Chinese Navy Ships Seen in Waters near Senkaku Isles." Japan Economic Newswire, July 16, 1999.

Thayer, Carlyle A. "China's New Wave of Aggressive Assertiveness in the South China Sea." Paper presented to Conference on Maritime Security in the South China Sea, Center for Strategic and International Studies, Washington, June 20–21, 2011.

Tiberghien, Yves. "The Diaoyu Crisis of 2010: Domestic Games and Diplomatic Conflict." *Harvard Asia Quarterly* 12, nos. 3–4 (2010–11): 70–78.

Till, Geoffrey. "The Navies of the Asia-Pacific in a Revolutionary Age." In *Maritime Security and Cooperation in the Asia-Pacific toward the 21st Century*, edited by Dalchoong Kim, Seo-Hang Lee, and Jin-Hyun Paik. Seoul: Institute of East and West Studies at Yonsei University, 2000.

Tkacik, John J., Jr. "How the PLA Sees North Korea." In *Shaping China's Security Environment: The Role of the People's Liberation Army*, edited by Andrew Scobell and Larry M. Wortzel. Carlisle, PA: Strategic Studies Institute, US Army War College, 2006.

Toft, Monica Duffy. *The Geography of Ethnic Violence: Identity, Interests and the Indivisibility of Territory*. Princeton, NJ: Princeton University Press, 2003.

"Tokyo Rattling Drill Bits over Disputed Gas Fields." *Yomiuri Shimbun*, April 2, 2005.

"Tokyo to Talk Gas Extraction with Beijing." *Nihon Keizai Shimbun*, September 26, 2005.

"Tokyo Will Fight for Senkakus." *Yomiuri Shimbun*, July 8, 2012.

Toppan, Andrew. "World Navies Today: Chinese Scientific, Research and Experimental Vessels." www.hazegray.org/worldnav/china/aux_othr.htm.

"Torture, Anger Overshadow Family Reunion Festival for Relatives of Detained Chinese Fisherman." Xinhua News, September 22, 2010.

Toshiyuki, Lt. Gen. (Ret.) Shitaka. "Can JGSDF Operate as Marine?" *Sekai No Kansen* [Ships of the World], December 2012.

Tretiak, Daniel. "The Sino-Japanese Treaty of 1978: The Senkaku Incident Prelude." *Asian Survey* 18, no. 12 (1978): 1235–49.

Tritten, Travis J., and Chiyomi Sumida. "Local Officials Stir Dispute over Senkaku Islands." *Stars and Stripes*, January 5, 2011.

Tsukamoto, Kazuto. "Japan, China Seal Deal on Gas Fields." *Asahi Shimbun*, June 19, 2008.

UNCLOS (United Nations Convention on the Law of the Sea). 1994, Part XIII. www.un.org/Depts/los/convention_agreements/texts/unclos/cl osindx.htm.

"Unless the Prime Minister Protests over the Chinese Survey Vessel, It Will Create Problems for the Future." *Sankei Shimbun*, May 11, 2010. World News Connection 201005111477.1_b89b02896f7c91d7.

US Department of Defense. *Annual Report to Congress: Military Power of the People's Republic of China 2006.* Washington, DC: US Government Printing Office, 2006.

"US Fudges Senkaku Security Pact Status." Kyodo News, August 17, 2010.

Valencia, Mark J. "China's Push for Offshore Oil: A Chance for Joint Deals." *Straits Times*, September 25, 2004.

———. "Domestic Politics Fuels Northeast Asian Maritime Disputes." *Asia Pacific Issues* 43 (2000).

———. "The East China Sea Dispute: Context, Claims, Issues, and Possible Solutions." *Asian Perspective* 31, no. 1 (2007): 127–67.

———. "Energy and Insecurity in Asia." *Survival* 39, no. 3 (1997): 85–106.

———. "Maritime Confidence and Security Building in East Asia: Recent Progress and Problems." *Ocean Policy Studies* no. 3 (2006): 27–45.

———. *A Maritime Regime for North-East Asia.* Hong Kong: Oxford University Press, 1996.

Valencia, Mark J., and Yoshihisa Amae. "Regime Building in the East China Sea." *Ocean Development and International Law* 34, no. 2 (2003): 189–208.

Van Dyke, John M. "North-East Asian Seas: Conflicts, Accomplishments and the Role of the United States." *International Journal of Marine and Coastal Law* 17, no. 3 (2002): 397–421.

Vasquez, John A. "Distinguishing Rivals That Go to War from Those That Do Not: A Quantitative Comparative Case Study of the Two Paths to War." *International Studies Quarterly* 40, no. 4 (1996): 531–58.

Vivoda, Vlado, and James Manicom. "Oil Import Diversification in Northeast Asia: A Comparison between China and Japan." *Journal of East Asian Studies* 11, no. 2 (Summer 2011): 223–54.

Walter, Barbara F. "Explaining the Intractability of Territorial Conflict." *International Studies Review* 5, no. 4 (2003): 137–53.

Wan, Ming. "Japan's Party Politics and China Policy: The Chinese Fishing Boat Collision Incident." Paper delivered at conference Democracy and Diplomacy in East Asia, University of Tokyo, September 16, 2011.

———. *Sino-Japanese Relations: Interaction, Logic, and Transformation.* Stanford, CA: Stanford University Press, 2006.

Wang, Jianwei. "Territorial Disputes and Asian Security: Sources, Management and Prospects." In *Asian Security Order*, edited by Muthiah Alagappa. Stanford, CA: Stanford University Press, 2003.

Wang, Stanley D. H., and Bing-yi Zhan. "Marine Fishery Resource Management in PR China." *Marine Policy* 16, no. 3 (1992): 197–209.

Watanabe, Takashi. "Four Chinese Warships Pass through Waters off Okinawa." *Asahi Shimbun*, December 2, 2011.

Watkins, Eric. "Japan, China Dispute Field." *Oil & Gas Journal* 103, no. 4 (2005): 30.

———. "Japan, China in Stalemate over Maritime Boundaries." *Oil & Gas Journal* 102, no. 42 (2004): 28.

Weeks, Jessica L. "Autocratic Audience Costs: Regime Type and Signaling Resolve." *International Organization* 62, no. 1 (2008): 35–64.

Wegelin, Florian H. Th. *Marine Scientific Research: The Operation and Status of Research Vessels and Other Platforms in International Law.* Leiden: Martinus Nijhoff, 2005.

Welch, David A. *Justice and the Genesis of War.* Cambridge: Cambridge University Press, 1993.

———. *Painful Choices: A Theory of Foreign Policy Change.* Princeton, NJ: Princeton University Press, 2005.

Wendt, Alexander. "Anarchy Is What States Make of It: The Social Construction of Power Politics." *International Organization* 46, no. 2 (1992): 391–425.

Westlake, Adam. "Secret Meetings Held in Shanghai between China, Japan Officials." *Japan Daily Press*, October 24, 2012.

White, Hugh. "Caught in a Bind That Threatens and Asian War Nobody Wants." *Sydney Morning Herald*, December 26, 2012.

Whiting, Allen S. "China's Japan Policy and Domestic Politics." In *Japan and China: Rivalry or Cooperation in East Asia?* edited by Peter Drysdale and Dong Dong Zhang. Canberra: Australia–Japan Research Centre, 2000.

Wiegand, Krista E. "China's Strategy in the Diaoyu Islands Dispute: Issue Linkage and Coercive Diplomacy." *Asian Security* 5, no. 2 (2009): 170–93.

Wirth, Christian. "Ocean Governance, Maritime Security and the Consequences of Modernity in Northeast Asia." *Pacific Review* 25, no. 2 (2012): 223–45.

"With Eye on China, Defense Ministry to Bolster Southern Flank." *Nihon Keizai Shimbun*, October 9, 2007.

Woodard, Kim. *The International Energy Relations of China.* Stanford, CA: Stanford University Press, 1980.

Woolley, Peter J. *Japan's Navy: Politics and Paradox 1971–2000.* Boulder, CO: Lynne Rienner, 2000.

Wu, Guogang. "China in 2010." *Asian Survey* 51, no. 1 (2011): 18–32.

Wu, Peng. "China's Regional Security Interests and Corresponding Strategic Countermeasures." *Ta Kung Pao*, June 30, 1999. World News Connection FBIS-CHI-1999–0701.

Wu, Xinbo. "The End of the Silver Lining: A Chinese View of the US-Japanese Alliance." *Washington Quarterly* 29, no. 1 (2005–06): 119–30.

Wu, Zhong. "China Shelves Island Dispute, Yet Again." *Asia Times*, December 17, 2008.

Xia, Liping. "The Prospects of China-Japan Relations." *Korea and World Affairs* 31, no. 2 (2007): 204–21.

Xiao, Guan. "Claimant Countries Concerned in the Nansha Dispute Seeking to Capture Sea Areas by Force Triggers Arms Race." *Zhongguo Tongxun She,* August 25, 2010. World News Connection 201008251477.1_64a200cff1031585.

Xin, Sheng. "'Justifiable Defense' Irregular: Behind Japan's 'Suspicious Boat Incident.'" *Jiefangjun Bao,* December 31 2001. FBIS-CHI-2001–1231.

Xue, Chao. "Foreign Ministry News Briefing." *Beijing Review,* May 19, 1997.

Xue, Guifang (Julia). "Bilateral Fisheries Agreements for the Cooperative Management of the Shared Resources of the China Seas: A Note." *Ocean Development and International Law* 36, no. 4 (2005): 363–74.

———. *China and International Fisheries Law and Policy.* Leiden: Martinus Nijhoff, 2005.

———. "China's Distant Water Fisheries and Its Response to Flag State Responsibilities." *Marine Policy* 30, no. 6 (2006): 651–58.

Yahuda, Michael. "The Limits of Economic Interdependence: Sino-Japanese Relations." In *New Directions in the Study of China's Foreign Policy,* edited by Alastair Iain Johnston and Robert S. Ross. Stanford, CA: Stanford University Press, 2006.

Yamada, Saburo. "The Problem of Food Security in Japan." In *Food Security: Theory, Policy and Perspectives from Asia and the Pacific Rim,* edited by Anthony H. Chisholm and Rodney Tyers. Lexington, MA: Lexington Books, 1982.

Yamaguchi, Mari. "Japan Protests to China over Undersea Gas Drilling." Associated Press, February 1, 2012.

Yan, Ling, Su Wanming, and Zhang Daosheng. "Concern about the Metamorphosis of Fishery Boundaries." *Liaowang,* April 13, 2011. World News Connection 201104131477.1_502204bd69a8948c.

Yang, Fang. "China's New Maritime Interests: Implications for Southeast Asia." *RSIS Commentaries,* no. 97 (July 4, 2011).

Yang, Jiechi. "Q&A: Chinese FM on East China Sea Issue." June 24, 2008. http://au.china-embassy.org/eng/xw/t450705.htm.

Yang, Jingjie. "PLA Warships in Drill near Diaoyu Waters." *Global Times,* April 18, 2013.

Yokobori, Keiichi. "Japan." In *Energy & Security: Toward a New Foreign Policy Strategy,* edited by Jan H. Kalicki and David L. Goldwyn. Washington, DC: Woodrow Wilson Center Press, 2005.

Yoshida, Reiji. "Fukuda, Hu Put Focus on Future." *Japan Times,* May 8, 2008.

———. "Senkaku Intrusions Seen as Testing Abe." *Japan Times,* January 9, 2013.

Yoshida, Reiji, and Shinichi Terada. "Japan, China Strike Deal on Gas Fields." *Japan Times,* June 19, 2008.

Yoshihara, Toshi, and James R. Holmes. "Command of the Sea with Chinese Characteristics." *Orbis* 49, no. 4 (2005): 677–94.

———. "Japanese Maritime Thought: If Not Mahan, Who?" *Naval War College Review* 59, no. 3 (2006): 23–51.

Yoshikawa, Yukie. "Okinotorishima: Just the Tip of the Iceberg." *Harvard Asia Quarterly* 9, no. 4 (2006): 13–45.

Yu, Chunguang. "PRC Land and Resources Minister Interviewed on Security of Oil Resources." *Jiefangjun Bao*, July 20, 2002. World News Connection CPP-2002-07-20-000016.

Yu, Huiguo, and Yunjun Yu. "Fishing Capacity Management in China: Theoretic and Practical Perspectives." *Marine Policy* 32, no. 3 (2008): 351–59.

Yuan, Paul C. "China's Offshore Oil Development: Legal and Geopolitical Perspectives." *Texas International Law Journal* 18, no. 1 (1983): 107–26.

Zacher, Mark W. "The Territorial Integrity Norm: International Boundaries and the Use of Force." *International Organization* 55, no. 2 (2001): 215–50.

Zha, Daojiong. "Calming Troubled Waters." *Beijing Review* 51, no. 28 (2008).

Zhang, Haiwen. "The Conflict between Jurisdiction of Coastal States on MSR in EEZ and Military Survey." In *Recent Developments in the Law of the Sea and China*, edited by Myron H. Nordquist, John Norton Moore, and Kuen-chen Fu. Leiden: Martinus Nijhoff, 2006.

Zhang, Jian. "The Influence of Chinese Nationalism on Sino-Japanese Relations." In *China–Japan Relations in the Twenty-First Century: Creating a Future Past?* edited by Michael Heazle and Nick Knight. Cheltenham, UK: Edward Elgar, 2007.

Zhang, Jingwei, "China Adjusts Its Maritime Power Strategy at the Right Moment." *Ta Kung Pao*, December 29, 2008. World News Connection 2008122914 77.1_8c50031423a54f05.

Zhang, Wenmu. "Sea Power and China's Strategic Choices." *China Security* 2, no. 2 (2006): 17–31.

Zhang, Xinjun. "Why the 2008 Sino-Japanese Consensus on the East China Sea Has Stalled: Good Faith and Reciprocity Considerations in Interim Measures Pending a Maritime Boundary Delimitation." *Ocean Development and International Law* 42, no. 1 (2011): 53–65.

Zhang, Yunbi. "Beijing, Tokyo Agree to Hold Second Rounds of Maritime Consultations Later This Year." *China Daily*, May 17, 2012.

Zhao, Suisheng. *A Nation-State by Construction: Dynamics of Modern Chinese Nationalism.* Stanford, CA: Stanford University Press, 2004.

Zheng Wang. "National Humiliation, History Education, and the Politics of Historical Memory: Patriotic Education Campaign in China." *International Studies Quarterly* 52, no. 4 (2008): 783–806.

"Zhejiang Rejuvenates Fishery Industry." Xinhua News, October 24, 1997.

Zhou, Yongsheng. "Sino-Japan Ties Not Easy to Improve." *China Daily*, February 4, 2013.

Zou, Keyuan. "China's Exclusive Economic Zone and Continental Shelf: Developments, Problems, and Prospects." *Marine Policy* 25, no. 1 (2001): 71–81.

———. "Governing Marine Scientific Research in China." *Ocean Development and International Law* 34, no. 1 (2003): 1–27.

———. *Law of the Sea in East Asia: Issues and Prospects.* London: Routledge, 2005.

———. "Sino-Japanese Joint Fishery Management in the East China Sea." *Marine Policy* 27, no. 2 (2003): 125–42.

Index

Information in figures and tables is indicated by *f* or *t*. Information in footnotes is indicated by n between page number and note number.

www.ingramcontent.com/pod-product-compliance
Lightning Source LLC
LaVergne TN
LVHW050150080826
844660LV00002B/145

* 9 7 8 1 6 2 6 1 6 1 0 2 3 *